WHITE HOUSE HOBO
Diaries from my time on the Cinder Trail

James Aldrich

Copyright © 2021 James Aldrich

All rights reserved. No part of this book may be reproduced or retransmitted in any form or by any means without the written consent of the publisher.

Published in the United States by
Lost Souls Press
Colorado
www.lostsoulspress.com

ISBN: 978-1-7346553-3-9

DEDICATION

White House Hobo is first dedicated to my children. The raw material contained in this work would not have been possible without the loving support of Sally, Jimmy, and Wendy. The astute reader may notice that Sally was not mentioned during my time on the cinder trail. That's because I was not aware of her existence until years later—but that's another story. My children's understanding during the wanderlust times of their errant father will never be fully understood. They had the courage to forge through life when their father was not nearby.

This work is also dedicated to all those wonderful and fun-loving individuals that I met during my travels across this great United States of America (I have changed names so as to protect their privacy). It was my great pleasure to have known these people—and I thank them for sharing their energy with this American hobo.

I wish I could talk with, and perhaps even see face-to-face, those individuals who made this period of my life so very enriching, enlightening, and enjoyable. I have attempted to do this on several occasions. I learned that some have departed this earth but live on in my memory. Some have moved to places unknown. I just hope that while being so nice to me during my travels, they also benefited from their good treatment of this stranger who briefly entered their lives.

Contents

The Journey Begins	3
White House to a Boxcar	18
Three Gun Gumshoe	31
Political Sparks	42
North Platte Slammer	50
Presidential Politics	65
Cold Steel on a Texas Hotshot	73
Arizona Philosophy	86
Altar Cloth of God	97
Hobo's Vacation	105
Philosophy of Freedom	110
California's Iron Trail	116
Sullivan's Chicago Bar	131
Italo's Barber Shop	141
Long Black Snake and The Silver Cadillac	150
Pre-employment Vacation	162
Oil Patch in the U.S.A.	172
Boxcars and the General	183
Desert Challenger Landing	197
Ribbons of Steel	208
Alabama Mercenary School	217
The Devil's Playground	228

James Aldrich

The Journey Begins

The journey described in this story actually started at the end of World War II in 1945. Soldiers returning from many years of overseas duty fathered a class of children known as "war babies." The writer of this tale was just another one of those war babies. Some may even say I was an "out of control" war baby. Using the language of a veteran of war in the South Pacific my father would often warn me, "Now son, if you raise your head from the foxhole you might just get it blown off." Had I been in war, in an actual foxhole, my head would have been blown off at a very young age. In second grade I stood up in class and screamed at my teacher, Sister Mary Florian, to stop slapping my fellow classmates. In seventh grade Sister Florian was my teacher once again—this time I was the "teacher's pet" and nearly earned straight As. Some years later I got in a fistfight with a bully of a priest that was the Dean of Male Students at the Catholic High School—I won—earning me immediate expulsion.

At seventeen, after I had stuck my head out of the figurative foxhole one too many times, some nice judge at the Woodbury County Court House gave me two choices: reform school or the United States Marine Corps. As a super-patriotic young man, my chosen "punishment" was to go to the Marines and to Vietnam to kill the enemies of the United States of America and of all the freedoms that we hold dear. My lawyer, an ex-marine, worked with the judge to keep me out of reform school, and I headed over to the Marine recruiter. But after a few talks with the Sergeant, he said they thought that I might be a "discipline problem." Reform school loomed ahead but another kind gentleman, a Monsignor at my Catholic Church—whom I had served as an Altar Boy—intervened and somehow gained my entrance to Boys Town.

Boys Town was wonderful in that from the start it seemed like a fair-minded place to live and finish high school. On my very first night at Boys Town, several of us incoming students were sent to an orientation barracks. All day long some smart-mouthed gangster type verbally and sometimes physically hassled me. I noticed that the barracks counselor was quietly observing but did not attempt to intervene. The behavior continued all day but I maintained my cool. I attacked in the middle of the night—he screamed like a hungry baby. The counselor separated us and firmly told us to knock it off and go to bed. My first impression of Boys Town was confirmed when in the morning the counselor pulled me aside and told me the kid had it coming, and that he was surprised I maintained my cool throughout the harassment.

Following orientation, I was assigned to a very nice cottage with twenty other high school boys. We had house parents that lived with us and they seemed to have the same basic philosophy as the counselor. Individual responsibility was a big deal at Boys Town. We took pride in keeping our cottage sparkling like a military facility – and there were periodic "white glove" inspections. Everyone works at Boys Town and I was put in charge of a section of the dining hall. I had several other younger boys working for me. We had the responsibility to ensure the tables were set with food and drink and then cleaned and re-set after the meal. I liked my first-time management experience and felt good that someone had seen fit to give me the opportunity to lead.

Once I finished high school at Boys Town it was back to Sioux City, where I hooked up with my beautiful high school sweetheart. I worked at a concrete block plant, finished one semester at the local college, drank gallons of beer, and got in many fist fights. Crashing my Harley Davidson motorcycle ended my college wrestling career so I drank more beer and got in more fights. Boys Town hadn't completely cured my wild streak and I didn't see much of a future in my hometown, especially since the local police had taken a rather keen interest in my activities. I wouldn't go so far as saying I was run out of town but I decided to head north about 100 miles to Sioux Falls with my now pregnant lady for a fresh start.

Sioux Falls was nice. A truck-driving job at the local concrete products company provided income for our young family. Several months later, Les, the very slippery owner and manager of a mobile home-sales company offered me a sales job. I accepted and after a few months was made assistant sales manager. The job didn't last long as sleazy Les was embezzling piles of cash and was setting me up to take the blame. Criminal charges were brought and the prosecutor was able to see through the attempted setup. The friendly prosecutor very clearly told me that I was under no suspicion and that he planned to "put that dirty bastard away for many, many years." It seems Les had screwed many seniors out of their life savings as well as his self-declared best friend – me! On a cold, rainy and frozen sleet filed January day my sweetheart and new baby boy, Jimmy, loaded up a trailer, hooked it to an older Pontiac convertible, and headed for another new start in California.

A one-bedroom apartment and a job at an aerospace company working on the control and guidance system for the Minuteman Missile paid for bread and beans. My high school sweetheart gave birth to a beautiful baby girl, Wendy. And I actually, finished my education – at that time the colleges and universities in California were great and also inexpensive—obtaining an undergraduate degree in Physiological Psychology and then a Master's degree in Health Science specializing in biostatistics and epidemiology. It was about this time that my high school sweetie and I went our separate ways, a very sad time of my life. The breakup was all my fault—I was still the wild kid looking for meaning and purpose in my life. It was like another blow to my head as I peered from the rim of a foxhole.

With a big boost from my professor and Master's thesis advisor, I secured an entry level faculty position in the Department of Pathology at the University of Southern California School of Medicine. After a couple of years of putting in many long days (and nights), I obtained research funds from the Cancer Control Program at the National Institutes of Health in Washington D.C. The contracting officer in D.C. said it was remarkable that a non-M.D. was awarded funds to do clinical cancer research. I didn't realize it at the time but this fact represented the fertile soil in which future trouble would flourish.

It turned out that my co-principal investigator was not that interested in conducting research as he was familiar with the "criminality" of cancer research. All hell broke loose when I questioned proposed expenditures that were not listed in the grant proposal. Our research required that young women come to the clinic at the USC Women's Hospital for examination and evaluation. Our pilot study indicated there was no problem and women were happy to come to the existing clinic. My co-director wanted to open up a completely new clinic on some of the most expensive real-estate in the world—the "Miracle Mile" on Wilshire Boulevard in Los Angeles. This single expenditure would use almost an entire year of our research money but would add much to his prestige and standing in the medical community. I refused to counter-sign for the expenditure.

One night after work, after an especially troubling day, I met with the medical school's director of contracts and grants. Over a few single-malt scotches, at the nearby Holiday Inn, he confided in me: "Jim, you're having troubles because you're acting like you got money from the feds to do cancer research when what you actually got was a *license to steal* from the federal government, and your co-director knows this." Wow, what a shocker. I thought I was going to do some valuable research that might just benefit society and, more specifically, cancer victims.

Little ole me, now advanced to instructor faculty status, could not stand up to the power wielded by full professors, and it wasn't long before I was summoned to appear before the dean of the School of Medicine. In the dean's opulent walnut-paneled office, he forcefully demanded that I sign legal papers that would change my legal contract status from, "co-principal investigator" to "administrator." This would essentially remove me from the contract, so I refused to sign. With an angry look, he said, "I can't believe you are giving up the opportunities you have at this school." I didn't understand what he meant but was soon to find out. They somehow managed to remove me from the contract, and took control of my research project without my signature. It seems there was much corruption in cancer research and there wasn't any tolerance for someone lifting their head from the foxhole. Not only did I lose my faculty appointment, office, and staff but soon found I was not welcome in cancer research anywhere in the United States.

Taxi driver and politics were my next endeavors. Both were challenging. Being a taxi-man in Los Angeles was very interesting. Once I was cruising through the intersection of Hollywood and Vine and a fight broke out in the back of my cab. The two drunk guys were crashing from one side to the other in the back seat when suddenly it went quiet – one of the drunks had opened the door and pushed the other onto the busy street. In my rear-view mirror, I saw him sitting up and looking rather confused in the middle of Hollywood Boulevard. Then there was the time a crazy guy pulled a gun and pointed it at my head. I somehow managed to talk him out of pulling the trigger. Or when a scuba diver, perhaps high on drugs, pointed a loaded spear gun at me for no apparent reason. At the urging of my old friend, Norm, I started to carry a loaded .38 caliber pistol on my lap whenever I was driving the cab. Thankfully the pistol was never even brandished.

During this time, I became interested in politics, naively thinking that as an elected official I could root out corruption. I sought to defeat, in a primary, a firmly entrenched California Assembly member. I lost, but didn't give up. I decided to give it another try and just continued campaigning for the next two years. Perhaps the decision to run again was influenced by the unexpected fringe benefits resulting from being a candidate for political office. For some reason the female species appeared to be attracted to the excitement, the glamor, and the sheer thrill of politics. I grew to learn that the business of politics seemed to differ little from Hollywood—politicians were often treated as stars or, in my case, a potential long-shot star. Also, I really believed that if I would just be myself, dump the suit and tie, and wear my more usual blue jeans and Hush Puppies, I'd have a better chance at winning a seat in the California legislature.

However, I turned out to be wrong, and my second failed attempt at politics was followed by weeks filled with sadness and just plain feeling sorry for myself. As the emotional pain and suffering diminished, I decided to spend some time on the beautiful and isolated coast of Big Sur. It was in that place that riches, in the form of the jade gemstone, would hopefully provide funds for another political campaign. It turned out that the excursion to Big Sur failed to provide the anticipated piles of money. However, it did not fail to jump-start a journey that would enrich me with non-material goods—riches beyond my wildest expectations.

Nomad's Lifestyle

One cold and foggy morning I opened my eyes to the sights and sounds of thunderous waves crashing into the jagged coastline of California's Big Sur. Some magic of life's circumstances had brought me to that isolated seventy mile stretch of coastline to seek wealth. Seeking peace of mind and some meaning, some purpose, for my life was also somewhere in my thoughts. As so often happened with these types of adventures the wealth never did materialize. However, the search for peace and learning about my inner-self was brought to the forefront. The money-making venture on the California coast turned into an attempt to understand the *purpose of my life* and caused me to experience many surprising examples of the *value* that was to be found in all people. That value, or goodness, in people was often demonstrated by acts of kindness directed toward this wandering, wisdom seeking and later penniless hobo. Kindness and a journey seeking to discover the meaning of life, and in particular *my* life, is what this book is about.

Big Sur Jade Mining

I loaded up my smooth-running Rambler American station wagon with mining equipment and plenty of beans, and headed up the coast to the extreme southern tip of Big Sur, far from the main tourist centers to the north. I later learned that residents of this end of the stretch of coastline were called "south-coasters," often with a derogatory implication. Some people believed that south-coasters were less civilized than their fellow citizens to the north. I really didn't care, as it was the peaceful atmosphere and the valuable jade gemstone that brought me to the rugged area.

While exploring the beach of Jade Cove I met John, an ocean diver and fellow jade hunter, locals called him "frogman." Frogman advised me: "the big jade boulders are found in the deep water. But be careful when diving, it is easy to become tangled in the seaweed and the waves and currents are deadly." His advice seemed to be rather friendly for someone in competition for the same prize. I guessed he didn't feel I represented any serious competition since my search for jade had been limited to the beach.

I soon found that it could be quite lonely in that place, so I was happy to have my girlfriend (soon to be ex-girlfriend) visit my campsite for a few exciting and fun filled days. But then one afternoon she told me that she was heading back to the city. An overwhelming sadness smothered my spirit. If I stayed, I would be giving her up for good. But at the same time, I couldn't leave Big Sur. After she left my days were filled with hard work and my nights with loneliness. A few weeks later my brother Tom and my good friend Norm arrived from Los Angeles for a visit and to see if I had discovered my sought-after riches. Norm, a retired business owner from Van Nuys, noticed my sadness and told me, "Hey Jim – cheer up--I'll keep you company and help with the search for jade for a few days." My spirits were instantly lifted; the companionship felt like a spectacular sunrise.

The next morning, Norm and I set to work carrying about 150 pounds of equipment from the Plaskett Ridge base camp to a small and rocky beach located in the cove. A portion of the mile long hike included a narrow, winding, dangerous footpath down a ragged cliff face.

The following day, "Frogman" emerged from the much deeper water and spread his arms to show me the size of a jade boulder while excitedly saying, "You won't fucking believe it — I found a piece of jade that must weigh over three-thousand pounds." He then invited me to participate in the week-long project to raise it from the ocean floor and bring it to shore. That operation involved several friends from other parts of the coast. I was happy and somewhat flattered to be invited to be part of the jade-raising and recovery team. The team included another long-time jade diver, an interesting and multi-talented fellow, Don. He told me that a few years ago he had recovered a 9,000-pound jade gemstone that was on display at the Oakland Museum of Art.

The jade recovery work lasted for several days with team members arriving and departing from different parts of the coast and nearby cities. It began with several divers surveying the underwater position and quality of the boulder. Then we prepared strong fishing nets that would surround the underwater gemstone. I was assigned to the tedious task of untangling and removing the many knots in the nets. The nets then were tied together according to the instructions of the diving team. The divers then took the nets underwater and slowly but surely maneuvered the net around the boulder. It took many dives over a period of two days to complete this part of the operation. Once that was accomplished, metal tanks filled with compressed air and large flexible rubber air bladders were taken to the ocean floor. The bladders were securely attached to the netting, filled with air and the jade was floated toward the surface. Being a much less experienced diver, I watched this from the shore, accompanied by interested locals and curious tourists. Since the rocky shore, steep cliffs, and wild waves of Jade Cove would not permit the landing of the boulder, the next operation was to slowly tow the boulder south to Willow Creek where landing the boulder would be possible. This boat trip took several hours to travel the few miles, waves were big and it was always a worry that the boulder would slip from the netting and be lost in the deeper waters. The diving team worried about whether they could make it before nightfall – they did – but just barely. The boulder was resting, under water, with bladders attached for the night. My part would continue in the morning, helping to drag the boulder through the shallower water and then onto the rocky beach – the operation was far from finished. This part actually took another two days as there were thirty to forty yards of large boulders to cross before reaching the parking lot where it could be loaded onto a heavy-duty trailer. After many hours of hard work fashioning steel cables and constantly repositioning vehicles to pull the boulder over the rocks, we finally got the stone to the parking lot. The boulder was next taken to Gorda to be cut into thin slabs using a water-cooled six-foot-long diamond blade — I helped with this part of the project as well. The jade slabs were destined to become beautiful table tops, sometimes inlaid into native redwood. It was all beautiful local and one-of-a-kind art.

It took about three months to settle into the local environment in a way that provided just a tiny portion of the comforts that were part of my previous Los Angeles lifestyle. The serene ruggedness and hard work spawned a period when I would ask myself: "What the hell am I doing here?" In spite of the indisputable beauty of the surroundings and the many interesting people I met, I missed my former busy city life. Many times, I thought about leaving, particularly late at night while huddled inside my little shelter trying to keep warm. After one such night, I decided to throw in the towel. I packed up my camp, said my goodbyes, and headed back toward LA.

My trip south was stopped short when the Rambler's clutch linkage broke and stranded me and all my possessions many miles down the coast. With nothing better to do, I decided to hitch a ride back to my old campsite to the north. I was rather despondent when telling retired lumberjack and camp host Ken my sad story. With a broad smile he said, "Don't worry, Jim, tomorrow we'll get your Rambler with my truck, bring it here, and fix it." He and his friend Bill built a replacement part from old things we found along the highway, and it actually worked. In two days, the Rambler was ready to roll once again. By then I had calmed down enough that I decided not to give in to the cabin fever of a few days earlier, and determined to stay put in Big Sur.

I had caught cabin fever because time was still important to me. I thought that perhaps another path in the city would provide a quicker road to riches which would then lead to political success. I sometimes felt that time was being wasted and my life was slipping away. My mind was somehow overlooking the value of the time spent in that magnificent corner of our universe. The mind was racing toward an unknown future and was wiping out the *value* of the current moment.

The First Formula for Life

It was during that time of indecision, actually self-pity, late one night, while sitting by the campfire, that I somehow decided to snap out of it and to pull myself together. I asked some difficult personal questions concerning why I existed and just what the hell my life's purpose was. Much of my educational and professional experience had been concerned with scientific research and how to measure observations. Based on that mindset, I decided to seek the meaning of my life using logic and the scientific approach. The seed for the development of a Formula for Life (FFL) was planted. Living in the solitude of Big Sur somehow spawned the realization that such a journey into the inner self must be conducted with total honesty. Absolutely no purpose would be served if I failed to be truthful, especially to myself, when developing any so-called Formula for Life. Two principles emerged: I must be honest with myself; and the Formula must be personalized and applicable to me. Hopefully others might find it useful as well.

Shaking with excitement in the light of the campfire, I found paper and pencil and began to write a crude list of important things associated with my life experiences, both in the city and in Big Sur. The list would provide the basic items (variables for the scientist in me) for the development of the Formula for Life. In the dim light on that cold and peaceful evening I anxiously scratched out the following list of influences in my life.

- Basic Needs (BN), or the physical necessities of life, such as water, food, and shelter.
- You need either dollars or tradable goods to meet those Basic Needs.
- The costs (in terms of energy expenditure) for Basic Needs vary and are dependent on where you choose to locate the physical body.
- Freedom and independence are increased once Basic Needs were met.
- Since free land is hard to come by, dollars or tradable good are required to secure a physical place to put your body and build a shelter.
- In order to meet Basic Needs you must *expend energy* to pay for them.
- Once Basic Needs are met, the human spirit then hungers for more, such as intimacy and relationships. I call this next level of need Personal Growth (PG).
- In order to realize Personal Growth one must somehow acquire New Knowledge (NK). Acquisition of New Knowledge might also include relationships with family and strangers. Relationships were often associated with a reduction in independence.
- Basic Needs plus New Knowledge lead to Personal Growth.
- Visions of the future results in setting of goals. Certain actions must be taken to "Accomplish Goals" (AG). This also requires an expenditure of energy.

From these basic insights a simplistic formula emerged that would serve as a starting point in my quest to find some meaning for my existence. That initial Formula for Life was:

$$FFL = BN + NK \rightarrow PG \rightarrow AG$$

FFL = Formula for Life
BN = Basic Needs

NK =   New Knowledge
PG =   Personal Growth
AG =   Accomplishment of Goals

This writer expects some snickers from the reader at such an over-simplification of the meaning of my life, but for this philosophical newcomer it only represented a starting point for an excursion into the unknown. Armed with those new insights I stayed in Big Sur for several months and managed to fulfill my Basic Needs, gain some New Knowledge and realized some measure of Personal Growth. The Formula for Life was laid aside and the journey through life continued.

A New Campsite

The welcome at the little used Forest Service campground started to grow sour. Even though the campgrounds were mostly empty during the week and often the same on weekends, "Smoky the Bear" wanted me to move. It was a bitter pill to swallow but I had no choice. I stalled my eviction as long as possible. Then moved my base camp to the side of the highway and lived inside the Rambler, which wasn't so comfortable. The following few weeks found me moving around, but always camping near Highway One in the Pacific Valley area. Some of the more friendly locals told me about a secluded ridge and beach near Willow Creek just a few miles to the south. Rare white jade was said to be on the beach, and there was a place to hide the Rambler away from the road. It looked great. The difficult footpath from the cliffs to the beach would make it impossible to transport the diving equipment. That was fine, since my new interest was in the smaller pieces found in the shallow waters and on the beach. I would forget about the boulders and concentrate on jewelry-sized pieces. In fact, I made enough money to satisfy my Basic Needs by selling jade to the tourists. I made small jade gemstones into earrings and necklaces, which I then sold from five to twenty dollars each. It must be remembered that at that point in my life twenty dollars was a substantial bit of change. My jade jewelry enterprise was easily paying for beans, beer, and gas for the Rambler.

The Willow Creek mining camp was fantastic and soon became my hiding place. The locals had long ago named the place "Broken Truck Ridge," or BTR for short; no one could remember the origins of its name. The heavily loaded Rambler moved slowly along the short rough road and disappeared into the cover of the squat, windblown trees. The Rambler and I were well hidden from the prying eyes of tourists and more importantly the Forest Service. I excitedly explored the ridge which overlooked a magnificent bay where Willow Creek flowed out of the mountains and into the dark blue waters of the Pacific. The terraced ocean floor and the swirling sage green waters of the creek produced stunning patterns as the creek water mixed with the deep blue of the Pacific. The cliffs and beach to the south were composed of dark black lava rock and stood in sharp contrast to the white water of the breakers. Off the south point of the bay was Cape San Martin, a large island mass of symmetrical rock that was the dominant feature of the majestic bay. During my stay on Broken Truck Ridge, I sometimes thought it would be nice to have a place on the rocks of San Martin. My more practical hutment was high on BTR, located on the northern side of the bay that jutted sharply into the waters of the Pacific. Here the winds rose from the ocean in an almost constant flow of clean, cool salt air. I quickly located a central spot on the ridge among the short windswept trees and begin work on a new encampment.

For several weeks prior to finding Broken Truck Ridge, I had traveled the coast selling jade and meeting interesting people. During the early weeks of my adventure I met Cindy who was traveling the country with her sister. Her visit had resulted in many pleasant memories. She returned after making a sightseeing trip to San Francisco. By the moonlight we headed for the beach on the other side of Highway One. At the side of the highway we decided to fall into the deep cool grass and kiss to the sound of passing cars. We were there quite some time. Finally, we crossed the highway and headed through the short trees and down the moonlit path. It wasn't long before we once again fell to the ground for more kissing. We never did reach the beach. Cindy stayed for several fun days and then headed for LA to visit my friend, Dan Van Meter. I suspected that Cindy was getting tired of the primitive Big Sur lifestyle — or perhaps of a certain jade miner.

Once again, I was alone on Broken Truck Ridge, but this time it was a pleasant feeling. I made the long trek to the beach and was surprised to find great piles of nice lumber on that isolated beach. I carried a heavy load of the two-by-fours to the campsite, and then another and another. They were the perfect size for building my little shelter. Later I learned that many years ago a lumber barge had capsized far out to sea. The lumber had washed up on shore for many miles of the Big Sur coast.

The shelter on Broken Truck Ridge was simple but functional, the frame was sturdy and the heavy canvas from an old army tent provided shelter from the wind and coldness of winter. During one of my lumber gathering trips I spent time looking for beach jade and found some of the unusual white pieces, which had gone unnoticed by others because of the beach's isolated location, and because the ridge was blanketed with a particularly virulent form of poison oak. It seemed to jump at you, hungry for human skin, as you walked past it on BTR's little used trails. I soon learned that if I wanted to stay on the ridge, part of the price would be a few serious bouts with this poison. It was impossible to avoid the greasy, oily bane of that vine-like plant. I clawed and scratched my skin just thinking about the nasty stuff.

I decided to take a trip to Los Angeles to talk with an attorney friend about filing a mining claim on Broken Truck ridge. Later I talked with brother Tom, who said he would help stake the mining claim, and then I returned to Big Sur to start work. Tom arrived a few days later and we set out to fulfill the legal requirements, including marking the boundary corners with buried bottles containing maps of the claim. To do this we were forced to tramp through the bush and the poison oak. After we finished the boundary marking, I went to the county courthouse in Salinas and filed the claim. Tom stayed behind and guarded the camp as some locals were threatening to attack. They actually raided the camp but Tom, an ex-army 82nd Airborne trooper, drove them away. When I returned to BTR the effects of the poison oak were just beginning to show, and by midnight we were both madmen. The constant itching was driving us crazy and we were both covered with the oozy, oily rash. There was no sense in both of us suffering so we decided that Tom should return to Los Angeles for medical attention. In time my body built up a natural immunity to its effects, thus helping to establish myself as a local. I was discovering that outsiders were not easily accepted on the south-coast, either by people or nature.

Filing the official mining claims on Broken Truck Ridge started all kinds of fireworks; the local resident Indians said I was on a sacred Indigenous burial ground. The Forest Service said the land was exempt from mining claims because of a law dating back to the late 1800's. Other locals just didn't want an outsider around and felt I was bringing heat down on their marijuana growing operations. A rather pleasant and cheerful California Highway Patrolman even stopped by BTR and warned me that there were rumors that I would soon be dead if I didn't find another place to camp. Later that same week a smiling Salinas County Deputy Sheriff came by to see if I was "still alive," as he put it. A few days later four men from the Forest Service stopped by to issue a ticket for what they called an illegal mining claim. It was a very interesting couple of weeks; there was no possibility of getting bored. I found myself once again not following my

Dad's foxhole advice.

Gorda and Tortilla Flats

A few weeks later, a character known as jade Ron came to my camp with the peace offering from the locals, an invitation to a party in Gorda. Gorda was a small town, situated about five miles from Broken Truck Ridge, with a population of about twenty attention-grabbing characters. Nearby was Tortilla Flats, another ridge on which sat a single cabin where a lady by the name of Becky and her teenaged son lived. I had met her once before when she stopped at my camp. She had sent jade Ron to invite me to the community party so that the citizens of Gorda could meet me. The party was fun and I seemed to get along fine with just about everyone. I could say one thing about the townspeople of Gorda, they sure didn't beat around the bush as their questions to me were direct and to the point. The party continued into the early morning hours, at which point Becky, the host and star of the party, walked part of the way with me back to BTR. That night I finally started to feel somewhat accepted by the fascinating "south-coasters."

The next week I went back to Salinas to file more mining claim paperwork. I also had to appear at the U.S. Army Base of Fort Ord before a Magistrate on the illegal-claim citation issued by the Forest Service. I pled not guilty to the charges, and the case was sent to trial in San Francisco Federal District Court. Before heading back to the solitude of Broken Truck Ridge I went to Sacramento to use the library to prepare for my trial.

I was back on the ridge for a couple of days when late one moonlit night Becky stopped at my campsite on her way to her Tortilla Flats cabin. She had been partying at a nightclub to the north and was feeling no pain. Becky was not at all interested in discussing the beauty of the night. It was a hot time on BTR that star filled night, after which I spent a couple of nights with Becky at Tortilla Flats and then headed for Los Angeles to discuss my recent legal problems with Joe, my attorney friend. Joe had been in contact with the clerk of the court at Fort Ord about my case, and was informed that the Judge had ordered me to vacate the claim until the matter was settled. I was surprised, but not too worried, as I had been spending my evenings with my lovely new friend, Becky.

I was in LA about three days when Becky flew down from San Francisco to spend time with me. After our stay, Becky and I had a leisurely drive from LA to Big Sur while making frequent stops to celebrate our newly discovered young love. I went to BTR to work on my mining claim and while there six Forest Service men dressed in green battle fatigues came rushing into camp and in a very aggressive and threatening manner told me "get the fuck off U.S. Forest Service property." Not being in a particularly good frame of mind at that time I spontaneously told them "you all get the fuck off this ridge or I will place you under citizen's arrest for trespassing." I had a very long shotgun slung on my shoulder and more than a little fire in the eyes. I then walked toward the highway. I was ready to defend my mining claim no matter what it took. Thankfully, the Forest Service "assault" team fell in behind and followed me to the highway as they verbally protested and castigated this very pissed-off and distressed miner. Two days later I was in Gorda, sitting at the counter of the town's only restaurant leisurely sipping a cup of coffee when one of the local redwood loggers came rushing up to me. The young man excitedly informed me that, "I just saw your Rambler being towed south on Highway One in a convoy of Forest Service trucks and SWAT type black SUVs in front and back." As it turned out the local forest ranger had called the Forest Service's SWAT team into action. They had descended on my mining camp. They took everything: mailbox, shelter and even the carefully selected and fine-looking rocks from around the campfire. The long-barreled shotgun and antique Smith and Wesson .32 caliber pistol, hidden in the Rambler, were also confiscated. I must say they did an efficient job of disappearing my humble mining camp. Once the SWAT team had secured my campsite the Forest service workers built a huge barrier to block the lane leading to my campsite. The following day a couple of the special agents from the campsite raid came looking for me at the Tortilla Flats cabin. Through the locked door they said they only wanted to issue another citation, but Becky immediately answered and rather forcefully sent them away. Becky and I drove thirty-five miles south to Cambria to get the impounded Rambler. The claim business was beginning to get complicated, downright dangerous, and expensive.

Becky invited me to make a new camp at Tortilla Flats, and I went to work preparing legal briefs for the upcoming court appearance in San Francisco. To make a long story short, when my case finally got before a judge, I lost. The San Francisco judge ordered me to "cease all mining work and immediately vacate the claim." The judge made it perfectly clear that my Broken Truck Ridge mining claim was indeed located within a special land area and that Congress had withdrawn the land from any new mining claims. As the court proceedings concluded, the judge told me: "Perhaps you should have been born a hundred years ago, during the pioneer days of the early West." I took the words as a compliment. The entire month-long court experience was an excellent example of the acquisition of the New

Knowledge that was part of the Formula for Life.

So now I was living the high life with Becky at Tortilla Flats. It wasn't too long before I suffered a broken leg at a wild mountain party. It was from a friendly skirmish with another liquored-up party goer as we tumbled over a cliff, necessitating a seventy-mile trip north on the very curvy Highway One with Becky driving her rather cramped, vintage Karmann-Ghia. We arrived at the emergency room in Monterey at three in the morning. There was no orthopedic doctor on duty so it was another hour before a rather pissed off and gruff, half asleep doctor arrived. He quickly set my leg, threw on a heavy plaster cast and sent Becky and me into the early morning dawn. With the Rambler now dead and my leg in a plaster cast from hip to foot, Becky gave me a ride to Los Angeles. It was there that I spent time with several friends and shared tales of my many adventures in the Santa Lucia Mountains of Big Sur. The time in Big Sur was one of the most educational periods of my life; there was no way to put any kind of dollar value on that fantastic learning experience.

A short stay at Mike's house in the San Fernando Valley, an old friend from my political days, resulted in meeting a couple of young ladies at a neighborhood party he was hosting. Late into the evening, when party goers had departed, I convinced Marlene and her blond Swedish friend to help me take a shower. The Swedish girl held my broken leg while Marlene lathered and rinsed the rest – a rather nice fringe benefit of a broken leg. That little exercise was filled with good-natured laughing and just a little kissing. It turned out that Marlene would become an important part of my journey through life, but more on that later. I stayed in Los Angeles for a couple of weeks before catching a plane to recuperate at my little sister's farm in Cape Girardeau, Missouri.

White House to a Boxcar

I arrived at the Cape on a sunny Saturday afternoon and sister Jeanne was waiting at the small local airport. We busily chatted as she drove the fifteen miles across the small Missouri town and into the beautiful countryside to her farmhouse on Wind River Lane. The heavy plaster cast for my broken leg had been on for about four weeks and something was definitely wrong. There was often a painful grating sensation where the broken bone should have been healing. My sister, a nurse, insisted that I see a doctor for x-rays. I nearly fainted (really) when my untrained eye saw the x-ray pictures of the bone still very much broken with ragged ends lying next to one another. Surgery would be required. I had the operation the following day and began my recuperation in the able hands of Jeanne and her friend, a nurse named Bunny. Both just happened to be on the medical staff at the hospital. Bunny made my time at the hospital enjoyable; we were destined to become close friends.

Thoughts of Philosophy at the Cape

The Cape was a quiet little town on the banks of the Mississippi, a nice place to reflect on the time recently spent on the California coast. The full-length cast for my broken leg greatly limited mobility and offered me plenty of time to read and accumulate New Knowledge consistent with my Formula for Life. Since the Cape was a university town, I had access to plenty of reading material in the beautiful university library. Politics, science, and philosophy were the areas that attracted most of my interest. Throughout my reading I looked for knowledge that might relate to the embryonic Formula for Life. Much of the philosophical reading confirmed many of my personal thoughts concerning reality and my Purpose of Life. Introspection led me to question the value of seeking New Knowledge through reading, as much of the material seemed to confirm what I already thought I knew. How about that for a large dose of arrogance? Many of the underlying principles of the works I read appeared to be founded on the belief that human beings should have a good time during our brief stay in this reality. Such a philosophy agreed with my outlook on life but the various authors never seemed to come right out and say it. As I saw it, the message was that we should enjoy everything our Creator had given us, while at the same time not infringing on the rights of others to do the same. Perhaps reading was a way of justifying my current lifestyle by providing evidence that I was not alone in my belief that we should always strive to *enjoy* ourselves. It also seemed reasonable to conclude that at least some portion of our Purpose of Life was the accumulation of energy through the learning process. When we accumulated such energy, we were actually adding mass, in the form of mental images stored in the brain, and hence Personal Growth was the result. Such stored energy might then be used to increase the probability that pleasant visions of the future became a reality. Unfortunately, many people felt that such behavior was selfish. Many individuals I met in my travels appeared to be very suspicious of a philosophy which was based on and encouraged individuals to strive to enjoy their life. I could see that a new component in the Formula for Life was emerging; I simply called it "Enjoyment of Life" or "EOL."

In my mind, I needed further justification for spending so much time in the library and reasoned that the New Knowledge (energy) resulted in the expansion of the mind. Since the universe was expanding, according to known laws of astrophysics, one became part of that harmonious expansion while absorbing the energy of knowledge. Such an expanding knowledge base became part of a vision of the future. If one selected only New Knowledge that added to one's Enjoyment of Life (EOL), then as time passed, all thoughts (accumulation of mass) became enjoyable and there would be no regrets.

Before leaving for my Big Sur adventure a considerable amount of energy had been expended in the accumulation of material things. Those material items were obtained with the idea of enhancing my Enjoyment of Life. We all know that material possessions could certainly bring pleasure, but one must also understand that the value of any particular item rapidly decreased with the passage of time. Just think of the time you took possession of that new car or perhaps a boat – how long was it before the excitement diminished? We must also recognize and remember that in order to first obtain and then retain any material item we must expend energy; that was the price we paid.

During preparations for my move to the Big Sur coast I was forced to decide what to do with my possessions. They were still very important. I solved the problem by distributing possessions amongst friends with the idea of getting them back sometime in the future. Much was stored at Dan Van Meter's three-acre estate in the heart of the San Fernando Valley. Dan was an elderly gentleman, a political activists and friend who had supported my efforts to become a California assemblyman. As time passed the concern over those material things became less and less; the process of "de-materialization" was slowly taking place. I began to recognize that parting with my possessions was somewhat painful and thinking about losing "my stuff" tended to consume much of my time and energy. Having things scattered about in many separate places was stressful. For a long time, I kept a carefully maintained written inventory of my possessions and where they were located. Looking back I think the written inventory made it possible for me to mentally enjoy my possessions while traveling from place to place. The feeling was that I no longer had the responsibility for these things and therefore had more freedom to travel.

During that time of my life, I began to experience a new sense of freedom and enjoyment by virtue of not being attached to, and therefore not required to expend energy to maintain, my material things. I also realized that by asking others to watch my things required that they expend energy; I was only giving up responsibility and passing it on to someone else. I was beginning to understand that to be truly free from material possessions one must be willing to live without those things, forever. My mobile lifestyle, beginning with the Big Sur expedition, had rapidly led to a definition of what was required to meet my Basic Needs and yet maintain Enjoyment of Life. Any item to be possessed that did not fulfill Basic Needs, or perhaps New Knowledge in the form of reading material, would be considered as extra and unnecessary baggage.

I had already dispensed of my most weighty and valuable possession when the Rambler American had died and then was pushed over the cliff at Tortilla Flats, finding itself a new home in the Pacific Ocean. I had reached a point where my only material wealth would be the items that could be carried on my back. Before you start to feel sorry for such a poor soul you should understand that, to my amazement, giving up these material things increased my Enjoyment of Life (EOL). Wow—what a realization: less was actually more. For me it was a huge spiritual leap forward. Freedom and independence were instantly increased and the process of "de-materialization" continued.

I began to understand that when Enjoyment of Life was contingent on material things independence was reduced because you were required to expend energy to possess them. You ran the risk of becoming a slave to something outside yourself. The message was to possess things only as long as they added to EOL. That was not easy since you must be totally honest with yourself in order to balance the cost in terms of energy expenditure with the enjoyment you derived. Once enjoyment of something requires too much energy, then that material item should be passed on to a friend. After all, we are only on this planet for a short time, and the old adage "you can't take it with you" is certainly true. We are only caretakers in the physical world; the spirit does not carry gold into ethereal space.

The Cape

I found myself truly enjoying life in the small town of Cape Girardeau. The campus of Southeast Missouri State University, known as SEMO, and its 10,000 students, were a major factor in the city's atmosphere. The Cape was definitely a college town with its many bars and pizza joints near the campus, bustling during the academic year and quiet during semester breaks and holidays.

Nurse Bunny and I had been seeing much of one another as she frequently came to the farm to make sure that I was healing correctly. Bunny was not in the least bit shy and before long she hinted that her thoughts for the future included a long-term relationship, perhaps marriage. Talk of that sort of cooled off our relationship as I was not ready to settle down. In spite of that major difference, we did share a little red brick house under the Mississippi River Bridge that was a few yards from the riverfront. The time spent with Bunny at the Cape was some the most peaceful and serene I could ever remember. She was a wonderful person and it was always such a pleasure to spend time with her. Somehow, she always managed to have a positive outlook on life in spite of her high-pressure nursing job at the hospital.

In spite of the serenity of the Cape the energy of movement was upon me. I removed my leg cast myself, giving me a little more mobility, but I was still restless. The young lady I met in Los Angeles, Marlene, wanted to get involved in Washington, D.C. politics — the 1979 race for the presidency, between President Jimmy Carter and Ronald Reagan — was in full swing.

She suggested I join her. I decided I would go.

Presidential Politics in Washington D.C.

I picked a departure date and told Marlene, now living in Arizona, about my east coast plans. We really didn't know one another that well, so I wasn't totally convinced of her sincerity when she said she would pick me up and we would drive to D.C. together. It was a happy Saturday morning when I saw Marlene standing in front of the Cape Girardeau's Holiday Inn, her wide smile and long black hair blowing in the wind. I would travel to D.C. in style. Did I really deserve such a blessing?

After saying goodbyes, we left the Cape in high spirits, determined to make an impact in our nation's capital. It was a leisurely trip with many stops along the way to kiss and to speculate about our time to come. We spent our first days in D.C. at a cheap hotel on New York Avenue several miles from the capitol building.

During my political days in California I had met many of Carter's top campaign staff when I had organized a few dozen volunteers to work on a major and the final campaign appearance by President Carter in downtown Los Angeles. It was a successful event, and at the time, some of the staffers had suggested I check out campaign headquarters in D.C. So, Marlene and I made the trip to President Carter's national headquarters to see about work. We found out that there were no paid positions available. However, we both decided to stick around the HQ and do some volunteer work, which we felt would increase our chances of a paid position in the future. During the volunteer period I got to know many of the people that were scattered on the building's fourteen floors.

One of my more interesting jobs was working the main telephone switchboard. Answering the phone might appear to be rather unimportant but I gained a great deal of respect for anyone doing that work. One fantastic benefit was that you learned about the organization's structure and its relationship to the White House and its people. The switchboard position actually controlled much of the day-to-day activity of the entire national campaign. Remember, this was prior to e-mails and text messaging so almost all the non-printed communications went through the switchboard. A telephone conversation was most often the first contact people had with a president's campaign representatives. I very much wanted to do a good job.

It was a real challenge to keep the calls in order and to connect them with the correct people. When I first sat down in front of the ringing telephone and its blinking lights, I was truly terrified. I would surely make a fool of myself and the president's campaign. It was a pleasant surprise that, with a little practice, my mind could actually process all those blinking switchboard lights. Somehow, I was able to keep the blinkers and their contents and level of importance in proper order. I soon developed the ability to recall who was behind each of the blinking lights, whom they were holding for, and how long they had been waiting. It wasn't long before I became a real pro and actually enjoyed the hectic pace of the switchboard. I guess I should add that there was always a cup of fresh coffee close by and sometimes it contained a splash of brandy from my flask.

As the weeks and months passed, I spent time working on almost every floor and in every department of the national campaign headquarters. Each department had a distinct feel, which did not seem good for a unified approach to getting President Carter re-elected. The fund-raising department wanted my services and hinted at a paid position, but it didn't really interest me. I seemed to gravitate to the "wild gang" on the tenth floor where national campaign manager Tim Kraft, or Krafty, had his office.

Krafty was filled with a real zest for his work and life, and it was a pleasure just to be around this energetic young man. His head was most definitely above the rim of the foxhole. He had played a major role in getting Carter elected in 1976, and was rewarded with the White House position of Assistant to the President for Political Liaison. Krafty was on leave from the White House to manage the re-election effort. The White House Liaison's office, run by Diana was also on the tenth floor. Krafty and Diana made the whole floor interesting, and I decided that it was for me. It took a couple of months to gain the trust of the tenth-floor people. I started by working with Diana, a very serious hardball player. At times our conversations would escalate to an unpleasant decibel level. And sometimes standing face-to-face with clenched fists ready for combat. It wasn't too long before I took over some empty office space, somehow acquired furniture and a phone and settled in on the tenth floor.

As a volunteer I was not yet getting paid, so Krafty suggested I take over campaign security at the headquarters. It was not much money, but it supplied me with bread and beans and I didn't have to pay rent since I was able to sleep on Krafty's office couch at HQ and take showers in another office.

While I got more deeply involved in the campaign, my friend Marlene soon grew tired of it, and after a couple of months made the decision to return to Arizona to enroll at the Tempe campus of the University of Arizona.

One result of my work in Diana's liaison office was that I got to know White House Office (WHO) staff. One of the more interesting fellows I met was General Lee (not really a general but he did operate with a general's precision). He was a fine young man from Georgia working in the Executive Office of the President (EOP) and doing advance work for presidential excursions. I soon learned that he was a trusted member of Carter's inner circle. Trust at the White House was an extremely valuable commodity and was to be cherished and appreciated. The first level of trust was when you were accepted as not being a spy for political opponents or a foreign country and that you really wanted to get the president re-elected. The second level of trust involved the belief that, even with the best of intentions, you would not make some stupid remark, either verbally or in writing, that would embarrass the president. Somehow it appeared that I had earned both levels of trust.

Meeting the President

I talked with General Lee about a computer project I was designing that provided a systematic method for more control and awareness of the president's correspondence. The project was an outgrowth of some of the problems observed at HQ with political letters that required the president's signature. General Lee liked what he saw and told me that he wanted me to show it to someone close to the president.

Early one morning I met Dan at his beautiful office located in the Old Executive Office Building just to the west of the White House. Dan showed me around, introduced me to staff and we were soon walking down steps, through underground passages with doors being opened for us by Secret Service agents dressed in white uniforms. Before long we emerged at the palatial surroundings of the Oval Office. We then passed through another door where Dan introduced me to Susan, the president's personal secretary. It was exciting to meet Susan and discuss my computer project. Before long the president walked in and Susan introduced me. She told the president about the computer project we were working on. The president quickly scanned our work and told us, "Looks great. Keep up the good work." Later, Susan told me that she would help me develop the computer system, but that it would be most useful during the president's second term, after the campaign was over. Of course, there was no second term, and the computer project never came to fruition.

During that White House meeting Susan also told me she wanted me to be a White House commissioned officer in the next administration. She said the position wasn't powerful, but that it could be rather influential. For the next administration Susan wanted me as the "Special Assistant to the President and Director of White House Correspondence." Not bad for the "wild kid" from that little river town in northwestern Iowa. It looked like I just might be moving in a valuable direction. Susan told me that she would deliver any of my concerns or suggestions regarding the campaign directly to the president, and she even shared secret and sensitive information with me. I was clearly moving into a position of trust, and I began to think that the long hours at National HQ could result in a totally unexpected benefit of a job at the White House.

At the time, some friends of mine had been out of town and they let me camp at their condo overlooking DuPont Circle. It was late at night, close to midnight, and while walking along the concrete corridor toward their condo the positive events of the day seemed to overwhelm my soul. Several spontaneous "yahoos" loudly erupted from deep in my throat and then echoed off the walls in that concrete jungle. Out of the dark, from far above, came the reply "you must have had a great day" – a broad smile lit up my face.

One of the most rewarding and enjoyable projects for the president was organizing a campaign trip for the hotly contested New Hampshire primary. Over 100 White House and campaign staff signed on for the excursion. It was a logistical challenge and I eventually rented two Amtrak passenger railcars to transport the party north to White River Junction, on the New Hampshire-Vermont border. It was rather exciting when the "gold button," the train conductor, came to my seat and asked for the ticket that I had purchased (with campaign money) for $2,700. In mock sternness he stood over me and said, "I am told that you have the ticket for everyone in these two cars--I hope that's true otherwise there could be serious trouble." With a big smile I happily handed him the ticket.

Unfortunately, the train schedule resulted in us arriving at our destination of White River Junction at three in the morning. There had been heavy partying for most of the trip from D.C. and it was no small task to get the many drunks to de-train. To add to the confusion there was a blinding snowstorm as we left the warmth and comfort of the Pullman cars. Thankfully the three busses I had chartered for the occasion were waiting for us and, despite the wind-driven snow, everyone got themselves and their luggage to the correct bus. The buses then traveled east through the state following three different routes, dropping people at pre-arranged cities throughout the state. Three days later the procedure was reversed for the return to D.C. The entire operation turned out to be a real challenge and I was happy to see things went according to plan. We must have had some impact, as the president scored an important victory over Ted Kennedy, who dropped out of the race shortly thereafter. An unexpected bonus was a personal letter from the president expressing appreciation for my work in New Hampshire. I was sure Susan had something to do with that.

The spirit that rode those Amtrak rails was very special as we had a unified sense of direction. Sadly, that feeling of unity was a rare occurrence; my observation was that such feelings were rarely found in the president's campaign. The national campaign staff put in their eight-hour days, but most of them rarely committed themselves to go beyond that. Many were working only with the idea of getting a job at the White House. The regular White House staff often looked down on the national campaign staff, which was discouraging to the latter, and hampered the campaign. The majority of the regular White House staff were snobbish to the point of being rude. Both the national campaign and White House staff often looked down on the volunteers – and didn't hide it. Such a condescending attitude indicated that they were motivated by things other than enjoyment derived from working to fulfill the president's vision. For many of the regular White House staff, their jobs were only considered as a stepping-stone to a future career position. The inner circle comprised a third group and consisted of those few dozen individuals who truly believed in the president and his objectives. Those few people would manage to look others in the eye and urge them forward. They seemed to have a certain sparkle in their eyes showing that they believed in what the administration was attempting to accomplish.

The more time spent away from the D.C. campaign office, the less influence I had amongst the national campaign staffers. Part of my responsibility while working on the tenth floor was to report campaign irregularities. I would report directly to Susan who would then pass it to the president if she thought it required his attention. Following some work in the field I returned to HQ and found that I was no longer welcome. I had ruffled some feathers with a report I had giving Susan about large amounts of missing cash. My head was above the rim of the foxhole once again — my cover had been blown. The new Security Chief (hired by the individual I accused of wrongdoing) had just issued a directive that I was not to be allowed in the building. Since I was already in my office, I stalled the security people while trying to reach Susan at the White House. The duty officer at campaign HQ's that Sunday morning called the Washington, D.C., police to report that there was a trespasser in the building (me). In very short order they showed up to arrest me.

It was quite a scene and there would be no help from Susan as she was with the president in Spain. It was really nothing to bother Susan with anyway; people in my position were expendable, and it was just part of the game of politics. I managed to get out of the building a free man, but was forced to leave all my files behind. There was a long discussion as to whether I could remove my US flag from my office wall. I won that argument when campaign security contacted higher-ups; then one of the D.C. policemen helped me *tightly* fold the red, white, and blue. I had been evicted from the national campaign headquarters, but not the campaign, itself. I would be able to survive without the small salary and would surely have more freedom to work for the campaign on my own terms. In the strange world of politics my differences with the campaign's administrative section actually enhanced my position with Susan and the White House.

I decided to do some traveling and visited several state campaign offices. The new sense of freedom felt great and it was still possible to have a positive impact. I returned to D.C. for a short visit with some of my fellow workers but generally maintained a low profile. The time spent in D.C. was a rewarding experience, but it was also exhausting.

I left Washington with just enough money for a train ticket to St. Louis, where Bunny met me. I had a short, pleasant stay in the Cape. Bunny's thoughts of a more permanent relationship continued but I was no closer to settling down. I wanted to head for California, but had no cash to get me there. Gradually the idea of hopping a freight train began to take shape.

First Time Hobo

After saying good-bye to Bunny, I stopped to see Uncle Kenny, a wise old Navy veteran and man of the world. Kenny actually served as the "doc" for the first Navy base in Antarctica, which was known as "Operation Deepfreeze." I remember he would often take my brothers and I camping when he was home on leave from some Naval expedition. He would always have interesting and exciting stories about his latest adventure as a U.S. Naval Officer. He had a good chuckle when he found out his nephew wanted to catch a freight train to California. He called a buddy of his who just happened to be a train engineer for one of the local railroads. Kenny's engineer friend said that the Cotton Belt train, part of the Southern Pacific system, passed thru Scott City just eight miles south of the Cape. After leaving Scott City the trains went south to Pine Bluff, Arkansas, where there was a major freight yard with daily trains to California. It all sounded very good to me.

Uncle Kenny taught high school science about half a mile from the rail yards, so he knew exactly where to take me. We put my gear in the back of his pickup truck and headed for the tracks. I was filled with excitement and expectation of what was to come. Kenny dropped me at the rail yard and I settled in to wait for my first freight train. As I strolled around and explored the new environment, I met a teenager and we talked about trains. He said his name was also Jim and that his job was to prepare and then pass lunches to the crew as they slowed the train while passing through the city. I was amazed to find that he also knew Uncle Kenny, who was his science teacher.

The trainmen's lunches were hung in large wicker baskets on the arm of a tower next to the tracks. The "pin lifter" or brakeman would grab the baskets as the train roared past. Jim told me that the southbound would slow slightly to get the lunches, and I'd need to hop on quickly or else miss my chance. I prepared for a run and jump entrance, the tension mounted as the huge monster freight train rumbled toward my hiding place in the bushes. As it rolled past, I made a mad dash for the first open boxcar and threw myself and my gear into its dark interior. I found myself aboard and in for the ride of my life. With pride and joy I checked out the new digs. It was a very dirty and greasy boxcar, probably used to haul old machine tools. In spite of the filthy surroundings, I found it amazing that such a simple thing as jumping on a moving boxcar could bring such satisfaction and pleasure.

The train rolled easily along for a couple of hours before smoothly sliding onto a siding to make way for a northbound freight. We were far from any city, the sun had set and dusk was overtaking the countryside. Music drifted to the boxcar from a nearby farm; not far from the tracks a young girl rode a horse in front of a rickety old barn and disappeared behind a large stand of trees. It was like a Norman Rockwell painting in motion. The sensations were very stimulating, from the constant noise of the moving train, to the exaggerated silence while stopped at some lonely spot in the country. Following a short wait, the freight moved on for an hour or so until it stopped in a swamp where we spent the night. The delay was okay except for the continuous attacks by the very blood-hungry southern mosquitoes. I somehow survived the bug onslaught and was rewarded with a beautiful sunrise as the train jerked to a start.

My first train was not in a hurry to get anyplace, and it stopped many times throughout the day, dropping and picking up cars outside of Little

Rock. The freight continued to travel into the darkness and through many small southern towns; the smell of burning leaves, young people driving up and down Main Street and the neon lights of a carnival all impacted my tired brain. The good old USA passed before my eyes in all its glory. I would learn later in my train-riding career that it was truly a "wooden axle" train, meaning it was about as slow as molasses on a cold winter day. I managed to sleep for a couple of hours and then awoke in Pine Bluff's huge train yard as a very thirsty and dirty novice hobo. The train pulled deep into the bowels of the yard, clanked to a stop, and then there was a deadly silence.

I sat deep in the corner of the greasy boxcar not knowing what to expect. Thirty minutes passed and one of the Cotton Belt yard workers looked inside and said, "Hey, buddy, where you headed?" His friendly disposition was a great relief since my only exposure to such encounters had been via Hollywood movies, where the trainman usually beat the hobo with a huge nightstick and threw him from the moving train. The yard workers were sometimes called "knockers" since much of their job was to "knock" the boxcars into strings of cars which then made up the trains. That knocker told me that the boxcar I had called home for the last couple of days was going nowhere, and would be 'humped' back into the arrival yard. Most railroad yards had a raised portion called a hump, over which strings of boxcars were pushed so that they could then roll down the hump and be switched to certain tracks depending on their individual destination. That process was called "humping" the cars.

The friendly knocker pointed out a train sitting several tracks over and said it was going all the way to Los Angeles. The pleasant rail workers in Pine Bluff gave me a feeling of confidence and I ventured from the boxcar to find water and a place on the westbound. During the walk I met more workers, welders driving a small utility truck between the long strings of cars. We talked about politics and it turned out that one of the welders knew Jack, one of the people I worked with at the White House, that they had been classmates at Pine Bluff High School. The welders gave me a two-gallon plastic jug filled with ice cubes and water. They also pointed me toward a faster train that was also headed west to Los Angeles, and hopefully wouldn't have wooden axles. I found a shady spot near the train and used the cold water to wash the dirt and grease from my hot body. Fruits gleaned from my hobo education so far: always ride in a clean boxcar, and bring plenty of water.

I found a spot on the California train and settled in for the long ride west. After a short wait we started to roll. I began to relax and just enjoy the beautiful scenery that moved before me on the gigantic movie screen of the open boxcar door. Somewhere on the Texas plains the train developed serious problems, and one of the crew told me that a nearby train would get me there faster. I took their advice, saddled up and walked a mile or so to the second train and found a spot under a Marine Corps truck. The disabled freight that I had been riding delayed us for a couple of hours. Once we began to roll, however, it became evident that the new train was high priority. I was forced to hang on tightly just to stay aboard. I estimated our speed to be about seventy miles per hour, which is really something for a mile-long train weighing several thousand tons. There were many beautiful sights as we blasted through Texas, New Mexico, into the Arizona Mountains, and finally the California desert.

A Hollywood Friend

My first train ride ended in La Puente on the outskirts of Los Angeles, where a railroad detective yelled, "Get off my fucking train, you prick!" In spite of the rather rough tone and language the guy actually had a pretty good attitude. My first hobo experience resulted in a four-day trip from Missouri to California and I was feeling pretty good about it.

I walked and hitched the last twenty miles to reach the loving arms of Becky, who had recently left Big Sur to live in Hollywood. The ensuing hot shower was one of the most enjoyable ever experienced. That, along with many beautiful kisses and food revitalized my body and I felt totally satisfied in every way — at 'one' with the universe. Becky had planned a trip north to San Francisco to visit friends and relatives. She invited me to come along and within a couple of hours I found myself off on another adventure. Once again, the body was on the move but now in the company of a beautiful young lady and the comfort of a car. I was discovering that it could be difficult being a hobo, but the time-outs could be very rewarding.

We spent a week in and around San Francisco and then it was back to Hollywood. During that stop I realized how very pleasant it was to have escaped the crazy world of D.C. politics. The current environment was much more suitable for philosophical thought, and would give me the opportunity to reflect on my recent experiences.

Three Gun Gumshoe

Following a wonderful Hollywood/San Francisco stopover with my friend Becky I had to shake my head and ask myself whether such lovely treatment was really deserved. Regardless of the answer, I was ready to travel, so it was back to the tracks. I caught the first train out of the Los Angeles Union Pacific yard and ended up going in the direction of San Diego. Following several stops to drop off boxcars we arrived in the San Diego yards, the smell of the cool salt air wafting into my nostrils. I saddled up and walked about five miles to beautiful Balboa Park and relaxed while watching the city by the sea come alive for another wonderful day.

At dawn I called my sister Maureen, who lived nearby, and she told me to come on over. After we caught up on family news, I headed over to see our parents in Oceanside, about thirty miles north of La Mesa. It was a fun filled couple of days that included a warm bed and never-ending conversation. We said our goodbyes and once again I headed for the iron trail, hoping to go northward.

I waited a couple of hours in the Oceanside rail yard before catching a fast freight for an easy ride to Hobart Junction near Los Angeles. It was an invigorating ten-mile walk from there to the Glendale Southern Pacific, or SP, yards, where a train worker said it was possible to catch a train north. But first, I'd have to catch an eastbound to the Colton yards, about forty miles from Los Angeles near the city of San Bernardino, and then catch a northbound. I hoped to visit my children in Dunlap, California, as well as my cousin Tracy and her husband Troy, who lived in nearby Auberry.

I had a pleasant rest under a bridge in the Southern Pacific yard, then hopped a long eastbound freight and rode on the last engine in a string of six. This was the first time I had ridden in such a plush manner. It was exciting to feel the power of the diesel engines pounding in my ears as they struggled to pull the heavy train to the Colton yards. There were many fellow hobos in the boxcars behind. They appeared to be Latino and I suspected they were mostly undocumented immigrants looking for work in America. A couple hours later we arrived in Colton. In the "receiving yard" the other hobos jumped from the freight cars in droves, headed for the bush carrying their belongings in paper or plastic bags. I climbed down from the engine cab, adjusted my gear, and walked through the main yard toward the "departure yard."

The Colton yard was very large and by the time I reached the departure yard, several miles later, it was time for a rest. A friendly knocker told me which track the north bound would be on. Armed with that information I headed for the outskirts of the yard and settled down. A hobo "jungle" (camp) by the side of the tracks offered the cool shade of a group of large cottonwood trees and a safe resting spot. Soon a train started down the north bound tracks. I gathered my gear and jumped into the first clean boxcar. I was still unsure which direction the train was going since the Colton yard was very confusing. It seemed that the easterly departing trains could go east, north, or even swing one hundred and eighty degrees and head west back to Los Angeles. As it turned out I was blessed with a train that was indeed headed north – the knocker was correct. We soon passed through the city of Oxnard on the Pacific Ocean, then San Luis Obispo and over the mountains to King City. From there it was on to Watsonville and Oakland.

I spent the night in an Oakland boxcar on a train that was said to be going back toward Fresno, which was where I wanted to go. After sunup I ventured out to see why the train had not moved. A couple of friendly knockers in a little shack couldn't tell me anything. They gave me coffee and a full bag of cookies, along with some great conversation, but no information. I walked a few miles to a very quiet Western Pacific yard, looked around, and then hiked back to the Southern Pacific tracks. After talking with several knockers, I learned that the southbound train was called the "Tracy train" and that it would leave at five o'clock that afternoon. I waited around and talked with more workers to make sure the Tracy train was correct information. I had learned during my brief train-hopping career that the knockers did not always know what they were talking about, so it was always a good idea to get a second, third, even fourth opinion. When you heard the same information from three or four workers you could be reasonably sure it would be correct.

Formula for Life

Somehow my Enjoyment of Life (EOL) continued in spite of little food, cold nights, and the long delay in getting to Jimmy and Wendy's house. In fact, I was thinking more and more in terms of the *percentage* of time that I was actually living according to my Enjoyment of Life philosophy. The striving for increased EOL was certainly paying valuable dividends as my personal percentage had gone from an estimated seventy to ninety-seven percent EOL over the past several months. My peace of mind and serenity were in great shape. Since I had to wait the whole day for the train, I made a run to the liquor store and got a couple of cold beers. I then headed for a shady spot by the side of the tracks to relax and reflect on the past few days.

Around lunch time a couple of more experienced hobos came by and invited me to a place nearby to get some free coffee and donuts. The three of us went for lunch; there was fun conversation and plenty to eat, then we headed in different directions. Such brief friendships seemed to be a common occurrence on the tracks.

I made it back to the Southern Pacific tracks and found the "Tracy train." It would travel north for about seventy miles, swing through the Roseville yard at Sacramento, then turn south toward Fresno, before continuing on to Los Angeles. I walked the train and found a clean boxcar that was equipped with old lounge chair. I would ride in style! The knockers warned me to be on the lookout for some "asshole woman gumshoe" that got her kicks by harassing hobos. The story sounded a little fishy, but I stayed in the bushes and out of sight until the train started to move, and then caught the Tracy on the run as it rolled out of the Oakland yard. More than one head turned at highway rail crossings as my train wheeled by with me relaxing in the easy chair. The view from the speeding boxcar was beyond spectacular. Several hours later we rolled into the north end of the Fresno yards. A couple of the yard workers waved me over to their shanty and shared some iced tea, cheese, crackers, and lively conversation. Following this enjoyable experience it was time to find the highway leading to Cousin Tracy in Auberry.

From there I embarked on foot once again until I reached the highway to Auberry, where my cousin lived. I found a nice place to camp on the outskirts of town and decided to get some shut eye before heading for the mountains. At dawn I awoke and walked through the vineyards, stopping to sample the plump seedless green grapes. With my stomach full I could really enjoy the beautiful morning. I walked for a couple more hours and stopped at a little roadside fruit stand where the owner gave me half-dozen very large seedless oranges. Lunch was covered. Then I went over to the highway and stuck out a thump; an elderly gentleman and local rancher gave me a ride the rest of the way to Auberry.

Auberry with Tracy

My cousin Tracy came down the mountain to pick me up, and I showered, shaved, and was treated to a delicious Mexican style lunch. Tracy and husband Troy had two young children and another on the way. They seemed to enjoy life and had many good times living in the relative seclusion offered by the small mountain community. Troy was a "hightower" man for a large electric utility, building and maintaining the huge steel towers that held the high-voltage electrical wires, and earned a good wage for the difficult and dangerous work. The family atmosphere was pleasant and they made me feel very much at home. This novice hobo was pampered with the use of an extra bedroom for a rather nice and very private "jungle."

Tracy and Troy left with the kids for a planned weekend vacation, leaving me alone in the sweet solitude of the central California Mountains. I raised my red, white, and blue on a thirty-foot pole next to the house, where it looked beautiful flapping in the clear mountain air. I spent a day repairing my gear and fixing things around the house. After that I set out to explore the surrounding countryside. From high above the property, I gazed back at the flag waving in the gentle breeze and let the Enjoyment of Life wash over me.

I tended the chickens and worked in the garden as the morning sun rose to penetrate the mountain mist, then I sat and read and thought about the next stop on my exciting journey through life. I began to understand that we all have a power within us that enables us to focus energy like fine-tuning a radio station in a way that would permit us to receive and/or send a beam of energy in a way that added to our Enjoyment of Life. Plans for my departure began to take shape. I hoped to see my children very soon as they were only a hundred miles to the north.

Jimmy and Wendy

I got up before dawn to walk and hitchhike to Dunlap to see Jimmy and Wendy, which ended up being a five-hour journey. At the tiny town's post office-general store I stopped to ask where I might find my kids. The young lady at the store directed me to a house sitting on the other side of a field. It turns out the storekeeper then called to let Wendy know I was coming. To see her run across the field and then jump into my arms brought tears to my eyes. She had grown a lot in the months since my last visit and was full of happy energy. Hanna arrived and we had a nice dinner and then talked late into the night.

Jimmy, my son, was living in Ceres, another small community about fifty miles away. After spending the night in Dunlap I headed for Ceres. Jimmy was a strong young man of fifteen, working on a ranch and making money with the idea of buying a car. We had a nice swim in a fast moving irrigation canal (seemed dangerous to me but Jimmy laughed it off), then for a long walk to bring each other up to date on what had been going on in our lives during the many months of my absence. Jimmy was filled with common sense and it made me feel proud that he was my son. The couple he was staying with, Mike and Christy, were fine people and seemed to be a good influence on him. Christy fixed a great dinner and then we all retired to the living room for a couple hours of good conversation. Jimmy and I found a nice camping spot and spent the night under the stars. We fell asleep talking.

The next morning after a fine breakfast, some good hugs, and a little fatherly advice, I once again headed down the road. I left with a heavy feeling of sadness and yet happy knowing how both were getting along in this world. Seeing Jimmy and Wendy was much like a dream. There was a sense of non-reality that made describing my emotions almost impossible. I loved them both so much and yet was not willing to settle down to a more normal lifestyle. One thing for sure was that they both brought an *extra* measure of joy to this man on the tracks.

Back to the Tracks

I headed to the nearest railroad yard in Bakersfield to see when the next train might be leaving, and lo and behold, there was a southbound just waiting for me. I made myself comfortable in a clean boxcar when a gumshoe appeared out of nowhere and rudely ordered me to identify myself. The guy turned out to be rather unfriendly; actually he was a total asshole. After checking my identification he told me "get the hell out of my yard and if I see you again I'll have your ass in my jail." I slipped into the surrounding darkness, happy to be a free man. I learned later from some more experienced hobos that the Bakersfield Southern Pacific yard was home of the infamous railroad detective known as "Three-gun Gumshoe." Old Three-gun's name came from the number of firearms he carried with him, and he was reputed to have a very itchy trigger finger. Three-gun seemed to fulfill my Hollywood built fantasy about what life on the tracks should be like. But I was young and brash and decided to hide in the shadows and, at the last minute, try to catch a freight train on the run as it exited the yard.

Within a couple of hours, I caught a train on the run, extremely happy to be traveling south on the tracks far from the clutches of Three-gun. It wasn't long before my boxcar was rolling into Los Angeles and, feeling just a little cocky after the brush with the Bakersfield gumshoe, I jumped off at the north end of the Glendale yard with a little extra flair and caught a city bus to visit friends in the San Fernando Valley.

Van Meter Estate

First stop was the Van Meter Estate in Sherman Oaks, one of the valley's more affluent communities. Dan Van Meter was a very interesting fellow, aged sixty-eight, who had helped with my campaign when I ran for state office in 1976 and 1978. He owned about three acres of land in the center of an area where land values had skyrocketed. Dan refused to sell even though he was offered many millions of dollars. Dan was one of the early residents of the valley and just didn't want to leave his homestead, which had become a green oasis surrounded by new office and residential-buildings. Dan's homestead was covered with the various things he collected over the years, that it was almost like a museum of the history of the San Fernando Valley. There was the horse drawn coach used by a Van Nuys High School teacher at the turn of the century. Many cars that spanned the last seventy years were tucked into old chicken coops next to file cabinets and antiques of all sorts. There was a forty-foot ocean going cabin cruiser "floating" under the tall eucalyptus trees. Dan was a unique character with something to say on just about any subject you wished to discuss. His main interest was in government and the foreign and domestic threats that faced our nation. We talked nonstop while walking about the property taking care of the animals that had taken up residence there. We talked late into the night. I opened my bed roll on the porch of the first cabin to be built on the property and fell into a deep sleep. The night passed quickly and soon the roosters announced the arrival of morning as sun filtered through the trees. It was the start of another beautiful day.

Enjoyment of Life

I called nurse Bunny who, to my surprise, told me she was engaged to be married. It became very obvious that she was not waiting around for this cinder walking hobo. There appeared to be no hard feelings. Many moments of diminished EOL (actually sadness) were felt over the next several weeks. It gave me another opportunity to more closely examine my EOL philosophy from a very personal perspective. I sometimes thought that the EOL philosophy was too self-centered. Perhaps it was the self-centeredness of EOL that kept us apart.

My situation with Bunny encouraged me to think about relationships and how they related to Enjoyment of Life and the Formula for Life. One aspect of maintaining relationships involved a construct called a "Space/Time Marker Value" or simply STMV. The concept of a STMV rested on the idea that everything in our environment had a potential to produce a measurable impact on our mind and/or body. Such impact left an impression and as individuals we were responsible as to the degree to which we were impacted and/or influenced. In other words all events occurred in Space and Time and had a Marker Value. The Value was determined by our ability to selectively absorb or shut out events that we classified as enjoyable or non-enjoyable. STMV's were different for each individual for it was impossible for any two people to have exactly the same experience. Thus, the importance or *value* of our experience became a very personal matter. People could not experience the *same* things exactly and to the *same* degree therefore the *values* we assigned to events were different. The size of such differences determined how successful people formed individual relationships and with the larger communities of man.

Hobo's Limousine Ride

I set out from the Van Meter Estate on a hike to meet brother Tom for breakfast in Northridge. As I walked toward Balboa Park a long black limousine pulled up next to me and slowed. From the open window, the driver said, "Hey buddy, you wanna a ride?" I hopped in, grinning from ear-to-ear, and got some interesting looks when the pleasant limo driver dropped me in front of the very busy Encino tennis courts.

Tom, his wife Doreen, and I had a nice breakfast and they invited me to stay at their place for a few days. The next morning we got up early and headed for Malibu Beach to do some fishing and managed to bring home a nice dinner. At dawn it was a short walk to my alma mater, California State University at Northridge, and I spent most of the day reading in the library.

I had a pleasant stroll on campus and enjoyed the beauty of everything our Creator had given us. It seemed to me that the value of the material world was mostly in the pleasant sensations that were elicited in the mind. The image of a magnificent tree could be visualized through the eye or by conjuring up a picture in the mind. Such mental activity could elicit the identical physical and mental sensations as when actually looking at a tree. It just happened to take more energy to form the thought-picture than to passively absorb the image through the eye. It was also our personal responsibility to either ignore or to absorb this energy through our sense organs. This was accomplished by carefully assigning STMVs to our observations, especially when they were perceived as valuable reflections of the physical world. By looking, really looking at the world reflections in slightly different ways, one's life could be made more interesting. Such "looking" would be practiced as my journey through life continued.

I saddled up late in the afternoon and headed out to visit some friends of mine, Mike and Bob, in the hills of Sherman Oaks, where a wild party was just getting under way. It got even wilder when someone produced a blue bottle of nitrous oxide —great fits of uncontrollable laughter ensued. At dawn I caught the city bus to the Glendale Amtrak Station, and walked from there down the cinder trail toward the freight yards. It was time for another adventure, and I figured this time I'd head Arizona-way to check up on Marlene.

Soon I was aboard a clean boxcar on an eastbound freight being lulled by the comforting sound of the steel wheels beginning to roll — hobo music. I relaxed and focused my mind to dwell on the just finished walk through the railroad yard and all the pleasant sensations evoked by the surroundings, giving it a high STMV. It occurred to me that we should all take the time and energy to recognize how easy it was to meld into a given situation and blend into its mental and physical environment. Such behavior made life a little easier and therefore less energy consuming. Sometimes you just had to take the time and energy to unravel the mind and put thought/ideas in order. Every path, or train for that matter, could result in an enjoyable and valuable experience and it was totally within our power to make it that way.

The Tracks to Arizona

The train rolled through the Southern California desert at an easy pace and stopped at a railroad siding called "Cactus Junction" to wait for cleanup of a derailed freight several miles ahead. The railroad van eventually arrived and the crew hopped aboard, leaving me alone in the middle of a hot desert.

The silence was unnerving, but I had no choice but to deal with it, since I was out there for almost two days before the crew came back and took it into Yuma, Arizona. I spent a day in that desert town, cleaned up in a railroad shack, and hopped a freight headed for Tucson, where I managed to catch the northbound. When the train slowed in Tempe, and I realized it wasn't going to stop, I had to jump for it. Unscathed once again, I walked the mile or so to Marlene's apartment.

We got up early and headed for the campus, she to her classes and the library for me. It was a gorgeous morning with the warm sun and gentle breezes filtering streams of light through the many campus trees. I felt a special union with all life that morning. It seemed that my reverence for my life was somehow extended beyond myself and thus all life became part of the current experience. Having such a point of view meant that "good" was to maintain life, to bring life to its highest *value* by sharing life and all it had to offer. Once we learned to make all life part of your experience it made life more enjoyable. Or in other words, it took less energy to enjoy our environment. We often failed to appreciate our Creator's gifts perhaps because we were eager for the next gift, impatient for the future and unable to enjoy the current moment.

I recognized that people and things were constantly directing energy at our senses and it was up to each individual to filter, receive and then assign values (STMV) to each incoming stimulus. The stimulus that failed to add to our life experience in an enjoyable way must be assigned a low value or simply not processed. By doing this, as we traveled through life, it was hoped that we would learn from past experiences. Such learning would then tell us where to place our physical body in relationship to enjoyable stimuli.

After a few days of wallowing in such stimuli with Marlene, she gave me a ride to the Phoenix train yard. We kissed goodbye and I settled in on an old wooden bench in front of a trainmen's shanty. Music drifted through the late afternoon air from some unknown source. The knockers were banging a train together somewhere in the yard. Before long I was on a boxcar rolling through the desert sand southbound on wooden axles. The train reached Tucson in the morning and while looking for an eastbound a Southern Pacific gumshoe spotted me. We talked for several minutes before he did his job and told me, rather sternly, to leave Southern Pacific property: "You'll go to jail for sure if I catch you in my rail yard again." We parted on friendly terms, nevertheless, and I left the yard and headed for the park.

Several hours later, in the dark of night, I snuck back into the yard and caught a train heading east toward Texas. It was a "hot shot," a fast train that stopped only for fuel and crew changes. My hot shot had a brief layover in El Paso then jerked to a start and we were east bound once again. The Southern Pacific tracks went through southwest Texas where the towns were few and far between. There was one little town of Sanderson that served as a fuel stop for cross country trains. While waiting during the fueling operation in the open boxcar I noticed several individuals laughing and joking in a park near the tracks. Some of the locals were having a beer party and waved at me to join them. After a few very cold beers, I learned that they were all off-duty railroad workers. The train let out one long blast on its whistle signaling that it was about to leave and the party was over for me. I walked to my boxcar with a bigger smile and an ice-cold beer in the cargo pocket. Another interesting town along the tracks was Valentine, which served as crew change point in that rather desolate part of Texas. Valentine looked like something right out of a Hollywood cowboy movie with its dirt streets and small wooden store fronts. It looked like it might be a nice quiet place to live, perhaps a place to settle for a while.

The train came to a stop on a railroad siding someplace near San Antonio. After a minute or so a small plane started to buzz the train—caboose to engine, engine to caboose and then back again. It wasn't long before a hand slapped the open railcar's door and a uniformed Border Patrol Agent effortlessly swung up and into my boxcar and asked, "Have you seen any Mexicans on this train?" Since he looked Mexican I told him, "Only you." He flashed a wide grin and without saying a word jumped out the other side to continue his hunt. Several hours later the train pulled into a small yard to pick up some boxcars and a heavy thunderstorm hit, providing an awesome display of nature's power. I disembarked in the Houston yard and scouted for a northbound, finally catching the "rabbit" train that was about to leave for Shreveport, Louisiana.

Sometime in the early morning darkness the train came to a stop in the middle of a pine forest. We sat on the main line tracks for about two hours for reasons that I could not discern. Impatient, I saddled up and headed for the front end to talk with the engineer. After a long and rather difficult hike it was a surprise to find only a boxcar where there should have been engines. It was very quiet with only the sounds of the night creatures in the air. I then hiked the entire length of the train to the back end to talk with the guys in the "crummy," or the caboose. A couple of guys were smoking on the back of the crummy and were surprised to see me emerge from the darkness. It was a relief to find that I was not totally abandoned. The trainmen assured me that the engines would return and we'd be on our way soon. Back at my boxcar, just as the sun was rising through the morning fog, we jolted to a start in that beautiful and serene pine forest. The "rabbit" arrived in Shreveport at about ten in the morning, and I found out from one of the geese (yard workers) that I could catch a northbound in that afternoon. I found a nice pond near the tracks and cooled my hot feet in the water and black Louisiana mud before catching the northbound train.

I arrived at the Cape in the early morning after a long walk from the railyard. My sister Jeanne picked me up and took me to the farm where we had a great meal of ham, beans and lots of cold watermelon. After the prior few days of nothing but dry oatmeal, everything tasted especially good.

Jeanne and I did some work in the garden, planting a row of giant California radishes while also picking a bushel of large red tomatoes. At dusk, we all retired to the screened in porch for a relaxing evening of conversation with Jeanne, Dave and their son Jerry. I made a camp in the basement and relaxed in Grandpa Oliver's rocking chair and just let my mind drift in this very restful atmosphere. A sudden storm hit with deafening thunder, great flashes of lightning and torrents of rain, and I opened the basement door to more closely experience the drama.

I sometimes wondered what people thought when they saw me walking, carrying my rucksack and leaving a normal life behind. Did they see a down-on-his luck hobo, a free spirit, unburdened by material goods, or a threat? Perhaps every individual saw something different. Could I project valuable energy that would overcome any fear people had of this mysterious track walker? And is it possible to discern the degree of positive energy in another person?

It was a quiet Sunday morning on the farm and everyone had gone to church, so I took a long walk down the lane, and then along the graveled creek bed with all the pleasant sights and sounds one might expect on a cool Missouri morning: church bells in the distance, birds chirping, a bellowing cow and the distant throbbing of Mississippi riverboats. Even in these bucolic surroundings thoughts of moving on entered my mind.

Political Sparks

It was a beautiful Monday morning when I hitched a ride with Dave into town. Visited with townspeople by the side of the river and then humped my gear to the Central Inn for a couple of early morning beers. Why not? I was on the move once again. My plan was to take a Cotton Belt train to St. Louis and meet up with my friend Don, a political operative, and perhaps do some work for Carter's Missouri campaign.

I caught a long slow freight into East St. Louis and then jumped on a shuttle train to cross the Mississippi and on to the Twelfth Street railroad yards. A couple of gumshoes spotted me in the yard, pulled me aside, and roughly searched my person and gear. I guessed that they were bored and had nothing else to do but harass a hobo. After those two jokers turned me loose, I walked toward St. Louis's Gateway Arch to catch a couple of hours of sleep on the riverbank. In the morning I visited the arch and watched a film on its construction before starting the five-mile hike to Carter's Missouri State campaign headquarters.

Non-Enjoyment of Life

I found a cool, green city park near the headquarters and tried to relax, but found myself troubled. Non-EOL, or unhappiness, had been slipping into my life over the past several days—a rather rare occurrence. I understood that such feelings could be pushed out of my mind but only with a tremendous amount of focused energy. Such non-EOL made me feel like running somewhere to hide, but where? Would establishing a base camp, a place to call home, erase the non-EOL? Would such a base provide a place to be near familiar objects, a place that would substantiate the reality that I had been someplace and would go someplace? The non-EOL seemed to be related to living a reality where time and becoming "successful" was important. Where would my body be tomorrow? Where was it yesterday? Did it really make any difference? No matter how hard I tried to think in terms of having no base, the thought of having someplace to go remained attractive. The vision of Valentine, Texas or some such place was comforting for my soul; such thoughts could not be denied.

Missouri Politics

I spent a couple of hours in a nearby shopping area with a couple of rather bright homeless men. We shared whiskey and had a great conversation about the world situation and U.S. politics. It was a very interesting discussion and motivated the decision to spend some time with the campaign before hitting the iron trail once again.

Gradually my Enjoyment of Life was returning. A special interest in examining non-EOL had encouraged me to keep tract of the amount of time that unhappiness was present. I estimated that such feelings had been present for about eight hours over the past few days. Walking to meet Don I began, more and more, to return to my more usual happy self and the humor of life once again infused my spirit.

Don and I had a good meeting and the dinner, conversation and beer all combined to rapidly accelerate the increase in EOL. To top it off one of the D.C. ladies invited me to stay with her while in St. Louis. While sharing the small hotel space we got to know one another quite well. Perhaps the body and spirit needed this kind of interpersonal attention once in a while. During my conversations with Brenda, I concluded that having a base, someplace to call home, would greatly reduce the amount of energy necessary to maintain EOL.

The Experiment

A crude "experiment" to evaluate the benefit of the projection of valuable energy was to think of extremely pleasant situations in the presence of others. I could then observe the effects on myself as well as on others. If the projection of thoughts had a positive effect on others then it could be observed and perhaps even measured. Such projection of pleasant thoughts could remain in the memory because of the high Space/Time Marker Value (STMV) that we had previously assigned them. The concept of STMV was related to thoughts and ideas and the effect they had on the physiological brain. The higher the STMV for a particular thought or experience, either internal or external, the more *impact* it had on the brain matter. That impact resulted because thoughts and/or ideas actually had a specific weight or mass. The mass was dependent on the amount of energy you put into such thoughts. You could therefore influence your future path by thoughtfully and carefully assigning STMVs to incoming stimuli.

Back to Politics and Trains

I spent the first day at campaign headquarters making phone calls and taking care of items on a "to do" list that had grown considerably since leaving California. The next day was much of the same, and per conversations with the D.C. Headquarters' I decided to head east. A final pleasant evening spent with Brenda definitely ranked high for STMV. She dropped me at the Twelfth Street rail yards on a dazzling sunshine filled morning.

The day before an older black gentleman running a shoe shine stand in the plaza had struck up a conversation with me. We had talked for a short time and I decided to spend my last bit of money for a shine on the black combat boots. We negotiated a price and I emptied out my pockets, literally, to pay him all of ninety-five cents. It seemed like a silly thing to do but it did bring EOL.

Later, as I walked through the railroad yard, someone called from behind a screen door: "Hey buddy, do you want a cup of coffee?" I climbed the short flight of steps, opened the door and stepped into a boxcar that had been converted into a kitchen on wheels. The Gangi cook, as the railroad crew cook was called, pointed to a large stainless-steel pot filled with a steaming black liquid. We sipped hot coffee and talked as he continued his work, making thick ham sandwiches and carefully wrapping them in wax paper. I wondered if he noticed my watchful eyes following his every move. He put a couple of the sandwiches in a crisp brown paper bag along with a generous handful of homemade chocolate chip cookies. We said goodbye as he handed me the lunch bag and wished me luck. I grinned and thanked him heartily and continued my hike feeling so blessed and happy with life at that moment, even after discovering that I'd have to hoof it all the way to East St. Louis to catch a train to D.C.

I started across the Mississippi River on the General Douglas MacArthur Railroad Bridge. Halfway across the bridge a heavy freight train slowly clanked toward me, and slowed to a stop with the "strawberry patch" (the caboose) next to me. An older, grey haired man slowly emerged and told me that the most direct line to D.C. was the Baltimore and Ohio Railroad, and that the yard for the B&O railroad was four miles down the tracks. As his train jolted to a start he hollered, "Are you broke?" Before I could answer he took out his wallet and handed me a dollar bill. We waved to one another as his train slowly jangled across the bridge. My smile was still growing. Just a few hours earlier I had no money or food; now I had both, thanks to the kindness of my fellow man.

It was almost noon when I got to the B&O yard and found a boxcar with plenty of clean cardboard with which to make a warm bed. I managed to get some sleep before we reached Cincinnati, waking occasionally to watch the small towns slide by—oftentimes the tracks ran directly down the main drag. At the Cincinnati yard some knockers told me I could catch the "cucumber"; I guessed it got its name from its destination of Cumberland, Maryland. The yard geese invited me to their lunch/break room since the "cucumber" was not due to "shine" (leave the yard) for several hours. As knockers came and went thoughts about my future and where this hobo was headed leaked into my head. However, this time non-EOL was not allowed into my thoughts. It was very clear that any vision of the future not adding to Enjoyment of Life *must* be instantly put out of one's mind, without exception. There was no reason which justified any kind of unpleasant vision of the future. While keeping that in mind, thoughts about getting a job and earning some money entered my mind—what a novel thought! The dollars could be used to improve my traveling gear and perhaps start saving to enough to purchase a piece of land on which to pitch a tent—a place to call home.

I spent the day with the Cincinnati rail workers, engaged in fantastic conversations, sharing lunches and having many hearty laughs. One of the men responsible for "making up" the cucumber said to relax in the air-conditioned lunch room. He said he would find a spot in a clean boxcar for my ride toward D.C. Later, as we approached the tracks the cucumber appeared to be leaving the yard and was rapidly picking up speed. The knocker saw the concern on my face and told me not to worry, he'd found me a clean boxcar and would radio the engineer to stop the train for an easy boarding. This was a first! As my pre-selected boxcar approached, the knocker radioed the engineer who then brought the train to a complete stop. He then handed me a newspaper and two dollars. "Use the money to get a chicken fried steak on down tracks," he said. People could sure be friendly and so very helpful – it was uplifting for the body and soul.

Throughout the day we lazily rolled down the tracks while stopping for many faster trains. Train riding was not exactly rapid transit, but I couldn't exactly bitch about the price. The knockers said that my slow train would be held up for several hours, but that a St. Louis hotshot would be coming through any time. It sounded like a good deal, so I exited the cucumber and found a place to relax while waiting for the fast train. On that train the engineer invited me to ride in the engine, so long as I stayed out of sight.

The B&O was part of the Chessie System; it had been the most fun to ride and the workers the most helpful. Maybe they admired me for having thrown off the shackles of society to live free on the tracks. Maybe they yearned for the same and wanted to live vicariously through me. The valuable energy projection experiment might have also played a role. Or perhaps they just felt good because their position in life appeared to be much better after seeing me on the tracks.

The engineer's chair in the second locomotive was comfortable and offered a great view of the countryside as our hotshot flashed down the tracks. We passed many trains which had pulled onto sidings to let our high priority cargo train sail on its way east. After we rolled to a stop in a small freight yard, the brakeman came back to my engine and told me that a new crew would soon be taking over and he handed me a few dollars for dinner. He warned me to stay out of sight until we left the next station since the gumshoes were "usually out looking for hobos on this hotshot." I hid in what the rail-workers called the "shitter" until the train was well on its way. As I emerged from my hiding spot I found a much older black man sitting in the brakeman's chair. He was startled to see me, but before long we started a pleasant conversation. Rufus told me that he had been riding the freights for most of his life. We rode together until the next crew change in Grafton, West Virginia, where he climbed off and cheerfully wished me "good luck" as the train came to a stop.

The three-thousand-horse-power engine was now all mine. The ride was much smoother than in the boxcars. The B&O tracks ran abreast of the very beautiful Potomac River for many miles and passed through historic "Harper's Ferry," a peaceful and quaint little town in the West Virginia Mountains. The train rolled on for several miles and came to a stop in Brunswick, Maryland where it took on yet another crew. Brunswick was a beautiful historic small town of about five-thousand souls that was founded in the late 1700s. The main part of the town was located between the B&O tracks and an inland waterway.

The train rolled through Silver Spring, Maryland, on the outskirts of D.C., early Sunday morning as a special steam-powered train approached from the opposite direction. Hundreds of people stood along the tracks to catch a glimpse of the old steam engine as it passed. The great plume of white smoke could be seen from many miles away, the magnificent sight was a special treat on that bright, sunny Sunday morning in our nation's capital. My train traveled on for several miles and slowed just enough for me to make an easy exit near the Rhode Island Avenue subway station. I had a few bucks in my pocket so I decided to ride the subway into D.C. It felt great to have found a way to get around our country with little or no money. America was still the best place to be, by a long shot.

The Capitol
I walked along the Mall toward the Capitol building, looking around and absorbing the many good sensations that seemed to be a natural part of this quiet Sunday morning. It was about six o'clock and the streets and pathways were deserted except for a few joggers. I had tried and failed to reach some friends to see about sleeping on someone's couch during my stay, so I kept my eyes open for a place to bed down for the night. Ended up at the Organization of American States (OAS) building which was near the Washington Monument. I found a place to sleep behind the Organization of American States building near the Washington Monument. The large covered garden area looked like a nice place to spend the night. Having found a "secure" campsite, I headed for the reflecting pool in front of the Lincoln Memorial to do some tourist watching.

 Nightfall arrived with a rapidly changing weather situation; storm clouds were gathering as I rushed for my bivouac at the OAS building and I got under cover just in the nick of time. The storm struck with thunder, lightning and lots of wind driven rain – but it was very pleasant in my sheltered spot, where I was awestruck by the storm's violence, especially after the hot, calm day. The Washington Monument glowed over the tops of nearby wind-blown trees. The surface of the large fish pond, directly in front of my campsite, seemed to be alive in a wild splashing dance of water. Somehow it was peaceful in spite of the crashing noise of thunder, flashing lightning and savage wind.

 I awoke in the pre-dawn darkness and crawled from the bedroll into the cool, damp air. Sitting on the cold stone and peering into the darkness a strange feeling of extreme confidence and yet loneliness entered my mind. The feeling was definitely related to non-EOL and therefore required some deep introspection to answer why it was present. It was as if my mind was flashing from non-EOL to EOL and back at lightning speed. I could not remember ever experiencing a similar feeling. It then dawned on me that it may be impossible to mentally and physically feel exactly the same as sometime in the past. From a purely physiological standpoint a feeling was impossible to duplicate since the chemical and electrical properties of the neurons and synapses were completely changed from one experience to the next. All of life was new—each moment in time was *never* the same!

Further thought brought me to the conclusion that part of the non-EOL feeling related to my physical appearance. Having not figured out how to stay kempt while riding the freights, I often was unshaven with dirty blue jeans and unpolished boots. Until I figured out a way to do laundry on the freights, I decided I would need to come to terms with my shabbiness. I decided to first teach myself how to overcome the difficulties of interacting with people and society while being dirty and unshaven. I would also learn how to equip myself in the future (with very little money) to make a cleaner and therefore a more respectful appearance.

I had learned to shed my worries about having no money. Perhaps total EOL would become a reality when the desire for such things as clean clothes and shaved face were also eliminated. I decided to overcome these self-perceived barriers to EOL by projecting valuable energy in spite of my rather grungy appearance. I spent the day talking with tourists while consciously radiating as much valuable energy as possible. It seemed to work. It was certainly possible to overcome outward appearances. The trick was to overcome non-valuable feedback, to somehow transcend the physical and to only think in spiritual terms.

I cleaned up in the public bathrooms at the Air and Space Museum. Having previously communicated by letters with a member of the director's staff at the FBI Headquarters, I called him to set up a meeting. Later that day I met with an FBI official with whom I'd corresponded regarding my concern about trains as a potential terrorist's target. He informed me that my concerns were worthy, but that the FBI was terribly short of field agents at this time because they had seven-hundred agents working on nothing but FOIA (Freedom of Information Act) requests. Can you imagine that? It seemed like a terrible waste to have full-time FBI agents working at clerical duties.

After the meeting it was a short trek to the Capitol, where candidate Reagan was scheduled to attend a large rally, then on to Lafayette Park, across the street from the White House, where I made some phone calls on the payphone and relaxed in the shade of a giant tree as the sun slipped beneath the horizon. The park became quiet as I dug into my dinner of beans and crackers. I wandered over behind the White House and sat down on the cold marble of the Memorial to the Second Armies War Dead and very soon fell into a deep sleep.

I awoke at dawn thinking about whether I should stay in D.C. or head west once again. After spending the day trying to get in touch with old friends and colleagues without success, I decided to get the hell out of the crazy city.

North Platte Slammer

It felt great to be on the move, walking down Rhode Island Avenue and on the way to the Baltimore and Ohio rail yards. It was late evening and the city was quiet aside from shouts from the shadows: "Hey boy what you doing? Where you going?" I was happy and relieved that it went no farther than words and learned only later that many of the neighborhoods I had walked through were considered unsafe because of open heroin use as well as rampant prostitution.

My immediate goal upon arriving at the yards was to get the hell out of D.C., but I wasn't going to risk life and limb by trying to catch any of the high-speed trains rolling by. After watching more fast trains speed past, I climbed the long staircase to an elevated terminal control tower to seek information. The railroad workers were very friendly, and after telling them California was my destination, they said they'd try to slow a westbound enough for me to hitch a ride. I found a place with good running room and hunkered down to wait. A few moments later, to my surprise, two female railroad workers emerged from the darkness and actually stopped to talk to this hobo. One of them was straight-up beautiful—she could have been on the cover of Playboy magazine! They truly seemed to be out of place in this dark railroad yard at two o'clock in the morning. We had a lively conversation, but my I failed to charm them into going somewhere and having a party. Nevertheless, I felt blessed as they excitedly talked and giggled and disappeared into the blackness of this otherwise gloomy train yard.

A train soon came roaring down the tracks, it slowed just a little and with an adrenaline-fueled burst of speed, I managed to pull myself into a boxcar.

Indecision and Non-EOL

The train stopped someplace in western Maryland, giving me a chance to take a breather and reflect on the value of being out of D.C. One of the most obvious benefits was that I didn't need to expend a lot of energy to project happiness, because feeling happy was more natural on the tracks and outside of the busy metropolis.

One valuable philosophical lesson I learned was that the state of *indecision* was definitely related to non-EOL. Non-EOL had definitely started to slip into my consciousness when I was hemming and hawing about leaving D.C. Happily, I figured out that the indecision was causing the non-EOL and I was able to correct the situation by biting the bullet and getting the hell out town. When such *indecision* was converted to a *decision*, unhindered Enjoyment of Life returned immediately.

Back on the Iron Trail

My freight train reached the pleasant town of Cumberland by nine o'clock. One of the knockers told me that one of the fast west bound trains I had missed the previous night had derailed, tossing thirty cars over the side of the mountain and destroying a mile of track. My guardian angel was with me once again. It would take two days to clear the tracks and make repairs, meaning I would be stuck in Cumberland for a bit. The delay didn't worry me in the least.

An old hobo sitting in another boxcar said he planned to pick the fall crop of apples. He had been doing it for ten years, but was worried that it might not last much longer because the farmers were hiring immigrant labor, instead. A bit later I stopped to talk to a middle-aged man who told me that he used to hop the freights like me, but that now he worked for the railroad.

I spent most of the day walking around the city and talking with several of its residents. They were friendly and very proud of their railroad-based community. There was a grandmotherly lady working in her yard who told me to help myself to her apple tree. It wasn't long before my rucksack was stuffed with big juicy apples, adding some variety to my hobo pantry which was stocked only with oatmeal. Back at the freight yard I learned that the mainline west would be closed for at least another day, but that I could hop on a slow train to Collinsville. I had the need to move, so I climbed aboard the last engine and settled in.

Somewhere in Pennsylvania one of the crew told me that the train I was on would go up to Chicago before heading for California. I wasn't excited about taking that sort of detour, but would stay on board unless something better came along. Besides, the northern route would give me a chance to visit my sister, Mary Kay, who lived in South Dakota. The train rolled right into the heavy industrial sections of Pittsburgh, where I watched the magnificent displays of blazing sparks and fires erupting from the steel mills in that dark night.

The train came to an unexpected stop in New Castle, Pennsylvania, so I jumped aboard another one, just to keep moving. At one of its many stops a friendly trainman hollered back and invited me to come join the crew in the engine. We shared some candy and talked about the messed-up politics of the world.

The steel mills of Youngstown were an impressive sight even though many looked deserted and were in various states of decay. Soon after we finally pulled away, the alarm sounded, an indication that I should head into the engine compartment to hide from possible gumshoes. While I was there the train sped up considerably. The sounds and vibrations generated by the three-thousand-horsepower engine were very stimulating. My body seemed very fragile as it huddled next to that massive engine. Inside my hiding place the engine sounded like a jet fighter roaring down a runway toward an afterburner takeoff. The friendly engineer soon came back to my hiding spot and told me that the gumshoes were gone and he was going to pick up another locomotive, making the train even faster.

It was just getting dark as we slowly pulled into the small railroad town of Willard, Ohio about twenty-five miles south of the Lake Erie shoreline. The train slid to an easy stop and I jumped from my boxcar plopped my tired body down on an old wooden bench with a couple of friendly yard geese. They brought me a hot cup of coffee and told me to make myself at home in the railroad shack. Would you believe that he even told me to help myself to sandwiches?

The Chicago bound train left Willard right on time and rolled west for a few hours before we stopped on the outskirts of another small town, where I jumped off and helped myself to the bounty of an apple tree by the side of the tracks.

Riding the freights is all about going with the flow, jumping from a slow train to a fast one, taking a northbound in order to go west, or vice versa. It's also about gleaning information from the geese in the rail yards. As chaotic as a big railyard can be, I usually was able to get to my destination, eventually. In some unknown railyard I was pointed toward a fast train known as the Country Club Special that was loaded down with military equipment. It got up to about seventy miles per hour—a true highballer!

We were traveling on a double track and another train approached from the west at what seemed to be an equally high rate of speed, which was an exciting and interesting sensation. At each stop George, the engineer, came back to talk to me and give advice on how to make my west coast connection. On his last visit, outside the Chicago yard, he handed me a peanut butter sandwich and warned me about the gumshoes in the yard ahead.

It was soon evident that George was correct about the gumshoes. And I spent most of my time in the Chicago yard hiding under boxcars and trying to stay out of sight. The air felt threatening and oppressive. With immense relief I finally found a spot on a train bound for Minneapolis. I crawled into the bed of a truck loaded on a flatcar and immediately fell into a deep sleep. Just before sunrise the train bumped to a start. I decided then and there to avoid the Chicago rail yards during future travels.

First Time Arrest by Gumshoe

The train made frequent stops and moved along at about thirty miles per hour through a relentless downpour. I huddled under some heavy cardboard-like packing material to stay somewhat dry and warm. By late afternoon we pulled into the Milwaukee yard and ground to a stop. The yard did not seem any friendlier than the one in Chicago so I stayed out of sight until the train bumped to a start after a short delay. About ten miles later the train stopped in the small community of Wauwatosa, where I spotted a gumshoe, looking mighty unhappy, walking my way. He saw me, pulled his gun, and with a shaking hand pointed it directly at me. He ordered me to get off the train and lie face-down on the rocky ground. "Put your fucking hands behind your back," he ordered in a shaky voice. Cold steel handcuffs were then snapped very tightly around my wrists. He gruffly ordered me to get up and go to his patrol car and pushed me into the backseat.

After about thirty minutes a grey-haired policeman, with sergeant stripes, pulled up in a local police car and joined the party. The gumshoe proudly presented me to the sergeant. So there we stood, behind an old warehouse next to the tracks, with the gumshoe and the policeman trying to sort out what to do with this criminal trespasser. "For Christ's sake, take the cuffs off," the sergeant said. The nervous gumshoe sheepishly removed the cuffs, muttering that he suspected that I was part of the notorious "salt and pepper" gang. That brought a chuckle from the calm and cool sergeant. The gumshoe insisted that the policeman arrest me for trespassing. The sergeant radioed his watch commander for instructions. With an apologetic tone, and perhaps a touch of sadness, he said, "I have no choice but I'll have to take you to jail." During the ride downtown, the sergeant told me he thought that the gumshoe was most likely a police academy dropout and perhaps on a power trip.

At the police station cops and detectives rifled through the political notes and White House documents I was carrying in my rucksack. They questioned me in a light-hearted way. They definitely did not want to lock me in their jail. The watch commander called a judge for advice as to how to handle the situation. Thankfully, the judge told them to turn me loose. The friendly cops decided that I needed to get cleaned up a bit and offered me the use of their locker room. The kindly sergeant proudly told me that "no civilian has ever used this locker room before--you're the first." After the truly privileged hot shower and shave, my enjoyment was very much in evidence.

The sergeant loaded me into the squad car—the front seat this time, and took me down to the tracks. With a broad smile he told me: "You now have two choices, but if you get caught on the tracks we'll both be in trouble."

I tried to thumb a ride on the highway for about an hour, got impatient and walked the short distance to the railroad tracks to wait for a slow train. After five or six hours, as it was beginning to get dark and cold, I tried my luck hitching again. Finally a nice, older couple picked me up. After they dropped me off, I got another ride with a friendly young couple, Jim and Ann, from Madison, Wisconsin—the locals called it Madtown. They had an ice chest full of beers and offered me one, then another and another. We had a lively conversation, lubricated by many beers, mostly about the life of a hobo. They dropped me off at the Portage rail yard.

After asking around I learned that the westbound 205 would be arriving soon, so I found a clean boxcar, stretched out, unrolled the bedroll and got some much-needed shuteye. It started to rain and the chill of the fall season had definitely arrived. However, my bedroll kept me comfortable on that cool, rainy and windy night. A few hours later the "205" pulled into the yard, but I soon found out that it would be going nowhere. It seems the heavy rain had caused a mud slide and all the tracks of the main line were closed. It was three o'clock in the morning, the rain and wind had stopped and all was quiet and peaceful, so I decided to take a walk around the area. I came upon an attractive young lady and her boyfriend quietly sitting in a boxcar, waiting on a southbound. "We like to ride the rails just for the fun and excitement – it's not the usual kind of date," the woman said. They both lived in Milwaukee, about seventy miles to the south, and said they enjoyed getting away from the city by riding the freights several times a year. The three of us sat in the boxcar for a couple of hours discussing philosophy, trains, and politics.

I headed back to the 205, which was just getting ready to leave. A little before sunrise the 205 and I were gently rolling through the beautiful Wisconsin countryside dotted by many lakes and rivers. We stopped at a village by a blue lake to pick up boxcars just as the sun was burning through the heavy morning mist; it was another wonderful Sunday morning and Enjoyment of Life was easily maintained.

Freight trains were a fantastic way to see the often-hidden beauty of USA. It was late in the afternoon as we crossed the mighty Mississippi at La Crosse and headed north toward Minneapolis. It took most of a long, cold night to reach Minneapolis and I began to look forward to getting west and south to a warmer climate.

Value in Everything

I spent the day in the Minneapolis yard before finally finding a clean boxcar on a train going southward and settled in for the ride. It was very cold. As we clanked down the tracks I thought about my experience with the Wauwatosa gumshoe and police. The memories brought a smile to my face as it was easy to identify the value of that situation. Some of the value resided within all the interesting people I interacted with. The evidence appeared to support my philosophy that there was Value in Everything (VIE) if you just looked hard enough. The VIE concept was turning into one of the basic tenets in the further development of my Formula for Life. VIE simply meant that every path could be a good (valuable) one; but that it was up to each individual to accept the responsibility to identify the value in *all* our life experiences. It was also each individual's responsibility to ignore any stimulus that might result in a non-EOL experience. Such non-EOL occurrences had the potential of spiraling one into a vortex of negative feelings. Sometimes individuals just had to summon up the energy, from within their spirit, when attempting to identify the value in every situation. The lesson was that if one actively sought to identify the value, they'd be rewarded by the discovery that there was indeed Value in Everything and Value in Everyone.

Back on the Road to Mary Kay's

In Willmar the knockers told me that a railroad bridge had been burned just outside of town. No south bound train would leave for at least twenty-four hours while it was being repaired. So, I saddled up and headed for the highway in the cool Minnesota night air. I walked for about ten miles before a nice farmer gave me a ride to Raymond, a small Minnesota town in the middle of nowhere. It was after midnight and chances of catching a ride were slim, so I walked to the center of that small, quiet town, then looked for a place to camp for the night.

To my immense surprise Raymond had a small railroad yard and while looking for a boxcar to sleep for the night, I heard a female voice call out from the darkness: "Hey, do you want to party?" Could you imagine the shock! I of course did not hesitate. Two young ladies emerged from the shadows and said they were going to party with some railroad workers and I was welcome to join. Mary Jo and Susie were full of energy and the three of us happily headed for the party talking and laughing in the cool night air. Mary Jo was good looking, in great shape and about eighteen years old. Her friend looked almost as good. They were both in the mood for a party. What a great example of how perceived misfortunes, such as a burned-out railroad bridge, could change within the blink of an eye. One minute I was very much alone, walking down the tracks cold and tired, and the next minute I found myself arm in arm with two lovely teenage girls headed for a warm spot and a party. Wow!

We walked for about half a mile to a string of old boxcars that had been converted into a bunkhouse for the "Gangi" crew. The three of us climbed aboard to the sound of loud music and soon discovered a wide variety of intoxicants floating about. Good feelings completely filled the living quarters with a lot of spirited conversation that continued into the morning hours. It was about three o'clock in the morning when Mary Jo wanted to move the party to her house. The girls, myself and two of the "Gangi" crew stumbled from the warm old boxcar. After a short walk we reached Mary Jo's where the party continued.

The workers left at about five in the morning. Mary Jo invited me to sleep on her couch and of course the offer was happily accepted. Mary Jo lived in the house with her older sister, a younger brother and her two-year old daughter. After we talked for some time she headed for her bedroom and I fell into a deep sleep on her warm and very comfortable couch. The morning arrived all too soon; hot oatmeal for breakfast and lively conversation and what appeared to be a sincere invitation for a return visit. With the railroad bridge still out, it was back to the highway.

Mary Kay's

I arrived in Brookings at one in the afternoon, following three rides and many miles of walking. No one was at Mary Kay's house, so I made myself comfortable on her front lawn. A couple of hours later Monique and Robert came home from school and were quite startled to see this hobo camped on their front lawn. As they carefully approached, they recognized "Uncle Jim" and we all had a good laugh.

Mary Kay invited me to tell her English students about my political and hobo experiences and I gladly accepted. The class asked many questions about my philosophy of life, experiences in D.C. and riding the freight trains. The give and take atmosphere in the classroom was especially stimulating. The students were bright and ready to ask many challenging questions. After class I walked to the library to check out the facilities and perhaps do some reading. To my surprise there was an atlas of major U.S. railroad routes. A shiver of excitement moved through my spirit as all the people and places visited on those ribbons of steel poured into my brain.

Space/Time Marker Value

Thoughts turned to the EOL concept and its relationship to Space/Time Marker Values. A scale of minus ten to plus ten might be a good way to visualize the values of stimuli which had the potential to impact our brain. The great range of EOL experiences could not be denied. But how important was the concept of such a scale to individual behavior? If such a scale did exist the theory would allow for a neutral state at zero. What would that look like? It could be a transitional state from non-EOL to EOL. Such a zero stage might indicate a particular situation that should be carefully identified and evaluated. Perhaps such a zero state represented a time of growth through which we all must pass. The concept of assigning weights to levels of EOL experiences certainly fits the STMV concept. The higher the value, whether on the minus or plus scale, the more impact the event had on the physiological brain. Such careful processing of inputs (stimuli) was where individuals assigned STMVs to virtually everything in their environment.

Back to the Tracks

Another great night of peaceful sleep and Saturday morning arrived with the family going about their business. As much as I enjoyed the visit, the time had come again to hit the iron trail. Joe had a goose down filled ski jacket which he donated to the cause of keeping me from freezing. Mary Kay gave me a very short haircut while Monique and Robert looked on.

Monique made a couple of sandwiches for my cargo pockets. Then I headed for the tracks.

There was not much action at the Brookings railroad yard, actually none; it looked like Interstate 29 would have to take me south. Two rides later I was in Sioux City, Iowa, my childhood hometown. I walked along the railroad tracks and looked for a train west and hopefully toward warmer weather. It seemed rather strange to be back in my home town waiting for a freight train. I guess I had come full circle. I wondered what my past teachers and friends might think of this hobo.

After a couple of hours, a slow train came lumbering into view and I hopped aboard, first stop, Fremont, Nebraska. There, a knocker told me that one of the "birds"—another name for a fast train—was going to Los Angeles, while another was destined for Oakland. Both were hot shots and traveling on high priority schedules. I caught the "5053 bird" and five very cold hours later arrived in the Union Pacific yard in North Platte, one of the largest rail yards in the world. It was nine in the morning and the sun felt good on my cold and frozen body.

Jail Time in North Platte

When I waved to some knockers in the yard I got very sour looks in return, which was very unusual. I didn't let it get to me, though, and sat down on a flatbed car and had a peanut butter sandwich for breakfast. As I dined, a black Blazer pulled up next to me. A gumshoe emerged and politely asked me to get off his train as he held up a bright silver badge and identified himself as a Union Pacific detective. After he checked my identification and examined some of the political papers, he decided that the local sheriff should check me out. The sheriff then explained that he wanted the local FBI agent to talk to me, but since it was Sunday morning the agent wasn't available. He said he'd have to hold me in a cell overnight. The jailer also happened to be an engineer for the Union Pacific, and informed me that his company had a zero tolerance for train riders. Now you tell me.

My fellow inmates bitched about the food. I thought it was great, but did not share my feelings. Following lunch everyone headed for their bunks and immediately went to sleep. I guess that was the pattern: eat and then sleep until the next meal. Our section of the jail consisted of three cells which housed four prisoners each, a connecting hallway, a room with a shower and a picnic style table. It was very quiet after lunch and the mournful sound of a distant train whistle drifted to the cell. Not being able to sleep, I took the few steps to the next room, sat at the table and made a conscious effort to make the most of this uncomfortable situation. In keeping with my philosophy, the *value* in the current situation should be identified. It required a tremendous amount of energy to find the value in being locked in jail.

The current predicament would be used as a learning experience and as a test for my Value in Everything and Enjoyment of Life philosophy. What was the value of being locked in jail and how was EOL possible in such a place? Well, it was a nice day and through the bars of an open window beautiful trees could be seen swaying to the rhythm of a gentle wind. There was a nearby church with silver spires glittering in the afternoon sunshine. I decided there was no reason why I couldn't enjoy the situation. I decided to put the time in jail to good use by writing and planning for my next move. My friend Dan Van Meter once told me about his time in prison and how it was possible to imprison a man's body but not one's spirit. You were the only person in control of your spirit.

One question to resolve was whether the time was enjoyed because there was no choice or because it was desired? That was probably a moot question but worthy of pursuit from a philosophical stand point. What happened to EOL philosophy once your physical freedom was taken away? You made the best of the situation and reached within your soul to find a higher order of freedom. The very act of reaching within myself raised my spirit. The jail experience must be demonstrated to be compatible with Enjoyment of Life. The non-valuable tendency of being locked in jail was to say that society locked me up and this treatment was not deserved. But then, having freedom of choice, I was the one that decided to illegally ride the train. Perhaps my arrest had something to do with paying the price for having the fun and excitement of traveling the iron trail. One might even get used to being locked up once in a while, however it might not be something to brag about. To avoid further arrest, plans were made to take to the highway, at least until miles were put between me and the Union Pacific railroad.

How could the EOL concept work in the jail situation? That seemed to be the overwhelming question. The mind must be put to work and start the de-materialization process. The spirit must rise above the physical body. How could energy be expended in a manner which would alter reality for myself and cell mates so as to enhance EOL? Extreme care had to be taken in assigning STMVs to everything happening in jail. The non-valuable aspects of being locked up with a bunch of not-so-nice individuals would be ignored. My emphasis was to identify any value which might be found. Some valuable points that immediately came to mind were: 1) air out the combat boots, 2) do some writing, 3) examine EOL philosophy in a unique situation, 4) test my ability to de-materialize, 5) meet some different people, 6) relax in a controlled environment, 7) reflect on the past month, 8) enjoy hot showers, 9) plenty of food and, 10) shelter and warmth. In other words, time should be taken to recognize my blessings!

The red, white and blue could clearly be seen floating in a gentle breeze. It looked good. It was mid-afternoon and the radiation of valuable energy appeared to be working, judging by the reaction of some of my cell mates. They seemed to be cheering up a little. I sat in jail writing about my thoughts and observations. Why bother to write? One reason was that it helped to organize thoughts and make sense out of one's reality. Writing also represented an interface between body and soul, a connection between mind and physical reality. Such thoughts were definitely related to the fact that my body was locked in a jail cell.

It was late afternoon; church bells rang in the clear Nebraska air. I soon heard the rattle of the jailer's keys and my mind flashed with the hope that he was *not* coming to set me free. It was a strange reaction. I was locked in jail but still free! It turned out that I wasn't being released. Later that evening I took a long hot shower in anticipation of the next day's release. I wanted to be clean for hitching on the highway.

At about eight in the morning, after a breakfast consisting of a sweet roll and coffee, the jailer let me out for a short walk to the sheriff's office. They decided to forget the FBI and had contacted the Secret Service because of all the White House materials they found in my rucksack. The sheriff and old gumshoe had a Secret Service Agent on the phone and while he questioned me they listened in on the conversation. The many questions regarding White House personnel and procedures convinced those listening and the Secret Service that I was who I said I was and not some crazed hobo who had murdered the "real" owner of the documents. Following several minutes of questioning they told me to wait outside the office while my fate was decided. In a few minutes the sheriff and the railroad gumshoe emerged from the office and told me that I was free to leave as soon as they got my gear together. Hurray for the Secret Service!

I loaded my gear into the gumshoe's blazer and we headed for the highway. Once again, I was in the front seat where the good guys ride. The gumshoe offered to stop at a grocery store for supplies. He told me, "You are by far the most interesting hobo that I have ever arrested and it is a pleasure knowing you. He said, I shouldn't tell you this but the Secret Service had plenty of good things to say about you." Old gumshoe dropped me at

Interstate 80 which went directly to Denver. It felt fantastic to be standing there in the bright morning sun, a free man waiting for a ride to the west. A night in jail certainly made one appreciate freedom.

Two rides later I was within two miles of Carter's Denver campaign HQ. I met a nice guy at the HQ by the name of Ramey who seemed to be in charge. We talked about D.C. politics, had a couple of beers and then headed for an Irish pub downtown near the tracks. Ramey was a very interesting fellow who had spent twelve years on the D.C. police force and then served as the sheriff in a small southern Illinois County. We had a remarkably interesting conversation. We openly shared past experiences as well as our plans for the future. We walked several blocks to the tracks together and with a firm handshake said goodbye. I was once again on the cinder trail.

I jumped a Union Pacific (yeah, I know, but there was no choice) freight headed north and passed through Greeley and toward Cheyenne, Wyoming. My plans for a warmer southern route were rapidly disappearing.

In Laramie the yard geese said my train wouldn't leave for several hours so I decided to look around. I walked to a beautiful park and relaxed in the late afternoon sun underneath cottonwood trees gently swaying in the cool wind. I saddled up and headed for the train yard with hopes of catching a freight to Ogden, Utah, then on to sunny California. The yard was quiet and not a single train left until one in the morning. It was a wooden axle freight which took most of the night to reach Rawlins. It was freezing cold on the open flatcar but the beauty of the stars and moon in the crystal-clear mountain air made it all worthwhile. The train stopped on the outskirts of the Rawlins yard in the pre-dawn darkness. As dawn approached the train began to move west and was happy to be on the roll once again. To my surprise we only pulled farther into the yard. My flatcar stopped directly under the glaring lights of the main railroad station building. No place to hide and visions of jail rushed through my head. I quickly grabbed my gear, jumped to the ground and briskly walked into the early morning shadows.

A couple of knockers said that a Pacific Fruit Express would soon leave from track three and would be headed for the warmth of the California sun. I walked the train and found all the rail cars tightly closed. Being determined to hop that train I got into one of the empty refrigerator cars. It looked a little greasy but I somehow managed to make a nest with some cardboard.

The scenery was fantastic. Many of the trees had taken on fiery autumn colors which seemed to vibrate in the glow of the bright sun. The tracks followed a mountain river through a spectacular canyon with many steep cliffs of granite. The Pacific Fruit Express moved fast. Following a few quick stops it arrived in Ogden's Riverdale rail yard. It felt great to get my feet on the ground after riding in the cramped and dirty refrigeration unit compartment. I walked to a little liquor store near the tracks to pick up dinner, a can of beer and a can of beans.

It was after midnight, very cold and the prospect of catching a hot shot or any train for that matter was not looking good. The workers had no information about a west bound train. That was a strange yard, not really unfriendly knockers but certainly not helpful. Finally, I gave up, built a campfire on the outskirts of the yard and waited for a ride.

My hobo jungle was set against some large boulders which somewhat shielded me from the icy wind. I somehow managed to fall asleep for a couple of hours and at three in the morning a south bound began to rumble toward my campfire. I caught it on the run as it was definitely leaving the yard. Once again my ride was on another open flat car with no shelter from the freezing wind! In less than an hour we arrived in a very friendly Salt Lake train yard. The knockers offered me steaming hot coffee and a place to clean up. Feeling refreshed with good coffee and conversation I explored the yard as the sun rose from behind the beautiful Mountains of the Wasatch Range. I camped next to the tracks where the knockers told me that a hot shot should soon begin its journey to California.

It wasn't long before the hot shot pulled onto the main track and came to a stop. The entire train was made up of flatcars loaded with truck trailers except for one open boxcar directly in front of the caboose. I was pleasantly surprised to find it loaded with clean packing materials. I climbed aboard and made myself a comfortable nest; thirty minutes later we were west bound on a beautiful sunny autumn morning.

As we rolled across the desert my mind wandered and thoughts of returning to St. Louis to take up Don's offer of employment in the campaign seemed to be a good idea. It would be ironic that Don and I would end up in Missouri working together on the presidential campaign. While working at the D.C. National Headquarters I recognized that Don was willing to do whatever necessary to get the president re-elected. In my opinion, he was one of the few individuals that truly believed in what he was doing.

We pulled onto a siding to let another train pass and the gold button walked to my boxcar. He jokingly asked, "Did the yardmaster put this one boxcar in the train just for you?" We both had a good laugh.

Percentage of Time Experiencing EOL is Increased

I had been thinking about increasing my estimate of the percent of actual time that the EOL state of mind was present. Since the percentage was at ninety-seven percent, the last few percentage points required the ultimate effort at being honest with one self. While doing my best to maintain objectivity, I declared ninety-eight percent Enjoyment of Life! It was a big decision; it meant that ninety-eight percent of the time I *must* truly be enjoying life. I had to live up to this new standard while striving to eliminate the remaining two percent of non-EOL.

The train passed through some very beautiful country just east of Caliente, Nevada. There were many rivers that ran along the tracks that carried cascading white water from the surrounding mountain canyons. We passed directly through a small settlement called "Little Springs." It was nestled at the mouth of a wide canyon and looked like a nice place to spend time. Someday a return visit might be in order.

A Steel Coffin in Las Vegas

My train arrived in a brightly-lit Las Vegas around midnight. Some friendly yard geese informed me that the train would continue on to Los Angeles in a couple of hours, so I decided to catch some much-needed sleep in my clean and comfortable boxcar. As I slumbered some yard geese *shut* and *locked* the boxcar door. It was a very strange and terrifying feeling to awake in pitch dark, not knowing where I was and then discovering that I was locked inside a boxcar. Was it a dream? Actually, it was a living nightmare accompanied by visions of my parched bones rattling along the steel boxcar floor. When my heart started to beat once again, I picked up a large piece of wood and started to pound on sides of my large steel coffin. Luckily the train was standing still and through small tears in the metal skin it was evident we were still in the Las Vegas train yard, not at some empty desert siding. I began to frantically look around for a way out of that death trap and potential oven, knowing I had to escape before the train started to roll. After what seemed to be an eternity (actually a couple of hours) three workers approached my boxcar with wrecking bars in hand. The feeling was indescribable as they opened the large boxcar door. I jumped to the ground, profusely thanked my liberators and then got the hell out of the yard. I just wanted to put as much space as possible between my body and that boxcar. It was once again fantastic to be free.

Following a brisk and bouncy, good-to-be-free walk through the brightly lit streets of downtown Las Vegas I slowly made my way back to the yard, hopped a west-bound freight and was once again happily rolling toward Los Angeles. It was a nice ride through the Mojave Desert and then through Barstow and on to Hobart Junction in Los Angeles. Once in L.A. a gumshoe greeted me as I jumped from the train, with: "Leave UP property." I did just that and caught a city bus to brother Tom's place in Northridge for lots of good conversation and relaxation. Still interested in the political campaign, I made several phone calls to the president's campaign people to find out what was going on that week. I learned that the President's son, Chip, was visiting the San Fernando Valley HQ.

A couple of days later I headed for campaign HQ in the San Fernando Valley and met several people that were involved in my political campaigns for the California Assembly in 1976 and 1978. The get together was fun although some of the supporters of my prior political opposition behaved in a rather childish way. For some reason the people putting on the party, old political enemies of mine, thought I should not be there. The Secret Service personnel were professional as always and asked that I leave. After stuffing myself with the delicatessen type goodies I was happy to comply and caught a bus to Altadena in the beautiful foothills of the San Gabriel Mountains and to the home of beautiful Becky. It had been a long time since we had been together. Good food, good conversation and many, many good kisses! What more could anyone desire on any particular day? We had an exciting few days together but then the feet started to itch for that cinder trail. We said our goodbyes, and I saddled up and headed for the Glendale yard with hopes of catching a freight to St. Louis and more work on President Carter's campaign.

Presidential Politics

It was a pleasant walk through the Glendale rail yard and a couple of knockers told me that "smoky," a daily eastbound, would be leaving soon. I climbed into a clean boxcar and waited to begin my eastward journey well supplied and very much looking forward to a leisurely trip. Following a short wait of thirty minutes the almost subliminal high-pitched sound emanated from the train's steel wheels. It was that wonderful "hobo music" once again.

Two hours later "smoky" arrived in the Colton yard, where the engines disconnected in the receiving part of the yard. I saddled up and walked about six miles to the departure yard where I found another eastbound, the only car on which to ride an empty auto rack which would provide little, if any, shelter from the cold autumn wind.

The track-four train got me to Yuma, Arizona. My initial destination was Tempe and my friend Marlene. But the best route was to go to Tucson first then head northward to Phoenix. It was a great ride through the Sonoran Desert, and I arrived in Tucson at nine a.m., twelve hours before the next train to Phoenix. It was a beautiful day so I walked a couple of miles to a large city park and while I was relaxing at a picnic table, Jose, an illegal Mexican citizen living in Tucson, struck up a conversation. He said he was looking for construction work. His English was good and we talked for some time. Jose suggested that we go to a nearby market to get some head cheese. When the goat-head cheese was combined with my bread and apples we had a fine picnic lunch in the park – just like "normal" people. We talked for a couple of hours while slowly eating our lunch. After Jose left, I met several other hobos in the park. All seemed to be nice guys and supplied many brief but pleasant conversations throughout the day.

A dazzling Arizona sunset hung over the mountains as I walked back to the yard. I saw a train moving through and I caught it on the run, not sure if it was going to Phoenix or back towards Yuma. Luckily it turned out to be Phoenix-bound.

Tempe Once Again

The train didn't slow much in Tempe but I went for it anyway, leaping onto the rocks next to the tracks and tumbling to a rough stop. I peeled myself off the ground to find that I was scratched and bruised, but had no broken bones. With a painful limp I walked the mile or so to Marlene's. Despite the aches and pains pride welled up within. After all, I had survived a rough and tumble exit from that fast-moving freight train.

Marlene had several students at her apartment working on a class project. I dropped my gear, said hello to the group and headed for the shower to clean up and wash the blood from my wounds. After what seemed like a very long time they stopped work and everyone left. We were happy to see one another and brought each other up to date. The next morning, she headed off to classes while I used the solitude to ponder my existence.

My mind turned to philosophy and how my Enjoyment of Life outlook had been so very rewarding. It was becoming easier to share my philosophy and accompanying valuable feelings with others. A smile could be a simple way to radiate EOL in a certain direction. A smile could be considered as sort of a body/soul interface and thus a good way to share such positive feelings. Actually, EOL could be thought of as a quiet feeling of satisfaction with your current life situation. It was a pleasing and comfortable emotion. Such feelings could range from total delight, which implied a high degree of obvious pleasure that was openly and enthusiastically expressed. Or perhaps joy that was keenly felt, sort of an exuberant feeling of inner happiness. EOL could also extend to a quiet personal feeling of satisfaction. For me, the entire range of feelings was contained within the concept of Enjoyment of Life.

Marlene's Parents and Campaign HQ

It was a magnificent Saturday morning in Tempe with Marlene. We had a nice morning together and after breakfast she went to the Tempe ASU campus and I headed for the tracks and, for a change, walked the rails without my gear. That evening Marlene's parents had us over for a delicious and very spicy native Korean dinner. The raw squid was not my favorite but somehow, I managed to swallow a portion of the rubbery stuff. Marlene's mother was from Korea. Ted, her father, was a soldier in the Korean War, where the two met. After dinner Ted and I drank beer and watched the Kansas City Royals defeat the Philadelphia Philly's baseball team. It was a pleasant evening as Ted was full of interesting conversation which included many tales of his experiences during the war.

I spent the following day at the president's campaign HQ in Phoenix writing letters and making phone calls. Late in the afternoon several high school girls came to HQ to do volunteer work. They sure livened up the place and provided many stimulating conversations. The young girls were very interested in learning about my experiences with the politics of D.C. and the White House. They stayed for hours and before they left one cute little blond came over to my desk, gave me kiss on the cheek and simply said "God bless you." She then quickly disappeared out the door. My guess was she enjoyed what she heard in my tales. The rewards of living according to the precepts of EOL were great! Marlene came to the office in the early evening; we worked for a few hours and then left to visit one of her best friends. We had a fun time and managed to drink a full fifth of Seagram's whiskey. Her friend, Dawn, was a real beauty and full of great conversation. We had a delightful dinner together and then they gave me a ride to the rail yard so I could catch the Tucson-bound train.

I stumbled down the tracks in search of a safe boxcar on that beautiful Arizona night. Somehow this now very drunk hobo managed to reach an open car, crawled inside and waited to roll south to the Southern Pacific's mainline in Tucson. My arrival time at the yard was perfect; I had just settled into my nest when the train jerked to a start and began its trip south, arriving in Tucson at four in the morning. I walked to the small neighborhood park at trackside and caught up on much needed sleep. Upon awakening, I struck up a conversation with a young first-time train rider, and told him that I would teach him the basics. The kid was relieved and happy as he was very apprehensive about hopping the train and the unknowns of being a hobo—"scared shitless" was the term he used. It was not long before we were bouncing along the tracks toward El Paso, Texas. We shared some delicious beans and much conversation along the way.

We arrived in El Paso in the middle of a tremendous rain storm. My train riding newbie friend elected to stay in the dry boxcar and take his chances, but I was feeling restless so I headed out into the rain in search of a train. I managed to find a hot shot that was ready to roll toward St. Louis and climbed into the shelter of the last engine. I got off in Valentine to stretch and look around in one of my favorite Texas towns.

We reached San Antonio after a rather long ride. The train was being broken up so I hopped on another and within a few minutes was east bound once again: Houston, Tyler, Pine Bluff, Arkansas, where a friendly knocker called "Spooky" gave me a ride in his utility truck to a faster St. Louis train. I hopped aboard an old broken-down switch engine being taken to the St. Louis junk yard. It turned out that the retired engine was rather uncomfortable and dirty with no flat, un-greasy place to lie down. I climbed on top of a small control panel in an attempt to get some shuteye and fell into a fitful sleep only to be awakened by the sound of the engine's whistle. During my restless sleep my feet had gotten tangled in the whistle cord and it was blasting the old engine's whistle, probably waking half the town. It was a good thing no gumshoe was prowling about.

Started to get sick with diarrhea and stomach nausea. As one might guess a slow, bumpy ride in a greasy old switch engine was no place to be heaving your guts out and for good measure a serious case of the shits. I managed to keep control of the situation until we reached the now familiar freight yard at Scott City, Missouri, where the train pulled onto a siding. We spent the day there which gave me a chance to talk with the local residents between bouts of sickness and short naps. My young high school friend, Jim, still passed lunches to the train crews and it was good to see his familiar happy face.

By late afternoon that "milk wagon" was ready to roll so I climbed aboard the old greasy engine still feeling sick. There was no other place to ride. I fashioned a portable toilet from a two-gallon plastic water jug which would ease the pressure, at least from an intestinal viewpoint. An hour before sunset we bumped to an awkward start and that old train was once again on the way to St. Louis. We crossed the Mississippi and then turned north to gently roll along the river flatlands of Illinois as the sun hung low in the western sky. We traveled for an hour and pulled onto a siding just as the sun slipped below the horizon. It left behind a beautiful sunset in the scattered autumn clouds. The illness was still with me and it required large expenditures of energy to maintain even a small degree of EOL. But it seemed that my personal philosophy of life would survive another real-life test.

The greasy switch engine reached East St. Louis around midnight. It was three in the morning when I got to St. Louis proper so it was another night of camping under the stars. There was a large city park near the campaign HQ and the green grass felt great after the prior days in that old greasy switch engine. After a few hours of pleasant sleep, I headed for Brenda's place. It was a relaxing visit just spending time getting my gear in order and then preparing for duties at the campaign HQ.

I arrived at the Missouri campaign HQ at eleven in the morning. It was exciting and encouraging to see that Scott, the state director, had things buzzing with excitement. Phones rang incessantly and people came and went. I worked late into the evening. I called Brenda and she let me know that she no longer had room for this wandering hobo at her place. Scott told me to camp out at HQ until I could figure something else out.

The following evening, we all piled into cars and drove to the Checker Dome Stadium to pass out political leaflets. There was a large crowd at the stadium because the St. Louis Blues were playing a hockey game. The leaflets announced a rally which the president would attend at St. Ann's shopping mall. Once back at HQ some of us decided to pass out more leaflets in a couple of targeted residential areas.

Within the metropolitan area of St. Louis there were many smaller communities referred to as "private neighborhoods." These communities were separate from the city and had their own private police forces. We met some of these police officers that evening and had to choose our words carefully to make our point. The police understood and let us enter their communities. I guess we used the correct words. When finished it was back to HQ for a good night's sleep.

The next day was filled with advance work with Scott and Don for the upcoming presidential visit. The president would be here tomorrow and much remained to be done. I had noticed that many of the volunteers seemed to regard much of what we did as unimportant. It appeared to be a rather dangerous attitude so late in the campaign. But perhaps they had a point and it was my patriotic view that was wrong. The following day I rode with Scott to St. Ann's Mall just two hours before the president arrived. We did the standard "walk through" with the Secret Service protection detail. This was the walking route the president would take from his limousine to the stage. It even included a ladder, up a loading dock, and into a back door of the shopping center.

The rally was a tremendous success with hundreds of local residents attending. I stayed to help close it down while Scott headed for Air Force One, riding with the president in his limousine. I helped the Secret Service fold the American and presidential flags, remove the presidential Seal from the lectern and place everything in their individual aluminum carrying cases.

I had arranged for Vice-President Walter Mondale to visit Cape

Girardeau, so I headed south to do some advance work. This time I forsook the iron trail in favor of a campaign-provided new Thunderbird.

It was early morning on a beautiful day cruising south on Interstate 55 feeling happy and looking forward to meeting friends and getting things going for the vice-president's visit. The day was busy getting the word out and making arrangements with the media, and in the late afternoon I drove to my sister's farm. She was surprised to see me in a new Thunderbird and looking affluent.

The next morning, we all went to the airport to see how things were going with the final preparations. The vice president was due to land in less than two hours. Everything was going smoothly as spectators, media and the Secret Service all went about their business. It was a special thrill to watch the vice president's plane circle the airport, then land and taxi toward us knowing that he was there because of my initiative. The rally was a great success and he was back in the air within two hours. Then it was back on the road toward St. Louis and the madness of big city politics.

In political campaigns you wanted to reach as many people as possible so you concentrated your efforts wherever individuals gathered. There was such a gathering at Bush Stadium where the St. Louis Cardinals and Dallas Cowboys were having a football game. A dozen campaign workers and myself passed out thousands of pieces of literature that detailed the president's platform to the football fans. We got about four hours of exercise on that beautiful Sunday afternoon. Then it was back to HQ with Scott and Don for more phone calls. We worked late into the night and the end of this campaign was looking very attractive.

Monday was busy; many new volunteers were coming and going throughout the day. In the evening many of us went to manufacturing plants and shopping centers to put literature on the windshields of parked cars—what a dirty job! After everyone went home, at two in the morning, I decided to cruise the streets and put up some remaining posters. At sunrise, back at HQ to straighten up the office and to prepare for the "get out the vote" effort. It was Election Day. I was needed at the International Seafarers Union Hall to help get out the vote. Late in the afternoon we started to get news the election was not going our way. Returned to the state HQ and met with the Missouri gang to watch the returns on television. The Carter people were stunned to see Reagan winning. Don was pissed off, much more than anyone else. He paced up and down the hallway, cursing and punching the wall. I can't really blame him as he had worked the hardest of just about anyone. Many of the others were only along for the ride and a possible

White House position. I decided to stay in St. Louis for a couple of days and help close down the campaign, while most of the staff headed in all directions as quickly as possible. There was no sense of unity and I began to form the opinion that it didn't matter who was in the White House.

Thursday afternoon found me back in a Forest Park. Scott had given me a plane ticket to California and some cash. I set out for Iowa in the Thunderbird in order to return the car to the dealership that had loaned it to the campaign. On the way out of town I called one of the ladies that had volunteered at the Maryland Plaza Headquarters just to say goodbye. Sally was glad to hear from me and invited me to her home for a home-cooked dinner. Afterward she very easily convinced me to delay my departure until the next morning. We had a great time recalling the campaign – and sharing many, many kisses.

It was a unique feeling to be traveling with money in my pocket and driving a new car. I decided to stop at a little tavern in the small town of Lovilia, Iowa, where I drank a couple of beers with the locals and had a good time. In Knoxville, Iowa, I stopped and talked with a young couple who said I had to visit the Yo-Yo Club. How could such a personal invitation be ignored?

It wasn't long before the evening patrons started to arrive and the beer began to flow. A couple of hours later a young lady by name of Katie asked me to take her to a party. We left in the Thunderbird and had more great fun with the locals. The party broke up at two in the morning. I started out for Des Moines but only drove a few miles before pulling into a roadside park to sleep it off and get a few hours of rest.

Arrived in Des Moines early in the morning, and called "Big Al," an interesting fellow who had helped with the president's campaign in St. Louis. He drove a new white Cadillac and was absolutely full of energy. We met at Ho-Jo's Hotel, which he built during his contractor days, and had a great breakfast and good conversation. Al told me that there was no hurry in returning the T-bird to his dealer friend and asked me to hang around for a couple of days. He had some interesting business to take care of and said he could use some company.

That evening Al took his family and me to a nice little old-fashioned restaurant in the country. Later that evening, on the spur of the moment, Al decided we should all visit and spend some time at his cabin in Northern Iowa on Clear Lake. We had a fun day at the cabin with Al proudly showing me his large collection of one-gallon bottles of booze. He had over a hundred of the unopened bottles that had long ago stopped being produced. They must have been worth a small fortune. The funny thing was that Al didn't drink. He just liked to collect the rare bottles of liquor as he traveled in the small towns of the Midwest.

The following day we drove to a small airport where he hired a pilot and plane to check on some of his business interests in South Dakota. We had a nice breakfast in the airport lounge and the three of us took off in the early morning sun. We were traveling at one hundred twenty miles per hour at three thousand feet and the ride was smooth, not quite as bumpy as the freights.

It seemed a little strange to be smoothly flying over my sister's house in Brookings while not long ago it was a bumping boxcar on the rails directly below our flight path. We landed at the small airfield in Clinton, South Dakota. It turns out that Al had purchased the salvage rights on thirty-six miles of abandoned Milwaukee Road Railroad tracks. He owned the railroad ties, tens of thousands of them, and was desperately trying to get them out of the ground and stacked before the winter freeze. If he failed it would cost many thousands in lost profits. Al rented a car and off we drove to check on the progress along the old track bed. Thousands of ties were stacked in huge bundles at various places waiting for shipment to various cities, but many were still in the ground. Al got his workers fired up and it looked like they would get the job done on time.

Spent a quiet evening at Al's home sewing on my train gear and talking with the entire family. The next day we had a lunch of hot dogs roasted over burning leaves in the front yard. My spirit was calling for change so it was time for departure. I said goodbyes and loaded the gear into the Thunderbird and drove north to return the car in Mason City. I also decided to cash in the plane ticket and pocket the money. I'd be heading west on the iron trail once again.

Cold Steel on a Texas Hotshot

It was late at night, by the side of the tracks in Mason City, Iowa. It had turned cold, perhaps in the low-thirties and I found myself huddled inside a large cardboard box waiting for a train. A knocker told me a westbound train would be by around three. I didn't know if I could wait that long. It was after midnight and fighting off the freezing cold was taking all my energy. With the return of the T-bird my campaign responsibilities had come to a close and despite the cold it felt good to be on the tracks and free once again. I fell into a fretful sleep and was awakened a few hours later by the sound of powerful diesel engines, music to my frozen ears. The train's powerful engines stopped right next to my cardboard box hutment. A brakeman jumped from the cab and in a loud and cheerful voice he said: "Howdy. This train is headed for Kansas City." My destination exactly. He informed me that all the cars were grain hoppers and then invited me to ride in the cab of the rear engine. A minute later I was sitting in front of the locomotive's cab heater thawing the cold flesh and bones. It was great to be back on the friendly cinder trail.

After the train's crew added a few more grain cars, the train picked up speed and highballed south and west. Mike, the brakeman, came back to talk with his hobo passenger. He also showed me how to turn on another cab heater and the lights. The railroad had been kind of a home for me and perhaps always would be. We continued down the tracks for an hour or so and came to a stop on a siding due to a sort of traffic jam in the Des Moines yard. Our train would be held up for at least a day. The brakeman invited me to the lead engine for some fried chicken and hot coffee. We had a lively political discussion. They thought it was pretty funny that a "hungry Democrat" was riding the rails. We had many hearty laughs and one of the crew suggested that perhaps the Republican party might be worth considering—given my current situation.

The brass buttons called for a taxi to take them the twenty miles to the main Des Moines freight yard. They told me to be cool and act like part of the crew and go along for the ride. We unloaded our gear from the taxi's trunk in a very busy downtown train yard. One of the brass buttons invited me to ride in his personal car to the departure yard which was several miles away. While driving he told me, "We are now working for the Rock Island Line and we are worried about losing their jobs." It appeared that the Chicago and Northwestern railroad was trying to buy them out.

The conductor let me out next to the mainline tracks where a train proudly sat with all engines softly rumbling in the early morning mist—it was a most beautiful picture. I hopped out and headed for the grain train and climbed aboard the last engine. Within a few minutes we were moving toward Kansas City. It was just another good connection. Inside the locomotive's warm cab, I started to think that winter travel on the freights just might be possible as long as I stuck to the engines.

We reached Kansas City as the sun was rising above the endless flat plains and Lady Luck struck again as our grain train stopped on the outskirts of the Atchison, Topeka and Santa Fe Railway Company yards. That line would take me to California. A friendly goose led me to the appropriate train and I began my search for a clean boxcar. It was an easy ride throughout the day reaching Wellington, Kansas, late in the afternoon, where I decided to see about catching a faster "pig." The pig train found was composed of all truck trailers loaded on flatcars. Such trains usually had the highest priority and were also called birds, jets and hot shots.

Less than an hour passed and we were highballing west. The brakeman came back to the engine and we had a long discussion about the history of trains and how they helped to make America great. Several hours later, following a "rolling crew change" (the train didn't stop), an uptight and unfriendly brakeman came back to "my" engine. I tried to ignore his grumbling as he checked out the engine's gauges. A few hours later, just as we rolled into Amarillo, Texas, a couple of gumshoes rousted me from sleep. They casually told me to collect my gear and get off their train and off the railroad's property.

I headed for the tree line but the pig train was still sitting in the yard and seemed to beckon me back aboard. So as soon as the gumshoes disappeared in the darkness, this track rider circled around toward the front end of the train and slowly worked my way back into the yard. I barely managed to climb aboard one of the flatcars as the "pig" was rapidly picking up speed and quickly departed the yard leaving the gumshoes safely behind.

Cold Steel

The train was made up entirely of truck trailers mounted on specially designed rail cars which only had a narrow band of steel on which to ride. The wheels of the railroad car spun inches from my head and there was no shelter from the icy wind. Before then I had always hoped the train wouldn't stop. But this time I screamed and screamed again for it to stop so I could get off, even in the middle of nowhere. Unable to change positions, forced to lie in one spot on a cold steel slab under a truck trailer, I began to wonder about the wisdom of catching that train. It wasn't until four in the morning that it slowed enough for me to get off, somewhere in the middle of the Arizona desert. The train was now traveling at four or five miles per hour, so I saddled up and hit the ground running toward the front of the train in hopes of finding a warmer spot. I ran until my lungs felt like they would burst then threw myself onto another slab of cold steel. Then I caught my breath and repeated the process. My body was warming but progress toward the engine was not good. After doing this "run and flop" routine for several minutes the train came to a complete stop. The welcome sun peaked over the horizon. I moved my sweaty and yet frozen body into the locomotive to soak up the warmth blowing from the cab's heaters and decided then and there to detour south to visit Marlene in Tempe. As we slowed in Winslow, I jumped from the moving train. I soon managed to catch another, but turned out not to be south-bound. My hopes for a Marlene visit were dashed.

The freight had wooden axles and stopped to pick up and drop off cars throughout the day and night. We crossed the mighty Colorado, passed through Needles, a crewman told me to get off the train. I did, then jumped back on. Finally, we reached Barstow. It felt great to get my feet on the ground. The Barstow yard was large and rather imposing and I figured that it might be wise to keep a low profile. I spent the day on the outskirts of the yard then crept back to the main yard after dark, which was well lit with many powerful search lights. It was a real guerilla type operation with me running, jumping and throwing gear over chain link fences. Once these obstacles were breached, I crawled through ditches and metal culverts to finally reach the departure yard. After four hours of this evasive behavior, I was once again rolling toward Los Angeles on an auto rack filled with deluxe pickup trucks. One of these trucks was not locked. I sat in its cab and listened to country music about freight trains from the Bakersfield AM station. I switched trains at Hobart and ended up in the City of Vernon, just a few miles south of downtown Los Angeles. Vernon was the smallest incorporated city in California, having a population of just a little over 100. It was heavily industrialized and had a reputation of corruption within its city government.

I saddled up and left the relative security of the train yard and started on a midnight walk through the mean streets of Los Angeles. By breakfast time this happy hobo was at Becky's house on the southern slopes of the San Gabriel Mountains.

Altadena was a pleasant town on the southern foothills of the San Gabriel Mountains which had somehow managed to avoid being annexed into Los Angeles. It seemed to have a sense of freedom not present in the more centrally located and heavily governed areas of the Los Angeles basin. In the early days the slopes above Altadena were covered with bright red-orange California poppy flowers so thick and vivid that they served as a navigation aid for the early explorers arriving by sea.

Becky appeared to be especially happy with my visit. Our lively discussions offered a welcome change from the solitude of the tracks. Becky did not embrace my EOL philosophy but was willing to discuss it and would try to understand how it worked. A visit with Becky was always bound to be stimulating no matter the twists and turns it might take.

Enjoy Our Creator's Gifts

It began to be apparent that it might be wise to remind ourselves to enjoy each moment of life to its fullest. We must appreciate everything our Creator has given us—and be thankful for those gifts. Sometimes it was advisable to store some of the excess valuable energy for future use. It was a matter of training oneself to maximize the absorption of valuable energy by assigning it a high Space/Time Marker Value (STMV). In other words, you should always strive to absorb all the positive energy (happy, good stimuli) in any particular environment. My travels provided many opportunities to experience enjoyable times which gave me the raw material for the much-desired valuable energy. It was often amusing and valuable to think about the enjoyable events that had become commonplace in my stream of history. There were many enjoyable times in my recent past and by assigning them high STVM values one could accumulate energy and thus grow.

It was a quiet morning in Altadena. Becky had left for morning classes at Pasadena College where she was studying land surveying. A cool morning breeze was blowing through the two large open windows facing the San Gabriel Mountains. The incompressible number of life's everyday events somehow placed my body in the space/time of that day in Altadena. It was impossible to attribute any particular circumstance of life that placed me there. Could it be that it was the normal pursuit of Enjoyment of Life that had placed me in such favorable surroundings?

Since arriving in Altadena my rucksack had been undergoing a downsizing as I got rid of unnecessary items. If an item was not essential to fulfilling the mission of meeting my Basic Needs and EOL, they were tossed out.

Becky came home for lunch in very high spirits. Somehow, she was convinced to take a long lunch and we had hugs and kisses followed by a quiet and peaceful lunch. After Becky left, I hiked up Lake Street, toward the crystal-clear mountains of the San Gabriel Range, in search of a place to do my laundry. The numerous communication towers perched on the highest visible peak, Mount Wilson, could be clearly seen in the bright afternoon sun. As my laundry tossed and turned in the laundromat machine I just relaxed, comfortably gazing at the powerful mountains. Total happiness was present – my station in life was wonderful. Not sure why but some poetry of William Blake came to my mind.

> Every night and every morn some to misery are born.
> Every morn and every night some are born to sweet delight.
> Some are born to sweet delight; some are born to endless night.

Experience in dealing with people of the "endless night" variety had taught me to be thankful that for most of the time my disposition fits in the "sweet delight" category. One thing that could be said was that at least for that exact moment, and perhaps ninety-eight percent of the time, it was the EOL state of mind. Throughout my travels people often tried to make an impact on my mind. Also recognized was that it was each individual's personal responsibility to control the magnitude of such impact. That was accomplished through the assignment of a value to incoming stimuli--STMVs. You must grow on your own terms and within your own space/time. Many, if not all, aspects of society were aimed at the control of STMVs in our everyday lives. We must gather power on our own terms, the guiding principle being to absorb the valuable energy offered by the Creator's universe. When recalling all the good times in my life it reminded me that EOL was the only logical concept providing an objective method of conducting my life. The message was to enjoy each God given moment to its fullest while not infringing on the enjoyment of others. That was the message that kept repeating. Tears, tears of joy, what do they mean? TACAMO (Take Charge and Move Out)! It was realized that having total control of my life was a basic component for having an enjoyable lifestyle.

The Mountains

Becky came home in the late afternoon; we spent several joy-filled hours together, then I saddled up and headed for the high ground to explore the mountains above Altadena. After getting through the maze of city streets I somehow ended up at Eaton Canyon, climbed to the canyon floor and followed it to an impassable water fall. I decided to scale the canyon wall, which turned out to be much more challenging than anticipated. During my ascent I had more than one close call with the grim reaper. One time my footing was lost, my body was out of control and sliding toward a two-hundred-foot sheer drop off into the canyon. Frantically, I clawed at the loose rock, but to little effect. Bloody fingers brought the uncontrollable slide to a stop with my feet at the very edge of cliff. With a wildly pounding heart, I carefully pulled myself upward inch by inch until I reached a safe place. I later learned that many hikers had been killed or severely injured at that very spot. Surviving that close call, the pursuit of EOL would continue for a little while longer.

Once off the rocky cliff face and on safer ground I climbed farther up the mountain at a leisurely pace. The many skyscrapers of downtown Los Angeles almost took on a surreal appearance in the light from the sun low in the western sky. The beautiful blue of the Pacific Ocean spread to the horizon. I found a good camp spot among large trees and settled into a soft bed of pine needles. To the west the sky was layered with red, orange and broad streaks of bright pink interspersed throughout. A glance to the south brought the now twinkling lights of the city with the endless snake of cars gliding down the many freeways. To the east a brilliant orange full moon was rising through the pines. As the night deepened the howling of distant coyotes lulled me into a tranquil sleep.

The rising sun filtered through the pines as billions and billions of sun beams danced in the morning mist. The dawn was slowly moving the electric lights of the distant city aside and the sun was now the master of the valley. The massive church at the corner of Sacramento and Lake Streets, near Becky's house, was clearly visible in the early morning sunlight. Downtown Los Angeles, Encino, Sunland, Pasadena and the Pacific Ocean were all spread before me in the morning light. I passively absorbed the energy of the sun as it warmed my body and soul. All the reflected energy of the spectacular sights around me elicited a moment of Total Serenity (TS)—at one with the universe.

I continued moving up the mountain until I reached another cliff like the one I had almost perished on the previous day. Not wanting to challenge the "grim reaper" twice in twenty-four hours, I embarked on a less heart pounding path to reach the canyon floor. It was worth the trip. A good size stream filled with crystal clear water meandered through the canyon. Many boulders, some as large as a car, were scattered about its shore as well as pockets of sandy beaches. The leaves of the trees lining the stream had turned to their brilliant autumn colors while bright green moss was splashed over many of the white boulders.

The morning sun had not yet reached into the canyon and the coolness of the surrounding air was invigorating. I explored one of the smaller feeder streams and discovered a beautiful grove of trees on a grass-covered plateau halfway up the canyon wall. I dropped my gear and enjoyed that small retreat from the world. I listened, really listened to the babbling of the small stream. Its voice was just as valuable as the wild rushing of this canyon's main stream. I hiked farther north and deeper into the main canyon. Rounding a sharp bend Mount Wilson popped into view; it looked very close in the clean clear mountain air. In reality it would take many more hours of difficult climbing to reach that summit. I'd leave that one for another time.

As I hiked deeper into that magnificent wonderland, I once again became aware of the rewards of living according to the principles of the EOL philosophy. Since the rewards were a constant, one was induced to continue that behavior. You understood that you were on a path best for you and perhaps, others as well. The lesson might be too be wary of those who attempted to direct you toward what they considered to be a better path. Of course, that did not mean that you should totally close your mind to advice. The point was that you must retain control in the assignment of STMV's to incoming information.

I continued my easy trek up the canyon and arrived, via the back door, at an old, abandoned Forest Service campground called "Idle hour." I followed the main stream to a point where it split into two separate canyons. The ruins of two stone houses sat on a flat spot near the stream. Who were those long-ago inhabitants and could they be my friends?

Where the two streams merged the waters had carved a large cliff into a shape that looked like a diving eagle. I found a nice campsite, where the colors appeared "alive" as they pulsed through the clear mountain air. My base camp was filled with the bright shades of orange and gold of autumn, the cool crisp blue of winter, the vibrant greens of spring and the bright sunshine yellow of summer. It was the perfect place to relax and reflect. The babbling stream spoke to my spirit; the tranquility was heavenly—Total Serenity once again!

The sun dropped behind the canyon walls and the day began to turn to night. The fire was lit and the beans were warming. Perhaps a return for a longer stay at this serene campsite would be in order. At four in the morning, I woke up cold and threw another log on the fire. The warmth from the blazing campfire felt great as the dawn slowly arrived in that deep cool canyon. After a hot portion of oatmeal, it was time to head back to the reality of civilization.

After several miles of hiking, I arrived at a National Forest Service campground and stopped at the office to find out about a trail that might lead to Altadena. The fellow on duty loudly barked out, without even looking up from his desk, "The whole forest is closed!" I told him I was trying to *leave* the forest, after which he reluctantly told me a way off the mountain which later proved to be incorrect. Farther down the path a Boy Scout troop leader was visibly upset about the forest being closed. He was being evicted from the forest along with his troop. He speculated that the closure was just another taxpayer rip off. We talked for several minutes and he showed me the trail that would take me to Altadena.

It was an easy downhill hike and it was good to get back to Becky's. We had a nice evening preparing for a Thanksgiving Dinner planned for the next day, which turned out to be fantastic. Afterwards we sat together at the big redwood table from Big Sur and watched the mountains take on the colors of the setting sun. A peaceful feeling permeated that time and space—it was as if the peace extended to the deepest part of my physical body and reached the very essence of my bones.

Reflections – Thoughts on Life

Time spent with Rebecca usually resulted in the stimulation of many different areas of thought. She was not at all shy about voicing her opinions. Sometimes it seemed that we talked too much! There were many different ways to communicate, all of which required different energy expenditures.

The best communication would require the least amount of energy and yet maintain effective communication. One way to accomplish that would be to use fewer words by thinking before you spoke. It might be summarized as the forceful, but conservative, use of language.

Using less verbal communication might be an interesting experiment. How about a vow of silence? That would allow one to conduct experiments on alternate methods of communication. No one had any right over your power of speech. It would be interesting to observe the different maneuvers of the mind that might result from the disciplined use of words. An atmosphere absent of verbal speech could be a soothing balm for the spirit and not talking could free up the brain for other activity. It would also further self-reliance because one might not ask as many questions. Some might be offended by such behavior, but it would be interesting to observe and explain

Becky stimulated me to think about the differences between the peoples on the earth. She strongly believed that all people should live on earth as one big happy family. In her view of the world there were no national borders and no need for a national defense. My view was that the world was populated with people having vastly different values and opinions. Furthermore, such differences were partially the result of one's physical position on the earth. An example of this was the type of clothing people chose. Clothing choices were always dependent on geographical location on this planet. Such differences encouraged people to form tribes and band together for their own survival. The influence of location eventually became part of their physical and physic make-up. Recent scientific advancements had suggested that environmental influences might also influence whether certain genes were expressed or remained dormant. We would be safe to also assume that environmental forces acting on any particular human were never exactly the same. But if a group of humans such as a tribe were in the same general physical space the forces were certainly similar. We could safely surmise that the differences for someone living in Alaska versus El Salvador would have had very different influences on one's spiritual and physical growth. The differences would intensify and expand as time passed. Adaptation would result and successive generations would grow in unique ways.

Since the world's population could not live in the same physical space there would always, at a minimum, be differences based on geographic location. Any attempt to unify the world would first have to recognize and possibly eliminate such differences. Until that happened the peoples of the world would always have separate tribes. These tribes, or nations, would then seek survival in the best way known to them. All we could hope to do in our world was to minimize the effect of the differences. Our political leaders should only encourage behavior which would first benefit the individual, then the nation, and finally the world. The family unit was also an important aspect since the socialization of an individual began with the parents. It was the parents that provided the environmental context for gene expression. One of the dangers facing any nation was when there was an "unnatural" alteration of the family unit, such as the economic pressures brought to bear on parents by government action. The citizens of our country had come to accept the fact that both parents must work outside the home to provide food and shelter for their offspring and governmental policy encouraged it.

My mind turned to the question as to how sensual experiences satiated our bodies. All things could not be experienced in exactly the same way. We and the many stimuli offered by our world are in a state of constant change and motion. Therefore, we can open the many different channels of perception, seeking new vistas—a constant search for New Knowledge. The search for knowledge fulfills our need to answer questions to help us make sense of our reality. The knowledge required to answer questions is based on our own and others' description of the physical world and how they impacted our sense organs. We store these perceptions in the form of energy and use them to expand or enlarge our own interpretation of physical reality. We can then move forward in life having a slightly modified foundation—hopefully for the better.

In one of Becky's many philosophy books I stumbled upon this quote by American poet Kenneth Patchen: "The size of the world was determined by the size of your dwelling: The smaller your house the larger the world." It seemed to apply to my current situation since my house was carried on my back.

Becky and I settled into a nice rhythm. She taught me basic sewing and I found that it was relaxing to create several stuff bags made from scrap material. It was nice. The ninety-eight percent EOL was certainly holding strong and it actually felt that it was moving toward ninety-nine percent.

Life had a rhythm all its own, much like sewing a piece of fabric. Sometimes you attained a smooth easy pace which felt natural and comfortable. You could do the same with life, you just had to learn to hold the fabric of life and move through it with a rhythm like the needle passing through the fabric—a synchronous feeling of serenity.

Everything was so very peaceful at Becky's. I spent much time at the Altadena Library reading and enjoying conversations with the librarians. It felt as if my finger was in the honey pot of life! It was strange—I found many pleasures for my body and the spirit in Altadena and yet something began to stir. Was it a desire for change?

I started reading "Siddhartha" by Hermann Hesse. It stimulated the philosophical portion of my brain. Hesse made an interesting and strong case that "time" was not real but only a concept conjured up in the human mind. Therefore, the dividing line between the world and eternity, between suffering and bliss, and between good and evil was an illusion. Hesse speculated that life was like a river and that "time" with its past, present and future was the same as flowing water. He said that knowledge could be communicated but that wisdom could not. Knowledge could be a wonderful thing and could greatly benefit us, but wisdom was something more as it was derived from one's very being. My thinking was similar in that I felt that wisdom was the result of the accumulation of energy once we absorbed knowledge. If you agreed with Hesse's concept that time did not exist and life was like a river, then you could also think of a stone by the side of a trail as being all things. It only appears to be a stone while you are looking at it, for it will eventually change. As the stone continued its lifecycle, its energy, which is locked in its very being, is directed in another way. Perhaps the stone would someday become a thought buried deep in the human brain. Herman Hesse believed that once we understood such concepts and then placed our existence within this framework, you would be well on the way to being a wise man. My thought was that all matter was congealed energy, therefore we as individuals became part of all energy and were destined to take on other forms. Hesse believed all energy was part of a cosmic law and the formation of a single stone was just as important as the birth of a child. Whenever matter was formed, energy was utilized and then incorporated into the structure being formed. Such a process involved the constant maintenance of what he called "universal equilibrium."

Such thoughts on the formation of matter and the conservation of energy were consistent with modern physical experiments. For instance, we knew that energy could not be created or destroyed but that it simply took on other forms. What were the basic characteristics of energy? What was the aura of energy which surrounded and permeated all beings and objects? How do things such as man and tree interact, how do they communicate? My thought was that a man and tree shared energy. The tree "communicated" with man by activating the man's doors of perception which could then stimulate thoughts. Was that not a method of communication or the sharing of the aura of energy? Let the trees, mountains, and streams communicate with our spirit. We were all part of everything in the massive scale of the universe. If one could truly recognize the value in energy, whether it was in the physical form or just a thought, you were communicating and sharing the aura of energy which had congealed into matter.

The comfortable and often pleasant feelings that resulted from being in familiar surroundings could be felt no matter where you were. That comfortable feeling happened when you believed in the unity of all of God's creation and how everything was "connected" through the sharing of energy. Thus, my favorite reading chair became all chairs; they were the same in terms of the effect they had in eliciting pleasant thoughts and EOL. For some, such feelings may seem to have a dulling effect in that everything in our experience became equal. However, for this philosophical adolescent the leveling of life's experiences appeared to provide additional opportunities for the rewards associated with the absorption of valuable energy. Another way to increase energy and hence growth was to open the doors of perception a little wider. Really "see" the mountains, "listen" more intently to the singing bird and "feel" the morning mist on your skin. The effects of such valuable energy were cumulative and continually added energy to the particular storage sites in our brain. Once we did that our energy base of knowledge was expanded and we actually grew in a positive way. You could say that we were on the road leading to wisdom.

One bright sunny morning the realization came that I had ceased working for the *illusion* of someday having a moment of glory. That moment of glory was now! The moment of glory was my energy, my life and having control over its direction. It was the ninety-eight percent Enjoyment of Life. We must live each moment of life in a way that would enhance that particular moment of glory—which was the present time. One must keep moving, mentally and physically, when you felt the flow of energy moving your soul. Ride the energy flow and one might even direct its flow in a valuable direction. As individuals we were all part of the universal energy supply and when we died we actually expanded--movement became less energy consuming. Physical limits were diminished and energy was liberated; we became part of everything.

Following several pleasant weeks on Lovila Lane, I saddled up and headed for the iron trail. The spirit was calling for movement. We had a pleasant breakfast, took a nice early morning walk and said our goodbyes, parting on strained but friendly terms. I spent the day running errands and seeing friends. Then, in the shadows of the late night, I made my way to the Glendale freight yards, to catch a train.

Arizona Philosophy

Caught the first train out of Glendale yard and it just happened to be old "Smoky." The new combat boots, picked up at the 146th Air Force Base, were breaking in nicely with just a few small blisters. The old trick of keeping them wet was working. It felt great to be back on the tracks and once again rolling east on the Southern Pacific tracks. The day turned to night and we headed into the desert with the train maintaining a constant speed of about forty-five miles per hour. The sounds and vibrations that came from the steel wheels as they rolled on the hardened steel tracks resulted in a continuous humming sound which was conducive to philosophical thoughts. It felt as if my spirit had become part of the energy of the powerful diesel engines as we moved as one across the desert floor.

I arrived at the old Tempe train depot and jumped from that slow freight. Unable to reach Marlene, I headed off to the library on the Arizona University Campus and read until I met a guy that seemed a bit spaced out. He told me that he had been traveling around the country for the past six years following a failed marriage and divorce in Oregon. We talked about politics and philosophy and found that we agreed on some things such as the many freedoms offered by our country—he appeared to be a real patriot. We discussed how in times of national emergency there was often a natural fear of the unknown, and how politicians sometimes exploited that fear or created their own in order to encourage citizens to give up individual freedoms. In such cases we were told to entrust others to make decisions concerning our individual security. When such deception was used to exercise "leadership" it was inconsistent with all the founding principles of our country. My original observation that he was a little weird was confirmed when he stood up, right in the middle of a sentence, and walked into the crowd of students.

It turns out Marlene was about to leave town for a few days, but gave me the keys to her place. I spent the afternoon by the pool and made an evening trip to the campus for some quiet reading. Sometimes it was good to recite a short prayer, turn down the brain and just flow with the energy. Confide only in those that would not abuse your confidence and/or misunderstand your words. The thought entered my head that every human activity, including work, should add to EOL. You must be able to identify the *value* in any activity. There can be no other reason for our existence on this earth! Activities such as work must be for our enjoyment.

With that in mind I started thinking about finding a job in a small-town hardware store. It would be a total change from my previous work experience. The idea of being able to organize physical objects was appealing—it could add a certain structure to my structure-free existence.

On the move again but only for a leisurely walk along the tracks without my fifty-pound house on my back. It felt good for a change to kind of flow with the energy unburdened with the extra physical weight. I realized that there were many different velocities of energy currents. Energy flow could be visualized as a river cascading over rapids which could lead to vaporization then once again condensing to become part of the eternal flow of energy. The river of life contained many different paths and personalities.

Went to the local store for some milk and paid for it with a pocket full of change. The clerk handed me back some of the money and told me in a bitchy way, "Twenty-five cents of this is no good, it's Canadian." I asked her why. She got rather nasty and very loudly said, "It's the law!" Later I realized that "it's the law" was often used in today's language of society. Perhaps it was a common excuse when people had to enforce a rule that seemed to be based on an unreasonable law. Many laws made little or no sense and were enacted to serve some special interest group. The types and number of laws which governed our daily lives were often incompatible with the notion of how citizens should live in a free society. I still felt that America was a great country but there was a system of laws that had been built over the past two hundred years which now threatened individual freedoms. Unfortunately, current law often did little more than ensure the expansion of the legal profession by increasing the number of causes for action. The lawyers and legislators even had a name for it – "CA" – meaning "cause for action."

The next morning, after a delicious breakfast of spicy Korean rice and zucchini, I went back to campus and relaxed in the shade of a large tree and wondered how many people would be quick to condemn my current lifestyle. Let them condemn it! Once we cease to be annoyed with the so-called moral views of others our minds can be freed from making such judgments. We can then expend energy watching and listening, which enables us to accumulate New Knowledge. Such knowledge helps us along the path to true wisdom. Once we become wise, we grow immune to praise and/or blame and reach peace within ourselves. Our very being is at rest. You are your only master. Control the direction of your mind and spirit and you will discover a wonderful power within yourself enabling you to live in peace. Always strive to be truthful with others, share your material possessions and do not be angry.

The accumulation of New Knowledge must lead to further joy (EOL) but how could this happen? The acquisition of New Knowledge seemed to be the only path which could lead to true wisdom. Could one person be wiser than another? What was true wisdom? Perhaps wisdom was different for everyone. One person's wisdom might be another's folly. It seemed to me that a wise man did not judge the wisdom of others. For me wisdom represented striving to be in contact with the spirit by searching for answers concerning our everyday existence. When in the "searching state of mind" I experienced Enjoyment of Life. A truly wise man could expound on the virtues of wisdom but would not force his views on those not sharing the same beliefs. Knowledge served as the foundation on which wisdom was constructed. Knowledge gave us the language enabling us to conceptualize and organize our thoughts. Such organization could then provide a coherent format for the writing of our thoughts. The written word would then further describe our reality--it was a way of making sense of our existence. Knowledge was a way of looking at the many dimensions of the world. It assisted us in relating to other individuals who may be wise in the same way we define wise.

Memories, memories, oh sweet memories! They were all good when you enjoyed each moment of life. Memories became part of the eternal flow of energy so they might just as well be pleasant.

Honesty

Be honest when you communicate with others and choose your vocabulary carefully. Being honest at all times might sometimes be difficult but it must be done. Speak and write in an honest manner or don't bother to open your mouth or place pen on paper. If a person is not proud of themselves then how can they take pride in what they do? The rewards of being honest first come from within. We must all form individual honest opinions concerning the meaning of our life; what is the purpose of our spirit? Honesty means you presented your picture of reality in a manner consistent with the reality perceived by those with whom you are attempting to communicate. This type of honest communication must be developed and learned, because it involves the perceptions of other individuals. It appears lawyers might learn more about honesty as their idea of reality is often at odds with the non-lawyer citizen. If lawyers fail to increase their level of honesty they soon lose all respect from those they should serve. The language of the legal profession is often distorted in a way that the perception of reality is slanted against the individual. The reason lawyers do this is to make money. I've got nothing against earning money, but it must be done in an honest, professional manner. Dishonesty in the legal profession could not only destroy individuals but possibly our society as well.

It was a breezy Sunday morning at the Tempe Train depot. I had a breakfast of big and juicy seedless oranges that I found scattered on the ground next to the Sunkist packing plant. The warming rays of the morning sun felt wonderful. A well-proportioned female jogger moved easily along the tracks which clicked my eyeballs to attention and brought a smile to my face. It was just another joy filled moment by the side of the tracks.

I awoke in Marlene's apartment at three in the morning, the full moon shining in the window. The sounds of a far-off train whistle, powerful engines and steel on steel drifted to my ears. Was it the power that was so attractive? What part of my spirit could be that power? What part of my spiritual self-existed as part of those steel wheels and ribbons of steel? The sounds of the train grew faint as moonlight filled the bedroom and was absorbed into my body and soul. Part of my soul seemed to drift out of Tempe as if it were somehow part of that late night mysterious train.

Reflections

Thus far blessing upon blessing has allowed me to experience many things during my life; surely more than if I had chosen a more stable lifestyle. I was a father, had been a faculty member at a university, published scientific papers, had mining claims in the San Lucia Mountains, worked for a president, ran for public office, and now was living on and riding freight trains. How did my life reach this point? Now, when people saw me, they saw a hobo. I no longer cared. What good were emotional interpretations anyway? The majority of people would think someone not displaying emotion would be very strange. How about the theory that there is only one emotion, that being, joy? Think, for one moment, that the human organism was capable of experiencing only that one emotion. My personal philosophy of life was partially based on the belief that there was some *value* in every human and spiritual experience. Within that contextual framework the single emotion of joy could range from painful death to a comfortable body in the state of happiness and perhaps even Total Serenity. At that time in my life, my personal range of emotion was very short, mostly happy while not letting thoughts of my future or past infringe on EOL. The concept of the existence of only one emotion fit nicely into my personal philosophy of life.

Over a period of years my material possessions had been steadily reduced—my house had grown small. However, sometimes, there was that feeling that that a place to put my "stuff" would be nice. Perhaps that feeling was somehow related to non-EOL? Sometimes the thought of getting my old files, notes and books together and putting them someplace where they would be "safe" entered my mind. Those thoughts were infrequent but they could not be denied. Responsibility for those "possessions" were given up, therefore the connection was weak, but it was still there. It would always be necessary to have some possessions.

One of the lessons driven into our minds as children and on into adult life was that we must accumulate things, and it was by these things that we measured our wealth or status. That philosophy put the community's needs above the individual since profit resulted when goods were accumulated. Was it possible that there were some members of society that might contribute in other ways? Unfortunately, many times such non-materialistic and individualistic people, such as hobos, were perceived as threatening to the regular order of society. If the majority of citizens held the hobo philosophy there would be little profit for those adhering to a more materialistic view of happiness. Our country's success was partially based on the concept of what we produced (as a nation) or what economists called the Gross National Product (GNP). Artistic abilities were of secondary importance and were not part of the GNP equation. Furthermore, the primary purpose of our educational system was to produce skilled individuals that would contribute to the GNP. Perhaps such early conditioning made it difficult to have a personal atmosphere conducive to creativity. Individuals such as hobos, and many artists, were constantly required to ask themselves whether they were contributing to the GNP and therefore to their society. Such self-questioning could lead to a feeling that since they were not contributing to the GNP they were not worthy of benefiting from society. That attitude could inhibit creativity for those not increasing the Gross National Product. Of course, there were many individuals able to overcome such hurdles and create, but often such creativity was not recognized. One thing that should be remembered is that the creativity of some individuals could benefit not only the individual but also society. All things considered, it appears that American society did a good job of maintaining a reasonable balance between its productive and artistic needs.

   I walked the tracks and soon found a little used hobo jungle, built a fire along slow-moving irrigation canal and relaxed under some large cottonwood trees. It was nice to get away from the comforts afforded by Marlene's apartment. However, it was also nice to have had the option of going back to silk sheets, warmth and my pot of beans. It was having the freedom to physically and mentally move which was essential to EOL that was so important for my spirit. It was the freedom of movement, which could lead to New Knowledge, which seemed to be the most important motivating force in my existence in that space/time.

More About EOL

Thoughts about my philosophy of life and EOL seemed to be stimulated by that quiet time by the side of that babbling irrigation canal. First, my emotional life was divided into five unique categories that are shown below. Next, I attempted to define of each of those five categories. It was an effort to use a systematic approach while trying to learn more about my motivation and chosen way of life. It was the search for New Knowledge about me. Once the emotional categories were defined the estimated percentage of time spent in each category could be determined. The percentage points given below only applied to me at that particular time. The reader could fill in values which applied to them while remembering the basic principle that you must be honest. The percentages and the five categories were as follows:

   0% Despondent, failed in life by missing opportunities. Just plain fucked up and there was little if any hope for a happy future.

   2% Uneasy with the future, looking ahead and asking, where was I headed? Looking back at the good times and wondering if there would ever be more. Was there a desire to return to a happy past or to a happy future?

   96% There was a quiet feeling of satisfaction and living for the moment while feeling good about my station in life.

   1% Delight that was obvious and demonstrated.

1% Extreme joy that was keenly felt, exuberant, demonstrated happiness. This was the Total Serenity state of mind.

If the reader chose to assign values for their own life then it should be remembered that the percentages could change with the passage of time. That's life! There is always room for improvement and one's "life profile" could be improved as one accumulated New Knowledge.

Another important consideration was how to erase non-EOL experiences from your memory? Negative experiences in our past were recorded in our brain and sometimes managed to return to our conscious thoughts. Such a return to an unpleasant past usually resulted in that non-EOL feeling. The first step to counteract such thoughts was to recognize their potential harmful effects. Following this, one must instantly expend the energy to put them out of the mind. If you could not learn a valuable lesson from the past non-EOL experience then there was no benefit from dwelling on it. Think of something totally different and pleasant. Moving into the future we must strive to assign all non-enjoyable stimuli an extremely low Space/Time Marker Value. If we could do that, they would have little impact on the brain and might never resurface.

Why was it sometimes difficult to identify the value in a particular situation while it was occurring? Perhaps it was because we were looking to the future for more of the same and didn't take the time to enjoy the moment. Was that the principal reason? Did we often look back and wonder--where had all the good times gone? Did such a feeling result because we knew, deep within our being, that we were not living up to our potential of one hundred percent EOL, or was it because we only looked back when enjoyment was not at the one hundred percent level? Of course, there was no doubt that looking back could be an extremely enjoyable, as it should be. The message must be to live *each moment* of life to the utmost and really, really, listen to what your inner self was saying. Listen carefully and enjoy all the sensations which our bodies had to offer through its many doors of perception. The message was loud and clear, live each moment, really live and experience life in a manner which enhanced your Enjoyment of Life. Be aware of your surroundings and the forces acting on the physical body and mental spirit at all times. We should strive to experience, really experience all the value offered by life. Let valuable experiences make deep impressions in the mind, smile and enjoy all that God's creation has to offer.

On Christmas Eve I found myself at the ASU library peacefully reading. I hiked back to a comfortable bed and the next morning walked to the Tempe train station. I was just about ready to saddle up and hit the iron trail. Perhaps part of the reason for the need for change was a desire to meet more of those complex creatures known as humans. It was a spirit within each of us which we called freedom which also encouraged physical movement. That spirit of freedom existed within everyone but was found in varying degrees. While locked in the North Platte slammer the difference between freedom of spirit and freedom of body was made very clear. Perhaps a totally free spirit existed only when you died. Even if death was the only way to experience total freedom it would be a good idea to continue to strive for maximum freedom as long as my body was still working.

Our spirit was carrying around a chemical bag. We called it a body. Sometimes it got heavy and also had certain energy requirements to keep it functional. Part of our mission on earth was to make the chemical bag a comfortable home for our spirit. A healthy body was important for the spirit. On the other hand, it was nice to experience the pure freedom of the spirit such as when your body was locked in a jail cell. Why was it not possible to experience a sense of total freedom at all times? One reason might be because it was energy intensive and took a concentrated effort to focus energies in a manner which allowed one to separate body and spirit. While the spirit was dwelling within the body the path of least resistance for communication with the surrounding world were the various channels of perception offered by our physical body. We had grown accustomed to the use of these sensory pathways and didn't wish to give them up, hence our instinct for survival.

The instinct for survival was the reason water was such a powerful influence on humans. Water was the most basic requirement for continued survival. Therefore, humans would always seek a place where there was water if they wished to continue on the journey of life. The next important physical need was either heat or coolness so the body water would not freeze or boil. Warmth or coolness could be in the form of clothing or shelter such as a cave. Food was the next item on the survival agenda since the body's machinery required energy and we had not yet acquired the ability to directly use solar power to fuel the body. After having met those Basic Needs we looked for more. We attempted to feed the spirit in order that it too might be comfortable and rest at ease. Fortunately, we were blessed with the ability to directly convert the energies of the universe into food for the spirit. Such "spirit food" added a new dimension to our existence and resulted in growth through accumulation of energy. Perhaps a more basic method of feeding the spirit was the ability to conceptualize ideas within the mind. Of course, such conceptualized "spirit food" was based on the prior accumulation of knowledge made possible by our sense organs. It was entirely up to each individual to select which stimuli they would store as part of their energy base of knowledge. The assignment of the Space/Time Marker Values must be an individual choice. Once we understood that it was our responsibility to assign *value* to incoming stimuli we would increase control over what our spirit consumed.

While still at the Tempe train station two teenagers zoomed by on dirt bikes, roaring down the tracks, bringing me out of my philosophical thought and into current reality. The happy boys brought a smile to my face and a nice pleasant feeling for my spirit. I suspected that the pleasant feeling was present because such fun had been part of earlier life experiences. Long ago I decided to feed my spirit by riding a motorcycle, hence "motorcycle spirit food." Our physical earth was a wonderful playground and provided an almost limitless supply of such "spirit food." I returned to Marlene's to work on the bean pot, they were delicious. Every pot was different and that one appeared to be especially good thanks to the Korean spices.

Saddle Up – Head for the Tracks

Late that afternoon I saddled up and headed for the tracks and another adventure. I missed seeing Marlene on that visit, but I had to move on. A large red, white and blue hot air balloon was just rising from a nearby vacant lot and we both moved toward the iron trail at about the same speed —a nice send off. I met a nice lady newspaper reporter at the tracks taking pictures of the old Tempe train depot. Karen worked for the Phoenix Gazette. We talked for ten minutes or so and she invited me to her house for dinner that evening with her, her husband Jack and their daughter Kathy. The four of us talked about politics, freight trains and philosophy until well after midnight before they gave me a ride back to the train station.

I hopped a northbound toward Phoenix where it would be much easier to catch a south bound to Tucson. I reached Phoenix in the early morning and soon caught a southbound, through Tempe, and headed for Tucson, where I caught a westbound. I arrived in Colton at three in the morning and found out I'd have to walk five miles to the Atchison, Topeka and Santa Fe yards to catch the San Diego train.

Some of my most enjoyable memories were associated with the physical act of walking. There was something about the fluid movement and getting close to the earth that resulted in a special impact on the brain. Perhaps there was a physiological reason since many nerves were found on the souls of the feet. After all there were not many people who would turn down a good foot massage.

During my walk I met a young man walking with his young son. We struck up a conversation, and I impressed them both by taking them aboard a running locomotive that was sitting on the tracks. Following this he invited me to his house to meet his wife, get something to eat and take a shower – wow! Ended up staying until after midnight. We had a great time, drank many beers, played pool and listened to loud music. They were a nice young couple, in their late teens and had a cute little house next to the honey factory where John worked. The tracks ran right in front of their house and John told me "you now have a place to stop whenever you are in these train yards." John was a beekeeper and took much pride in his work. His father had many bee hives scattered throughout the West and Midwest. John sometimes traveled to collect the honey and then brought it to the plant for processing. He taught me about the bee business as he enjoyed talking about his work. We also discussed trains, politics and philosophy for hours. His wife, Linda, was very friendly and fixed us a delicious dinner. John was a very interesting fellow and reminded me of myself many years ago. In many ways we shared a similar background.

Perhaps there were times during life when you should look at reality in a non-humorous manner, however; it should be done in a way that did not interfere with EOL. Individuals not having even a little humor tended to be mostly serious, sometimes grave, and carefully considered their every move. They were almost frozen in time since every decision was extremely important to their future. Living with that state of mind assumed one path was far better than another. Such behavior fit nicely into the second category of life experiences; it was the two percent of time referred to a few pages back. If we could release ourselves from thoughts of good, bad and judge our actions on what was best for the body and soul we once again would enter the serene stage of consciousness. Life could be like Thanksgiving dinner; you could enjoy savoring each bite or stuff it in while not enjoying each morsel. If you chose the latter you would certainly wonder why the pleasure lasted such a short time.

How did the feeling of Total Serenity and the theory of constant change coincide? This question might be approached in two ways: 1) serenity of the spirit and 2) serenity of the physical body. Could one be in a state of serenity while the other was not? Serenity was a quality that came from within--at least the most lasting kind. The physical body could be serene (warm, well fed etc.) while the spirit was not, in fact that was probably the state in which many people lived from day to day. Serenity of the soul could exist regardless of body condition. Serenity of the soul while having an uncomfortable body was difficult to maintain as it required tremendous amounts of energy. However; it could be done. While riding the freight trains many times the body was uncomfortable yet the spirit was made to comfortably rest.

John invited me to spend the night but I elected to stagger (from the many beers) along the tracks in the cold night air. Within a couple of hours, a running jump was accomplished for a ride on a south-bound Union Pacific. It highballed directly to Hobart Junction in Los Angeles. Next the "night coaster" was discovered. This train made daily San Diego trips and was due to shine in ten hours. While sitting under the Long Beach Freeway Bridge at the east end of the yard I saw some greenery growing along a fence. On closer inspection I found several tomato plants of two varieties, small cherries and regular – yum, yum.

Under the Bridge

Sitting under the freeway bridge, in that dirty hobo jungle, thoughts of sweet serenity and my current state of total Enjoyment of Life entered my consciousness. Those thoughts really felt good! It was as if that dirty, stinking hobo jungle became my campsite on the Altadena side of the San Gabriel Mountains. It was a feeling which came from my very soul—it was as if my spirit was at total peace. For that moment, I had been nowhere and would go nowhere for I was there in that space/time at peace with my soul. That feeling was rare – it goes beyond the usual Enjoyment of Life. It was the feeling of Total Serenity (TS).

I caught the "night coaster" in the early evening and had a pleasant ride to San Diego, where I went to my sister Renee's house for a visit. But the need to move was powerful and after a couple of days I went to the rail yards to see about a northbound.

Altar Cloth of God

Back in Altadena, where Becky seemed especially happy to see me, I headed for the only hardware store in town and put in an application. It was a family-owned business and the possibility of getting hired looked good. I also acquired a library card which made me feel more like a real citizen of the town. Thoughts of maybe settling down for a while entered my brain. It was indeed strange to have an address after such long time on the cinder trail.

Spiritual Thoughts

Our creations and accomplishments are for the enjoyment that is immediately available to us as individuals. We might decide to reflect on such creations or more likely they reflect on our spirit by way of our mind in some future space/time. Thus, if we create valuable things in thought or deed, they will return. Spirit, mind and body are words often used when describing humans in philosophical discussions. Mind and body are difficult to separate; together they form a system which provides the spirit with a method of communication and a way of enjoying our various physical senses. Such experiences provide a path for the spirit which combines them in numerous ways, in other words they provide, "spirit food." As we move through the world in a mental and physical way we are constantly re-arranging energy. We actually send waves of energy in all directions. We sometimes refer to this energy as an "aura." It is our responsibility to ensure that the energy is directed in a valuable manner. Energy is neither good nor bad for it knows no morality. It knows only of the constant flow and change in physical reality. Everything in our reality is composed of energy. Therefore, in the interest of mankind we should make sure all our actions and reactions are valuable. We should think more in terms of *value* of energy. Energy does not have the same value for everyone. Think of energy as a resource that provides the path to a way to acquire New Knowledge. The rational conclusion is that when incoming stimuli are valuable then we should keep our doors of perception wide open. However; sometimes the amount of incoming energy is overwhelming. At such times the soul and body need solitude.

When describing physical reality we often find it difficult to find the appropriate words to adequately describe the phenomena. When describing things such as "reality" the idea is to convey a common view acceptable to most listeners or readers. That is often difficult, sometimes impossible, since everyone perceives reality in their own way. Actually, it is impossible for two individuals to perceive the same thing in exactly the same way. This is because the photons of energy radiating from the information source are not the same. Additionally, those photons activate different receptors. The language used to describe reality is generally imprecise—a crude description at best. The language is generally understood by most people and hence we have different levels of knowing reality. An example: one might choose to stand in front of a beautiful mountain range and absorb the photons of energy radiating onto the optic nerve. Another level of perceiving the reality of the mountain might be to close the eyes and feel the air currents falling or rising before the mountains. That level uses the skin's surface to detect and describe the rock of the mountains where you might actually "feel" the energy of the mountains. Perhaps we might even "feel" electromagnetic radiation emitted by the sheer mountain mass impinging on some undiscovered receptor within the physiological body. It seemed to me that language sometimes became a barrier when trying to describe such realities. Sometimes words just don't exist to relate such experiences. Perhaps that is why language must be dynamic and subject to constant change.

What is the energy which moves curious men and women to the top of a mountain or deep into a dense jungle? Is it not the same energy that moved the sun through the heavens? Is it not the same force that moves billions of stars in the black void of the universe? Is it not the same energy that moves the wind through the trees and pushes the mountains skyward? Is it not the same energy that occasionally shakes the earth's crust and causes the mountains to erupt in fiery displays of molten rock? Such energy must have a physiological receptor someplace--perhaps where the body and soul interface. Some might refer to that unknown receptor as the soul of man. I felt it represented a physiological point between the brain and spirit.

Hardware Store

Becky told me that the hardware store called and wanted me to start work tomorrow and work four days a week. It looked like my wish had come true. It was a nice feeling. The idea of receiving a paycheck was interesting, especially with my Enjoyment of Life now being at 98%. It seemed that no matter what I was doing, working for the White House or a hardware store, I had to perform in the manner in which I wished to be remembered. You should be proud of whatever job you were doing. It is as simple as doing your best while still maintaining EOL.

After two days at the Hardware store everything was going fine, time seemed to flow smoothly. Learning about the hardware and where everything was located in a well laid out store was challenging and fun. The family atmosphere was terrific; they made me feel right at home.

Problems in Paradise

It was nice to be able to, or at least strive to objectively observe the actions of others. The ability to be objective was enhanced when the observer was in the state of heightened EOL or even Total Serenity. It was a matter of putting the spirit outside the physical being in order to witness a transpiring event. Such activity of the mind required a conscious effort and an extensive expenditure of energy. One of the things people often did was to make a small problem into a big one—Becky seemed to be doing exactly this. Many people were not aware of it when they were actually doing it. They somehow failed to see the direction of their own spirit and body. As a young man, I had what some might call a short fuse, leading me into more than a few physical fights. Later I learned to distinguish which threats were real, and therefore worth fighting over. That was part of the learning process on how to respond to a perceived or actual threat. Some people never learned.

Matters of principle endure—even in an atmosphere of constant change—it is the valuable energy which survives. Whenever a group of people get together and form a society its members are expected to contribute energy to sustain the goals and objectives of the society. The society will only be successful if the correct amount of energy is extracted from each of its members. If more individual energy is required than available, the result is an unhappy society. The citizens of such a society would be unhappy individuals and the society would suffer. In my opinion that argues against "self-sacrifice" as the cure for society's shortcomings.

Sometimes there is "magic" in the air—the conditions which govern that "magic" reside within oneself. Are such feelings related to joy, delight or perhaps serenity? The feeling is definitely related to all three and perhaps could be used to describe the combination of all three and the overall EOL feeling. Or could this magical feeling go beyond Total Serenity?

Surprisingly Becky decided to make some rather critical and harsh judgments regarding my basic philosophy of life. One evening when we were talking about EOL, she rather rudely told me, "You don't know what you're talking about. You're full of shit!" The forceful and animated way she said it gave me the distinct impression that it was something she had wanted to say for a long, long time. In my view it made no sense for her to criticize my perception of reality. The main reason was that no one would be in a better position to interpret another's reality other than that individual. At least that should be the case, unless there was clear evidence of mental illness. At this point Becky would argue for the "mental illness" interpretation. She calmly told me, "You're crazy!" She even informed me that she thought my state of Total Serenity was a weakness and represented the suppression of my conscious self. The more we talked the more obvious it became that her vision of reality was much different than mine.

The joyful feeling between us was just about totally gone. The philosophical mind was attempting to analyze that uncomfortable situation. The stop on Lovila Lane had been very nice, truly a valuable experience which had added greatly to EOL. However, the energy which once flowed so easily between us was no longer synchronous. If we remained together it would require an excess of energy expenditure. The energy required for the assignment of STMVs would result in diminished EOL. Getting ready to move to a more synchronous energy field was uppermost in my thoughts. In defense of Becky, it must be hard to share space with someone like myself.

Out the back door of the hardware store and down the alley there was the BBH bar. It was a hangout for the locals – mostly law enforcement and fireman. Friday after work it was my stop off for a few beers and conversation before heading back home to talk some more with Becky. We were trying to decide how much longer to stay together on Lovila Lane. Why did it make any difference when one left or arrived at any particular place? Why? There was no difference if you believed that time was a creation of man and not an actual reality. The only "safe" way to proceed was under the guidance the EOL philosophy. EOL was the only reality that could objectively evaluate such a situation. In any relationship it was the energy that must be shared with equal velocity and direction. It seemed that we had reached a point where we exchanged very little energy which caused a non-synchronous state. We definitely were not communicating during that time.

I left Becky's after spending the last few hours in pleasant conversation. Our break-up was very "civil." Somehow, there was a smile on my face in spite of our separation and not knowing of a place to sleep that evening. I decided to walk down Los Robles Street for reasons unknown. While walking and whistling I spotted Heather waiting for a bus. Heather was a student at Pasadena City College studying English and Art. We talked for several minutes and she invited me to stay at her small apartment in South Pasadena. I guess the radiation of positive energy must have been working. I stayed the night and then headed into L.A. for the weekend.

Upon my return to Altadena I went to see Heather again, but she was angry that I had stayed one night and then left. Maybe that was for the best, as freedom was especially important to me. So, I camped in various places near the mountains. My routine was to close camp in the morning, then go to the hardware store to shave and wash. It worked well. I had a job, but also my independence. But Becky's conversations and sweet kisses had spoiled me, and soon I was missing her beautiful company. It would be nice to have a female companion having the ability to move as this hobo. Of course, she would have to be self-sufficient. Was that really too much to ask?

The popular view of "reality" failed to take into account the concept of constant change. It was the constant change in all things which made "reality" more like a stream rather than any one static reality such as a lake. To deny the reality of constant change was non-scientific thinking. Change was one of the basic physical laws which governed the universe. Reality represented constant change. You might think of yourself as an ethereal being, in constant motion, moving within the universe made up of pure energy. Humans might try to stand together and move with and through the adventures presented by the reality of constant change. Life could be as good as desired, for life itself was a state of mind and how one chose to interact with all the energy available for the physical receptors. We all had the power to make life as good or as bad as we wished.

How various stimuli in our environment reached the brain was not of concern; the important thing was that the receptor for a particular stimulus must control the weight or value attached to each bit of incoming energy. The simple act of assigning such Space/Time Marker Values influenced our future path. As individuals we must be the final judge regarding the assignment of those values. By assigning such weights we could determine what things we chose to remember thus influencing our future interpretation of reality.

One morning after camping next to the frisky Los Flores creek, I stumbled upon an abandoned house hidden in a dense tangle of trees and bushes not far from the hardware store. The back door was open, so I went inside to look around. Broken furniture and magazines littered the floor, but I figured it might just serve as a shelter during my work week.

I went to the BBH Bar Friday night after work. After a few beers a nice lady sat down next to me and introduced herself. Rita told me that she recognized me from my political campaign in the San Fernando Valley. As we talked. I remembered her as one of my early supporters. We had a great discussion about those past campaign days and what we were both doing now. Our chance meeting once again reminded me that it was indeed a small world.

"Looking outward" from my newly found stability and relatively non-mobile position in life it became evident that many people were sort of "stuck in a rut." Of course, what was perceived as being "stuck in a rut" might represent something completely different for those being judged. Security and consistent relationships could bring personal joy, as there are many different paths to EOL. But at that point in my life, there was a need for frequent change. If early in life you were alert for all stimuli you could become an active receptor of information and thus grow through the accumulation of knowledge. People often "burned out" early in life and sought stability and security by shutting out new and/or alarming information. It was as if one's power of imagination, leading to the visualization of a different future, was somehow extinguished. It seemed to me that a more natural approach would be to acknowledge constant change in our environment. Such acknowledgement could then lead to personal changes where the magnitude and speed of change could then be controlled by the individual – not society.

The old abandoned house on Altadena Drive was a nice dry campsite for that colder and wetter winter season of Southern California. I cleaned out an area and set up a bed and covered broken windows with boards. The rent was reasonable (free) which would make it possible to save part of the paycheck for a little nest egg for a piece of land. I began to wonder if this sometime hobo would ever really settle down and live a more "normal" life. Even if I found a piece of land it most likely wouldn't lead to a more "normal" existence – at least that was my thought.

My chosen lifestyle did sometimes present certain challenges. It was stimulating to survive on the road and repeatedly gratifying to face and overcome every so-called obstacle. Actually "obstacles" became an opportunity to learn more than anything else—a problem to solve. Therefore, all challenges became enjoyable experiences in that they added to my energy base of knowledge. The candle light, maps, soft rug, food and the sound of the rain on the roof of the dilapidated house, all combined to make that place very special. I mentally pinched myself and assigned that space and time a high STMV. It was truly a comfortable campsite and required very little energy to maintain my Enjoyment of Life (EOL).

Becky called the hardware store to let me know some important looking mail for me had arrived at her house. Upon arrival, she made it perfectly clear that she retained her negative outlook toward my chosen lifestyle—no morning kisses were accepted. The mountains were crystal clear following last night's rain; the snow almost reached the top of Echo Mountain. Mount Wilson and the flats west of Millard Canyon were covered with brilliant white snow. It was fantastic feeling when walking up the hill for another day at the hardware store.

Modification of EOL

While sitting in the tranquil atmosphere of the Altadena library my mind drifted to thoughts of my Enjoyment of Life philosophy and how it might be better presented. The word "enrichment" came to mind. Enrich meant to make richer in some quality but not necessarily with money. The definition of "rich" implied something of high quality, well supplied, magnificently impressive, full and mellow in tone and quality and something highly productive. The idea of using different words to describe my EOL philosophy had been developing over the past year. Some people would react negatively and just stopped listening when they heard the word "enjoyment" associated with any Purpose of Life. How could anyone be so selfish as to go through life enjoying it?

I had to admit that the idea of changing anything about my EOL concept was met with much internal resistance. I was quite accustomed to the way it had developed. It was much like a comfortable pair of old shoes. EOL had certainly developed to the point where it did generate strong reactions when verbalized to others. To make it more tolerable one might think of "Enjoyment of Life" as being interchangeable with the phrase "Enrichment of Life." Having the freedom to move, and thus expose oneself to new stimuli, played a major role in both *enjoyment* and *enrichment* of life. Thus, Enjoyment of Life was a direct result of efforts to "enrich" it. Hence the concept of EOL could also be considered as "Enrichment of Life". Adding to the energy base of knowledge was both enjoyable and enriching for the body and spirit. Perhaps it was time to modify EOL in a way which made it easier to understand and therefore more acceptable. After all, constant change was foundational for my belief system and a basic principle underlying life. The idea that EOL should be expanded to include both "enjoyment" and "enrichment" was almost accepted. Perhaps E^2OL (E-squared OL) might be a better way to communicate EOL. I decided to give the idea some additional thought but was pretty sure it would be included in my Formula for Life.

I needed a vacation and there was going to be a workshop concerning military aid for El Salvador at Arizona State University in Tempe that I wanted to attend. My boss gave me the go-ahead, and on Friday after work, I saddled up, stopped at the library to see my friends, had a few beers at BBH and with a broad smile headed down Lake Street to see about catching "Smoky" for the ride east.

Hobo's Vacation

It was delightful to be back in the grittiness of the freight train yard. I soon spotted a train getting ready to highball in the direction of the massive Colton yard and settled in for the ride east toward San Bernardino. It was a pleasant morning; rolling down the tracks my mind drifted as if to review the many recent enjoyable times spent in Altadena. It was a feeling worthy of a high STMV.

It wasn't long before the train arrived in the Colton yard and I happily walked five miles to the crossover tracks to say hello to my beekeeper friend John and his wife Linda. They asked me to spend the night and this time I accepted. It was another fun evening with John and his family as we had much to talk about. The next afternoon found me gliding smoothly across the sands of California's Mojave Desert on a hot shot bound for Yuma then Tucson.

It was so pleasant to sit by the side of the tracks in Tucson, watching the sun rise and the many hobos emerging from the boxcars; freedom was such a cherished part of life. Some of the hobos stopped for brief and pleasant conversations. Hobos generally stuck together and shared possessions when they could. It seemed to me that when you shared knowledge with others you were actually sharing energy. It was knowledge which gave a sense of direction to energy. That morning, in that trackside park, it gave me a humbling feeling of satisfaction to share the energy of conversation with those Arizona hobos.

I arrived in Tempe the following morning. When Marlene showed up at her apartment that evening she was pretty icy and didn't seem at all happy to see me. Her attitude got much worse once we began to discuss the El Salvador meetings at the ASU campus. She was taking the position that the U.S. government was absolutely wrong in giving military aid to the Duarte government. From my point of view she was siding with the rebels, who were supported by the communists. Our opposing views resulted in some friction, but we managed to set it aside for many lovely kisses. We had no trouble when limiting our communication to kisses.

The next morning, after listening to the "so-called" rebel leaders from El Salvador, I concluded that these meetings were meant to push an ambitious communist agenda. The meetings raised money and provided a platform for their communist propaganda. The students were eating it up and appeared to believe every word. How could the State Department, FBI and/or the CIA allow these people to speak in our country?

One of the self-anointed rebel leaders went so far as to state that El Salvador was only the first country they would eventually "liberate." All of Central America and Mexico would eventually follow. The audience could clearly see his facial expression as he ended his list with Mexico. It was almost with a "wink and a nod" when he stopped before adding the USA to his "hit" list. For me the saddest part of the whole show was that most, if not all, of the students seemed to agree with his blistering tirade.

Most of the two-day workshop was designed to build support for the defeat of a military aid package for El Salvador; it was about to be voted on by Congress. The following day was much of the same propaganda. Only in a free America could such a spectacle take place. Marlene thought the rebels were great and we had a heated discussion regarding our very different views. Following that exchange she made herself scarce for the rest of my visit. She suddenly found better things to do than to spend time with a "rightwing redneck" as she angrily called me. She decided to spend the nights during my visit at her parent's house. We talked on the phone and made a sincere effort to work through our differences. She was upset because my voice was raised in the heat of our disagreement. She assigned my verbal display of emotion a high STMV and it definitely impacted her brain. Needless to say, she didn't like it, and as a matter of fact, my behavior didn't suit me either.

Such yelling behavior was actually quite uncharacteristic for me and therefore worthy of some analysis. Was that emotional display an example of the two percent non-Enjoyment of Life? Was it really enjoyable and enriching to shout at a fellow human being in an emotional outburst just because they held different beliefs? It is doubtful! There was no excuse for such behavior and it was definitely a manifestation of non-Enjoyment of Life. The value in that experience rested in the lesson taken away from that encounter – when disagreeing with a fellow human being don't ever yell in anger!

In spite of my uncomfortable situation with Marlene, energy was expended in a way to ensure an enjoyable hobo vacation. Tempe's Main Street was filled with people as the annual City Fair was in full swing. Many things stimulated my brain including many attractive ladies dressed in their hot summer outfits. I spent evenings between Marlene's and her neighbor Terrie's apartments. I tried to convince Terrie's friends to venture onto the steel ribbons for some fun on the cinder trail. It didn't work. Perhaps someday I'd find a woman who would want to travel the iron trail.

As we travel through space/time an individual has the freedom to seek synchronous energy fields, whether such energy comes from people or nature. When such an energy field is located it is nice to travel in unison; it makes the trip less subject to interference from outside energy forces. The last couple of days in Tempe were spent at the ASU library, sitting around campus or by the pool at the apartments. It was very relaxing and found it easy to enjoy myself with very little expenditure of energy. In spite of my brief bout of non-EOL, my time away from the big city was turning out to be a great vacation.

I headed down to the rail yard to catch a train, but had no luck, and found myself preoccupied with my behavior toward Marlene. We hadn't made up or even said goodbye. I headed back to the library to figure out a next move, then went to the Campus Union for some ice cream. Marlene was there! What great luck—at least for me. We discussed our earlier conversation regarding the rebels but in a much more civilized manner. We had a long talk and at least understood each other's position much better. She had not changed her view. She still strongly supported the rebels, which was certainly a legitimate position. I apologized for my earlier loudmouth behavior and she acknowledged that we were both very passionate on the subject. She walked with me to the bus stop and we parted company on friendly terms with hug and a very light kiss. There was no more—she was done with having this hobo in her life.

Returned to downtown Phoenix to see about catching the midnight train, preferably one with an open flatcar for a good view of the Arizona stars and sunrise. Solo train riding really did test one's ability to be alone. It kind of reminded me of the time spent at the mining camp in Big Sur. The rising sun greeted me in Yuma and a few minutes later a couple of polite U.S. Border Patrol Officers climbed into my car looking for illegal aliens.

I emerged from my hiding spot late in the afternoon and jumped on a fast mover as it left the yard. Once in the open desert several jet fighters swooped down and used that train as a mock target. They came in low and very fast. It was quite a display and was a great addition to the excitement of the day. You could actually see the pilots as they sped by on their simulated "bombing" runs.

It was a hot day, well over a hundred degrees, and the water canteens were just about empty. The value identified in that uncomfortable situation was that it reminded me once again about the importance of Basic Needs and how unimportant everything else really was in this world. Until you ran out of water in the hot desert you just didn't know what it was like. While we continued to roll toward the Colton yards a pair of Army Huey helicopter gunships swooped over a mountain ridge. They slid into positions on both sides of the train and flew from the caboose alongside until they reached my boxcar at which time they slowed to match the train's speed. At that point it was eyeball to eyeball with a couple of bad-ass looking Army chopper pilots. It was a fantastic break from the slow ride across the hot and waterless desert. After a minute or so the pilots and their mean olive drab machines continued up the length of the train, peeled off and disappeared over another ridge. Wow! What a show, hurrah for the U.S. Army!

The lack of water made the trip through the scorching desert seem as if it was taking forever—visions of water made me count every mile. My skin was dry and a pinkish color and I actually felt like passing out several times during that blistering trip. I knew from past experience that the Colton yard had many refrigerated water coolers scattered throughout the yard. Such thoughts took over my mind. We finally made it to the Colton yard and I stumbled out of my baking boxcar in a desperate search for water, finding one of the coveted coolers within yards—water never tasted so good!

I arrived in Van Nuys a few hours later. I had saved a few dollars from working at the hardware store and a new rucksack was high on the list of needed items. I found a U.S. Army pack that seemed to perfectly fulfill my needs. It was an ALICE rucksack. ALICE was an acronym that stood for "Army Light Infantry Carrying Equipment." It was beautiful! It felt fantastic on my back and could not resist taking off to spend the night in the bush with my new house. I set up camp right in the San Fernando Valley in a magnificent stand of eucalyptus trees next to the tracks. I listened to the powerful sound of speeding trains as they passed my campsite throughout the night.

I called my old friend Rocky and she made it clear that she would be extremely happy to see me. Rocky had accomplished what she had often voiced during our prior time together—she was now a registered nurse and working at a local hospital. She promised to be extra nice to me and, true to her word, it was a wild, crazy and fun filled night! She was really a calm and warm-hearted woman but that night she only wanted to party. There was no stopping her. Aside from the fun it was really special to see her and reminisce about the good times we had during my political campaigns. It was sad to say goodbye after such a short visit. We may have only spent the night together but the impact on my body and soul will last a long, long time.

I spent the next few days visiting with old campaign colleagues and friends before heading back to my Altadena campsite. This hobo's vacation was coming to an end.

Philosophy of Freedom

Once again, I found myself on the corner of Hollywood and Vine and the bus transfer point for my trips between the San Fernando Valley and Altadena. I stopped at my Korean friend's wig shop to say hello, then observed some Hollyweird-style humanity, and jumped on the Lake Street bus, arriving at my Altadena Drive campsite an hour later. It felt great to be back in my "peaceful shelter." Altadena had a small-town atmosphere despite its proximity to the beast of L.A. Following a good night's rest I walked leisurely to the hardware store.

Now that I was receiving a regular paycheck, I thought a lot more about how to make ends meet. Somehow the few dollars left in my pocket didn't seem like much when payday was three days away. On the tracks I could go for days with empty pockets without a worry. Now the thought of running out of money before payday caused anxiety—I couldn't understand why.

Since Becky and I had split, I'd developed a pattern of going to the San Fernando Valley for the weekends, so on Friday I hopped a bus and headed that way to visit friends and to set up a weekend office. After a long Saturday of sorting through files and arranging the office, I got restless and headed for the local beer joint to relieve my boredom.

A Wild Ride

It was after midnight and everyone at a friendly local bar was pretty well oiled up. It was a pleasant atmosphere, no bottles being smashed against the walls, lots of laughter and a few young ladies roaming around. Kathy caught my eye as she was seductively dancing with the jukebox. We struck up a conversation. She was feeling no pain and appeared to be open for some male companionship. At closing time, she offered me a ride to her place to continue the party.

As we took to the road my mistake became apparent as that fun seeking young woman turned into a very drunk driver. It appeared to me that she was trying to commit suicide as she sped down the road; often on the wrong side, sliding around corners, running red lights and generally driving like an out-of-control maniac. My romantic intentions rapidly cooled as survival instincts took over. I screamed at her to pull over. She just sped up. Finally, I reached over and grabbed the keys out of the ignition. She instantly turned into a wild-eyed tiger. She was furious and refused to let me drive. "Give me the fucking keys you no-good dirty prick," she yelled. Wanting to live to see the morrow, I held on to the keys, removed my stuff from the back seat, tossed her the keys and headed for my campsite as she sped off into the night. I would sleep alone, but felt happy to be alive and unharmed.

I awoke early and headed for the Operations Building at the 146th Tactical Air Wing to meet with some Air Force officers about my efforts at getting new "H" model C-130's for their unit. Then it was off to the Van Meter Estate, where I spent the afternoon organizing my many files that were stored in Dan's outbuildings. It was an enjoyable and relaxing time that triggered many pleasant memories of my 1976 and 1978 political campaigns. Dan fixed a great lunch and we had a good time discussing government policy and where we thought our country might be headed. We worked at solving the world's problems late into the evening and then I caught the bus back to Altadena.

After another week at the hardware store, I headed down to the Santa Fe Rail yards in in East Los Angeles to catch the "night coaster" to Oceanside, to attend my brother Tom's wedding that weekend. Once in the freight yards my spirit was at ease—to feel the thundering power of the passing locomotives and to smell the pungent aroma of diesel fuel was up-lifting. I jumped on a nice clean boxcar—the ALICE gear was fantastic and made jumping a moving train much easier— with both doors wide open. It was a rubber-necking trip south trying to absorb all the beauty through those two open doors.

As I was about to jump from the moving freight in Oceanside I saw a gumshoe scanning the train. I hid behind the boxcar wall as the train rapidly picked up speed. I stayed aboard, as I did not want to risk getting arrested and spending Tom's wedding in lockup. I hopped off in San Diego, where a little telephone work was successful in finding both Rennie and Tom, reminding me, once again, that all trains were good ones.

A Little Philosophy

During my travels, when I would speak to others about my personal philosophy of life, they sometimes would try to find something wrong with it—a flaw. One such attempt to discredit E^2OL was when they said that life would be boring if you enjoyed yourself all the time. How about that one? One critical individual even seriously suggested that "going around wearing a constant smile and in a happy mood would be boring." That particular person didn't understand that for me enjoyment existed as a continuum. The vast array of life experiences available along the total range of enjoyment could easily add plenty of spice to one's life. What was the purpose of man but to strive for perfection through the principle of Enrichment and Enjoyment of Life? What was perfection? What was our symbol of perfection? Our God? Our Spirit? To my way of thinking perfection was the one hundred percent E^2OL that resulted in Total Serenity. The more you understood your body and soul via the process of Enrichment and Enjoyment the better it was when dealing with both the spiritual and physical reality. We should strive to understand our attitudes and behaviors. Answers about one's own behavior could guide one on the path toward perfection. Perfection was the E^2OL all the time. It was a project worthy of a lifetime of effort.

College Philosophy Class

While working at the hardware store one day, I was surprised by a call from Heather. She wanted to invite me to her philosophy class since it was something that interested me. I arrived late for class and drew some unwanted attention attempting to sneak into the back row of chairs. The lady teaching the class had a charming and articulate manner.

The subject matter for that evening's class was John Paul Sartre. He seemed to endorse the belief that all of life was meaningless and therefore *nothing* mattered. My Enjoyment of Life philosophy had sometimes been accused of supporting that same belief. However, just because a belief that *all* paths were valuable did not mean the same thing as Sartre's "nothing matters" philosophy. That was because some paths required less energy than others to identify the Enjoyment and Enrichment of Life. As we traveled through the adventure of life, we acquired energy through New Knowledge and thus grew and changed thru that accumulation of energy. All choices were valuable! All paths could be glorious, even death. Glory in death belonged to those who chose to live by the E²OL philosophy. Such a person would live a life filled with joy to the very end. Look for the *value* offered by each path for there was always some blessing, some gift from our Creator waiting for us as we moved through the universe. My interpretation of the Sartre philosophy was that he found it difficult to see the value in simply enjoying one's life. Heather failed to show up for the class! What do you suppose she was trying to tell me?

Hobo's Beliefs

One night at the BBH there was a loudmouth drunk looking for trouble and wanting to fight. It wasn't long before the Los Angeles Sheriff's Deputies arrived and took charge of the situation. It was a pleasure to observe their professional behavior. They somehow managed to use just enough force to subdue the guy, remove him from the bar and leave the rest of us in peace.

It was logical to think that nations often behaved as individuals and therefore the same principle guiding the use of force might be followed by our nation's leaders. We often found that other human beings or nations displayed behaviors vastly different from our perception of how reality operated. However, when confronted with such behaviors it should be remembered that we should look for *value* as there certainly was Value in Everything. It was the individual or nation that must determine the amount of energy you wished to devote to finding that value.

Intoxicants

All types of intoxicants used by us humans enhance our ability to separate the body and spirit – usually a good idea under the correct circumstances. It must be remembered that the abuse of intoxicants could actually result in the death of one's body. Intoxicants just make it easier to take a vacation from current reality. It could be thought of as putting the physical reality of our world into its proper *subordinate* position. Once physical matter is subordinated it requires less energy to visualize future paths. The weight of physical reality is immediately removed. A path based on spiritual reality requires less energy than when thinking of the consequences of future or past physical actions. It is the freeing oneself from the constraints of the material world which set the spirit free. The realm of the spirit allows us to more easily live according to the Enjoyment and Enrichment of Life principle.

It should be remembered that when working in professions such as the military or police you are rarely permitted the luxury of such spiritual thinking. Perhaps that is one reason why intoxicants are such an attraction to off-duty military and police personnel.

Back to Physical Reality

Another Sunday night was spent at the Conservation District Office. The morning found me heading for West Los Angeles to look for old friends and perhaps spend some time soaking up the beauty of the Pacific Ocean. I ended up walking several miles down Wilshire Boulevard to the Pacific Palisades Park in Santa Monica. That beautiful Park overlooked the Pacific Ocean which sparkled in the afternoon sun. A slight breeze brought the taste and smell of salt water to my senses.

Experience, really experience the beauty in the world, let it permeate every molecule, every atom, and every thought and give it the highest Space/Time Marker Value. Such beauty could then fill your being and radiate – for it has actual physical mass. I relaxed and just let my body and spirit absorb the beauty of the wind, the eucalyptus trees, the ocean, the green grass and the many smiles of the people walking in the park. Let your spirit act like a sponge for all the valuable energy that filled the universe. Once you become filled with the energy of beauty you will have fulfilled your reason for being part of this reality.

Back in Altadena I camped under the stars in the General Farnsworth Park. During the night the strong Santa Ana winds hit with a vengeance! I love those winds and theorized that they were nature's way of welcoming me home. On an early morning hike, I encountered many tree limbs littering the streets. The mountains were crystal clear and vibrant with the brilliant green of early spring. I headed for the hardware store as the wind slowly diminished and the sun grew brighter; it was the start of another wonderful day.

Everything was so synchronous. It was difficult to understand why thoughts of leaving Altadena—of moving on to new places—were entering my consciousness. Perhaps the ease with such movement was based on an ability to blend with physical reality no matter where my body was. My spirit was healthy. Value was present whether the body was in the slums of D.C. or in San Gabriel Mountains. One could consciously open the doors of perception and let the valuable energy flow into the mind. One could discover true beauty while achieving the state of Total Serenity! We all had the power within us. It was another bright sunny morning and once again I sat in the alley behind the hardware store, reading the newspaper and waiting for another work day to begin. It had been interesting to observe my energy focusing on change lately—movement was in-the-air. It was as if my spirit sought new stimuli someplace, anyplace or every place in our wonderful country. Most likely that energy would lead me to our Nation's Capital via the northern train route. Fresno, Oregon, Washington, St. Louis and perhaps New Hampshire sounded like a reasonable itinerary; plans were very flexible at this stage.

I had a pleasant evening at BBH and camped under the stars on the lovely Altadena Library grounds, then awoke before dawn and took a long walk through the city as if to say good-bye. I told Paul, the hardware store owner, about my intentions to head East. He was gracious about it and understanding. The expression "salt of the earth" seemed to describe that family; they were the type of people that made this country great. I got up on my last day and spent time getting ALICE ready for travel. Becky and her son Shawn met me for lunch and to say goodbye; it was nice to part as friends.

I decided to spend one more night in pleasant Altadena and then "set sail" in the morning. That evening I sat on the library's beautiful lawn while watching the sun fall toward the horizon. I felt very much at ease with my decision to leave and actually felt blessed in that time and space. Altadena was still as enjoyable as on the first day of my arrival. Perhaps stopping in Altadena was giving my spirit a needed rest. And now my spirit was ready to seek out new experiences in a quest for Total Serenity. It was the energy of movement; a sense of constant change that encouraged me to seek some new adventure. Perhaps someplace existed that had an even more peaceful environment. Perhaps it was the solitude of the rails which was calling to my spirit.

California's Iron Trail

It was a bright and beautiful day in May in the Santa Fe railroad yard and I still couldn't decide which train to catch—north, south, east or west. As I approached the old hobo jungle at the south end of the yard a couple of gumshoes came speeding toward me in a cloud of dust. They drove right past me and wildly turned, with tires screeching, onto the street. Later the yard workers told me they were looking for some train riders at the north end of the yard. I figured I should keep out of sight while waiting for the "night coaster." I had decided to begin my journey with a visit to my parents in Oceanside.

Trackside Philosophy
My mind often meandered as I waited for another train. For some unexplainable reason (perhaps boredom) I used my knife to prune a large vine-like plant climbing a nearby fence. The pruning would undoubtedly cause a spurt of growth with new energy flowing toward the very top of the plant. The redirecting of energy was caused by removing the lower branches with their buds. The thought occurred to me that the same approach might apply to the human spirit. Once you mastered the ability to assign values (STMV) to environmental stimuli you became much like a well pruned plant. You could even say you were "pruning" your spiritual self. The valuable force of growth (spiritual enrichment) was not directed toward extraneous considerations (branches) and you were free to develop in the most efficient and beautiful manner. The "bud" of your psyche felt the spurt of power and blossomed to its fullest potential. There was a certain measure of comfortableness with that new analogy and the insight that it provided for my search to identify a meaning for my life. One thing for sure--it brought a wide smile to my face.

Rolling Down the Tracks

Later in the evening I found myself on top of an ore car that was filled with some black clay like material. We rolled south, me sitting on top of the world with the cool wind blowing in my face. Occasional sips of brandy made the ride even more enjoyable.

Upon arrival in Oceanside, I realized that I was as black as the "coal man" who delivered to our home in Sioux City. It seemed that the loose material from the forward rail cars had blown my way as we sped through the coastal towns of Southern California. It was just another lesson from the tracks. Called my parents and good old Dad came to the tracks to pick up his very dirty hobo son. Much to his credit he didn't appear to see the grime and was happy to see his eldest son. Spent a pleasant few days in Oceanside relaxing and enjoying the company of Mom and Dad as well as many wonderful cool sea breezes. The nearby Mira Costa College library provided raw material for the accumulation of brain food. It was a pleasant atmosphere on campus and the reassuring booming of the Marine Corp artillery range, twenty miles to the north, drifted to my ears.

Dad and I put up a flagpole, raised the stars and stripes and together looked at it as it gently waved in a cool sea breeze. A major part of my Dad's patriotism stemmed from his years in the Pacific during World War II. He was one of those disabled war veterans that spoke little of his Army Air Corp experiences. However, on occasion he would sometimes remind us kids of the horrific consequences of war. Guess you might say he was anti-war based on his four years on the front-lines of the Pacific.

Relaxed under the bell tower of Mira Costa; sunshine, brilliantly colored flowers, purple necked hummingbirds, cool ocean breezes and pleasant conversation with a nice female student, Marie, who told me she was a second-year drama student with hopes of someday becoming a movie star. During our conversation it occurred to me that her search for acting perfection was much like my attempt to find one hundred percent E^2OL. Talent and perfection were closely related in that talent represented society's judgment of another's search for perfection. She was a fine young girl and it did my spirit good to talk with someone so filled with excitement and enthusiasm about life and their mission on earth. God bless her as she unknowingly provided value and encouragement for my chosen lifestyle.

Following a very pleasant stay in Oceanside I decided to travel first class and caught the Greyhound Bus to Los Angeles and then the city bus to the San Fernando Valley. Landed at Tom's apartment, dropped ALICE and got ready for Rocky to pick me up for a date. Our date started by parking on Topanga Canyon Road where it overlooked the Valley—we acted like a couple of teenagers with no place to kiss. It was exciting and filled with scandalous fun! We passed the rest of the evening at her apartment where we reminisced about the good old days. Rocky told me she had just returned from Israel where she had completed advanced nurse's training. She was seriously contemplating taking her newly acquired skills to New Zealand and wanted me to go along for the adventure. I said I would stay in the good old USA.

A Short Prayer

I found some prayer books at brother Tom's place and one particular prayer seemed so very relevant to my wandering lifestyle. This short prayer by Saint Francis of Assisi also shared some aspects of my E^2OL philosophy. It read as follows:

> Lord made me an instrument of peace,
> Where there is hatred; I sow love
> Where there is doubt; faith
> Where there is despair; hope
> Where there is sadness; joy
> Where there is darkness; light.

What beautiful words to express a very positive outlook on life. The words point out that we should seek to counsel, understand and teach others. By sharing our knowledge/energy we also become the recipient of valuable energy.

Malibu

Glenn gave me a ride to Malibu Beach—for some reason it sounded like a fun place for my mind and body. It was a stunning sunny afternoon with a cool breeze. I stopped on the beach after a two-mile hike through the warm sand and thought about my next move, ALICE at my side. Later I walked south on the Pacific Coast Highway, PCH as it was called, and two cars stopped to offer me a lift. I turned down the first, as it was made by a gang who looked like drug-crazed killers, but accepted the second, from an active-duty Navy Seaman, exact opposite of the first. He was just starting a two-day pass from nearby Port Hueneme Naval Station. He was a nice young man from Pittsburgh that had fallen in love with the California coast.

He had many good things to say about his Navy job and was extremely proud of his work in the Navy. He let me out at the Malibu Pier. It was a nice feeling to really communicate with another human being—we had much to share about the government, politics and even shared some philosophical thoughts.

It was late afternoon on Malibu Beach, the sun was slowly sinking below the horizon showering the scattered clouds in a splash of golden sunshine. From the clouds spokes of multi-colored light filled the blue sky. It brought back memories of a time ten years earlier, after a shattered love affair, when I had walked that very beach with tear filled eyes and a broken heart. There was none of that on this night. I was alone, yes, but without desire—the mindset was that this time represented a sort of "gateway" for a movement toward a higher level of consciousness and existence! Such a higher level of existence encouraged the understanding that we are individuals (one-of-a-kind) in the existing spiritual reality. It may be true that we exist as individuals but we must also learn to get alone with, and respect, the individuality of our fellow travelers in this reality.

I found a quiet campsite near the beach. In the morning I made my way to Pepperdine University's Malibu Campus, where I stopped by a small Redwood tree. A bronze sign announced that it had been planted by President Reagan. The tree looked healthy and would be interesting to witness its growth in several years. The view from my higher spot on campus was even more spectacular and soothing for the spirit. I then found the library, where huge plate glass windows overlooked a majestic Pacific Ocean that was sending electro-sparks of then morning's light into my brain.

After another night spent in Malibu with my camp on the grassy bluffs between the Malibu Campus and the Ocean, I caught a bus to Van Nuys for one more night in the San Fernando Valley before hitting the iron trail once again.

Mike's Hobo Instruction

I had a restful stay at Mike's place. He wanted to take a train ride—hobo-style—north to Fresno as he had some relatives that he wanted to visit. We first took the city bus to the Glendale yards where we quickly caught a freight to the Colton yards. So far Mike was thoroughly impressed with my train catching abilities. As we walked eastward, we were stopped and questioned by a gumshoe who told us to get off his property. We quickly moved to a spot under a trestle and out of "his" yard where we could relax.

From past experience it was known that the north bound trains left on the tracks just above our hideout. We took it easy as we waited for a slow freight train that would take us toward northern California. The freights using that track were usually traveling slowly since there was a steep upgrade as they left the Colton yards. We waited for only an hour or so before a long slow freight rumbled our way. Mike's demeanor spoke of apprehension as the train neared our hideout; I assured him that he would do just fine even though we would be forced to catch it on the run.

We readied our gear, and perched in the rocky ballast by the side of the moving train while looking for a boxcar with open doors. A clean one came our way and I took off running with Mike close behind. We threw our gear into the open door and pulled our bodies up and into the boxcar and we were riding the rails in a northernly direction! Mike wore a big smile. The weather was cool which would make the desert crossing comfortable. The views were magnificent as we climbed the Cajon Pass, through the Blue Cut, where the San Bernardino and San Gabriel Mountains met. The train then smoothly glided into the Southeastern corner of the Mojave Desert near the small community of Oak Hill. Several hours later, after passing through Palmdale, Lancaster, and Rosemond, our freight train stopped in the small desert town of Mojave. Mike was hungry, he saw a small liquor store and told me "I'll make a run and get some food." "Okay," I said, "but if the train starts rolling, you'll be on your own."

Mike brought back a cold six-pack of beer, some delicious roast beef deli sandwiches and a bag of potato chips. How about that for roughing it on the rails? The two of us had a great party in that clean boxcar while watching the beauty of the Mojave Desert and then mountain ranges roll past our happy perch. The train pulled into the Fresno rail yards at two in the morning. Mike was giddy with excitement as his relatives arrived. We said our goodbyes and I headed on down the cinder trail on foot until I found a good campsite.

Awoke at about five o'clock and for some unexplained reason my spirit and body were in extreme synchronicity—it was Total Serenity once again. I thought it would be a great morning for a long hike. After passing through the town, I reached the quiet solitude of the many citrus groves that surrounded Fresno. A few more miles up the road I stopped to talk with a nice lady at a roadside fruit stand; she gave me several large oranges. It looked like the hobo would have a great breakfast! Further up the Auberry Road I found a fresh can of snuff and a recent Los Angeles Times lying by the side of the road. Was there some higher power at work that wonderful morning? My next good fortune was when a passing rancher stopped and offered me a ride all the way to Auberry.

In less than an hour, found myself sitting in cousin Tracy's living room having a pleasant conversation with her and her friend, Jan, both of whom were very pregnant. Tracy's young daughter, Trista had really grown since seeing her nine months ago. She was now a year and a half old and required constant attention as she got into everything in the house. Tracy and Troy were in the middle of a large landscaping job. So. the next morning, after Troy left for his job, Tracy and I worked in the yard.

It had been a wonderful and fun-filled visit, but the urge to see my children, miles to the north, nudged my spirit of movement. Once again, there was a realization that the level of importance of any physical situation was a matter of personal opinion and the assignment of its value that you gave it. It was the concept of Space/Time Marker Value (STMV) in my Formula for Life. That time spent in Auberry was very important for my spirit and deserved a very high STMV. There was a feeling of being surrounded by the spirits and energies of those who have inhabited that space long ago. It was the spirits of the early animals, Native Americans and right up to my son and daughter that had spent time at that peaceful place —it was so very soothing for my soul.

The following morning, I made some minor repairs to Tracy's car that I would be driving to Dunlap to see my kids and hit the road by early afternoon. I managed to spend only a few hours with Jimmy and Wendy. They were getting ready for a camping trip at nearby King's Canyon. Hanna and husband Joe were anxious to leave. It was a pleasant visit but much too short. Both children looked very good and were full of energy and excitement about life. They seemed to be getting along in life in spite of the wanderlust of their father.

After returning to Auberry, I met an interesting gentleman named Dave. He invited me on a private tour of a power plant where he was one of their top design engineers. The Kerckhoff power plant was one of a kind, as it was being constructed under the ground, and it required some very specialized drilling and tunneling equipment. Dave gave me a very extensive and impressive tour of the plant. We rode a seemly rickety construction elevator into a vast "surge tank" that was carved from the ancient rock. We next traveled through tunnels using a special electric vehicle to reach the underground "dome" room. That gigantic underground excavation, carved from solid rock, would eventually house the actual power plant. The most interesting and massive piece of machinery was what Dave called the "mole." It was being positioned to begin work on the five-mile-long main water tunnel. We climbed the fifteen-foot ladder to reach its control center which looked much like the cockpit of a seven-forty-seven jetliner. The rail system that was used to support the drilling machinery and to remove the tailings from the mole's diggings was one of Dave's first responsibilities.

One of Dave's friends was going toward Fresno so he gave me a ride to the city of Clovis, on the outskirts of Fresno and very close to the train yards. Before looking for a train I called Martha, an old friend from Big Sur. Martha now lived in the small town of Gilroy to the north. She told me that she would love to have me stop for a visit. I decided to go by road and quickly got a ride all the way to the edge of Gilroy.

I made a campsite in a grove of trees that was near the highway and surrounded by tall thick grass. Gilroy was known as the "Garlic Capital of the World" and the garlic smell did tend to snap you to attention; actually, its uniqueness made it a rather pleasant sensation. I humped my gear the last few miles into town, found a comfortable spot behind the old city hall, and watched the city slowly awaken. When I called Martha to tell her I was in Gilroy, she brusquely told me she didn't have time to see me. I said "okay " and "goodbye."

So, I continued my journey north toward Watsonville and Salinas, catching a highway ride with a retired Army intelligence officer who had worked at the Pentagon. We exchanged many interesting stories about Washington D.C. and its political infighting. The quick stop in Salinas brought back many memories of the Big Sur mining claims, the many hours spent in the County Assessor's Office and the Rambler American outfitted as a traveling home. The streets looked familiar. It was as if part of my spirit still moved in that town. If it were true that time only exists as a mental construct then a portion of my spirit would always be in Salinas. Perhaps the legal paperwork filed on behalf of my mining claim in Big Sur was my spirit made manifest.

The public transportation system in that area of California was quite exceptional. Regional buses took you just about anywhere for less than a dollar. I took one of the regional buses to Monterey. In Monterey, I talked with one of the federal agents that had raided my Big Sur Mining claim. During the raid they had confiscated my thirty-two caliber pistol and ten gauge goose gun when they impounded the Rambler American. The agent met me at Congressman Leon Panetta's office as I wanted to see about getting my guns back. The congressman and agent were polite and told me that the shotgun was destroyed (sure, someone was hunting geese with it) but he did return my pistol. It was good to get the pistol back as it belonged to my maternal grandfather; it had sentimental value as my mother gave it to me many years ago. It seemed it had saved Grandpa's life. "Diamond Jim," his nickname, was a banker and he had stopped an attempted armed robbery of himself using that little thirty-two pistol.

The Man of Jade

Called my friend Don, the Big Sur jade expert, and was pleasantly surprised when he cheerfully answered the phone. As a marine biologist he was usually off on some expedition as he loved to dive in far off exotic places. He invited me to spend some time at his place in nearby Pacific Grove. He had moved from Monterey since last visiting him. Don fixed a delicious dinner of freshly caught Abalone, salad and wine; what a special treat for a hobo. We brought each other up to date as we sipped wine in front of a pleasant fireplace.

Don decided that we should drive south on Pacific Coast Highway for a quick diving excursion on the south coast. We arrived in good spirits and I helped Don get his scuba gear ready for his dive. While Don was hard at work under the waves of the Pacific, I relaxed on Fisherman's Rock while totally enjoying the rhythm of ocean. The motion and sound of the waves somehow seemed to mingle with the many wonderful memories of Big Sur. The water was the same beautiful shades of green and blue which had so very vividly impacted my brain many times before.

Later we decided to drive up the mountain to reach the Alder Canyon Campground for a night away from the much busier main campgrounds. The drop into the canyon to reach Alder Creek was very steep and pushed the Volkswagen bus to its limits. Don took the road in stride and was much at ease as we dropped deeper and deeper into the canyon. The campfire, fresh abalone, bagels, wine and plenty of conversation made that canyon stop something to remember. Back in Pacific Grove, Don patiently taught me how to carve jade into gun handles for my grandfather's pistol. The handles were a little rough around the edges, but Don told me they were pretty good, especially for a first-time jade carver.

Mary and Ann in San Jose

Don and I headed up to San Jose to visit old friend Mary. Her young friend Ann happened to drop by just to say hello. Next thing you know we were doing the California hot tub scene in the starlight overlooking the brilliant lights of San Jose. Ann had a Master's Degree in Public Administration and worked for Apple Computer while being involved in political pursuits. I could easily envision her holding public office sometime in the future. Don and Mary left us alone and we continued on the beautiful road to bliss as our swim suits soon disappeared. We had a wonderful time together as she was an exciting and energetic young woman. We were so very synchronous. The energy she chose to share with me that night would be with my spirit for a very long time – perhaps forever! Yes, it was that much fun.

Early in the morning we fell asleep on my poncho while tightly holding on to one another. We only slept a short time, perhaps an hour, and she cheerfully told me she must go to Apple for a days' work. Even taking into account that there had been no woman my life for some time Ann had a super-large impact on my body and soul. It was a very special evening and morning deserving of a very high STMV. I hoped to see Ann once again and the sooner the better!

Hours later I was ready to head out on the cinder trail once again. That San Jose yard was very friendly, a real "bo park" as we hobos liked to call such places. I found a clean boxcar and had a pleasant ride north to the Oakland train yards where I switched to another train going toward Sacramento.

The past few days had been exhausting with very little sleep—poor me! I fell into a deep sleep nestled in a pile of clean smelling cardboard and awoke the next morning in the same place. I hiked through the yard and found a train going to Sacramento. It was slow, and I became impatient and jumped on a train that was slowly rolling south, the opposite direction. What difference did it make when there was value to be found in all trains? Now riding on an open flatcar, piled high with various sizes of shiny aluminum stock, with the cool wind on my face and a beautiful sunshine filled sky. The train slowly slid back through San Jose and a big smile magically appeared on my face as my mind focused on Ann. From San Jose we traveled through the garlic capital and then on to Watsonville.

Watsonville, San Luis Obispo, early morning coastal fog, morning sunshine, fresh green lettuce from a field next to the track, Camarillo and Oxnard. I was joined in my boxcar by a man who spoke almost no English. Musical sounds of distant church bells were drifting over the many rows of bright green lettuce heads on such a gorgeous Sunday morning. The weather was once again wonderful. Put a shine on the combat boots while my silent Spanish companion watched my every move with a look of fascination.

We soon began to roll at a slow rhythmic pace south toward Los Angeles. The two of us must have been a real sight of contrast for those driving on the highway which ran next to the tracks. I had a tight clean haircut, fresh shirt and spit shined boots; my Spanish buddy was very dark skinned, long hair, bearded with a red bandana tied around his head. We rolled down the tracks, our legs dangling in the wind.

Our train blasted through Simi Valley at sixty miles per hour while overwhelming my spirit with ripe memories of living next to these tracks on Agnew Street. There was absolutely no possibility of getting off this fast mover. We soon passed through the long dark tunnels in the Santa Susana Mountains, one about four miles long, and emerged into the stark sunlight of the San Fernando Valley. I jumped off when the train slowed on the outskirts of the Glendale yard. It was a professional exist (I didn't fall) as we were traveling fairly fast for such a smooth exit. I waved to my Spanish companion and then to the brass buttons on the caboose as the train clanked on down the rails, out of sight and into the center of the train yard.

I stayed with my friend Glenn that night, but at three in the morning my eyes opened wide and I felt a sudden urge to move. My two black limousines (combat boots) were standing by and ready to move out. Walking in the cool pre-dawn darkness my thoughts turned to any number of non-enjoyable futures for this wandering hobo. Such thoughts were not good and placed undo constraints on decisions and thinking; it was the non-E^2OL. One must be on guard for such non-productive and non-valuable thinking.

After a day of meetings and conversations with old friends and colleagues, I ended up adjacent to the Southern Pacific railroad tracks. Going north sounded good, if a slow train rolled up the tracks it might just get a passenger. If that didn't happen it would be a bus trip to Altadena for a quick visit. The bus arrived first so it was off to see the gang at the BBH, and then to Lovila Lane.

To my great surprise Becky was at home and actually invited me into her house. I left Becky's magic house Sunday morning after treating my mental and physical senses to the maximum. A broad smile was painted on my face when walking down Lake Street. I may have looked like a crazy man – given all the smiles. Happy songs were in my heart if not on my tongue.

I caught the first Hollywood bus and got off at Los Feliz Boulevard and climbed down a steep embankment to reach the Southern Pacific railroad tracks. The knockers told me a train was getting ready to highball. The only place to ride was on a special flatcar designed to carry hazardous chemicals.

Two large tanks, maybe two thousand gallons each, were nestled in a strong steel framework which would provide a flat place to lie down. The tanks held liquid Bromine which was a highly corrosive and poisonous liquid—what a pleasant bedmate! As we rolled down the tracks my bedroll was laid in the only place available, next to the tanks. The syrupy brown liquid could be clearly heard splashing around in the containment vessel. It elicited a spooky feeling.

We rolled north for several hours and came to a stop a little before dawn in the middle of a very large oil field. There was plenty to look at as many of the wells were burning off excess methane gas in towering plumes of multi-colored flame. The train was two miles long (usually a mile was max) with four lead engines and four more in the rear. That amazing train actually picked up speed as it climbed the mountains near San Luis Obispo. At one point it was possible to look far up the mountain to see the front of the train turning back toward me as we wound our way toward the mountain pass. At San Jose I was done with riding next to acid, so I made a jump for it. I made a nice morning walk to the Amtrak station, got cleaned up and finally managed to talk with Ann, who forcefully told me "wait right there--I'll pick you up in one hour." Then it was off to her house for a fun filled Sunday morning and afternoon. Late in the afternoon we visited the rose gardens in a nearby park and had more fun under the blanket. We fell asleep in each other's arms. The next couple of days were imbued with similar bliss, but when Tuesday morning arrived it was hobo time once again.

After a three-mile hike I found a train to Oakland, got situated in a clean boxcar and waited to highball north. It felt good to be back on the tracks, especially with the beautiful memories of my last few days with Ann. I relaxed on a pile of clean cardboard and waited for the tramp music from the steel wheels to fill my ears. As we started to roll, I spotted a boxcar with "Oliver 9-80" written in white chalk on its side. It was one of my autographed boxcars from several months ago. A touch of sadness echoed through my brain as we pulled away from San Jose. I missed Ann, already. She somehow reminded me that we must all strive to be ourselves and then take pride in our various ways of absorbing and expending energy. Ann provided an excellent example of someone living and working according to the E^2OL philosophy. Her attitudes and behaviors were so uplifting – it was a pleasure to be with her in that time and space. It was humble feeling to think she choose to share her valuable time and space with this wandering hobo.

My train was really moving and in less than an hour we were gliding into the San Francisco Bay area. My boxcar provided a gorgeous view of the Bay, city skyline and the Golden Gate Bridge – wow – the splendor was overwhelming.

In Sacramento, where the train stopped to set out some boxcars, the hunger pangs struck. I had eaten nothing during the past twenty-four hours. I hopped out and looked for a grocery store without luck. Then, walking forward along the train, I noticed a brown paper grocery bag sitting on the flatcar directly in front of my boxcar. As the train started to move, I grabbed the bag and climbed back into my boxcar. The grocery bag contained the following items: one-pound bag of oatmeal cookies, one-pound bag of Dutch fudge cookies, one large bag of potato chips, six tins of canned meat, and one can of SPAM (hoorah), one can of chili and two cans of Spanish rice.

I set up camp just outside the Roseville yard. Almost immediately an older hobo walked up and asked if I wanted company. He looked like a pleasant guy so I told him to sit down and take a load off. As we talked, he shared his bottle of beer, a jug of cheap wine and some fine conversation.

A morning train rolled slowly down the tracks toward my campsite. I collected some cardboard for a little extra comfort in my boxcar and ran to a nearby liquor store to get a couple of cold beers. Thus provisioned, I hopped onto the train and waited the signal to highball. It felt great to once again experience the freedom of the rails and to hear the tramp stories. We rolled through the stunning Trinity Mountains and followed the rushing Sacramento River just north of Redding. The crashing wild white water of the river could sometimes be heard over the train's powerful engines as they rhythmically conquered the mountains. The many greens and blues of the trees and vegetation flowed down the canyon wall to meet the magnificent white granite boulders on which the river flowed. That beautiful mixture of brilliant colors then disappeared into the thrashing river as it flowed along its granite chute.

We traveled for hours upon hours through that beautiful wonderland of forest and rivers. Majestic Mount Shasta would often appear on the distant horizon as we steadily rolled north. It was late afternoon; the sun was about to set and suddenly the clouds covering the mountain peak separated.

The train made it to Klamath Falls. The night was spent around a campfire with four other hobos—intuition informed me that it was a safe harbor. The elder hobo talked about "streamlining" which simply meant to travel light--usually with water only. We five hobos talked for most of the night. Many of the hobos felt that all train yards were hot – meaning, filled of gumshoes just looking to arrest a trespassing hobo.

As dawn arrived, I and five other train riders moved to the south end of that Burlington Northern yard. We could see a train sitting on the tracks which just looked like it was about to head south. I saddled up and walked toward the train with my campsite buddies and five newcomers in a single file line. There was only one open boxcar on the entire train so we all climbed in. In a short time, we were heading south. It was interesting to observe the social interaction among the ten of us riding in that single boxcar. Five of the hobos looked and acted like escaped convicts that would slit your throat for a dime. Diligence was the special order of that day! The other four, my camping buddies from the night before, were more of the "professional" hobo type and stuck to themselves. Anyway, no one bothered me and the conclusion was that just the right amount (not too much and not too little) of serene confidence had been projected.

By being confined in that "crowded" boxcar introspective thoughts about the Formula for Life and the E^2OL philosophy were stimulated. How much energy should one expend to be "alone with yourself" and without desire regardless of the physical environment? If we used our ability to Enrich and Enjoy our lives through the power of our mind then environmental influences over our feelings would be minimal, if any.

We passed through some of the most beautiful country ever seen by these eyes. As the sun dropped behind the mountains the tramps started to get their gear together. They were ready to jump from the moving train; it looked pretty dangerous as the train rolled along a cliff with only a narrow band of rocks on which to land. They started jumping off even though we seemed to be moving too fast. Thinking my new buddies were jumping, too, I jumped only to find that they stayed on board. The five rather rough looking characters that I found myself with left for a cabin farther up the mountain. I was alone in the wilderness as the train clanked down the tracks and disappeared into a tunnel. The silence of that place was overwhelming. I set out to find Keddie Junction, where it was said to be possible to catch an east bound. After several miles I saw one of the friendly hobos walking toward me from under an old water tank. He cheerfully invited me to join their jungle camp. I cleared a spot for ALICE and my bedroll. We all had a good laugh about my jump from the train miles too soon. It had been steadily raining but the old wooden water tank kept us and the fire dry. I shared some of my earlier grocery bounty and our main dinner course was hot chili, beans and rice.

Morning brought the smell of coffee and an invitation to the hobos'

White House Hobo: Diaries from my time on the Cinder Trail

mountain mining camp to pan for gold. I decided to wait, alone, to catch a slow freight. The four men were very interesting; all had worked many different jobs in their lifetimes and still did – at least when not being hobos. They were intelligent and clear headed. One stayed up all night as we talked about politics, philosophy and hopping freight trains. We exchanged much information about our backgrounds as well as more recent hobo stories. Since those were the first hobos that I had associated with, my thoughts were whether they were typical. Thus far, most of my time on the tracks had been done solo. Perhaps it was time to experiment with being a little more social.

I walked to the only store in that little railroad settlement, Kiddie Junction, and treated myself to a candy bar and tin of snuff. The settlement was named for the civil engineer that designed this unique mountain junction, which is generally recognized as one of the great engineering accomplishments of all time.

Back at the tracks, two very fast trains sped by, with no chance of getting on either one. I asked some rail workers about a slow train and they said I'd have better luck a few miles away at Paxton Junction. I reached Paxton Junction late in the afternoon and sat up a cozy camp beneath some tall pines by the side of the tracks. I was only just getting settled in when two young boys about fifteen years old visited my camp. We had a long discussion about my travels; they had many, many questions. We said goodbye and in fifteen minutes they returned bearing big smiles and a large paper bag. They both seemed very happy as they handed me the bag containing: two thick ham and cheese sandwiches, cookies, fig cake, oranges, potato chips and two cartons of milk. How about that, dinner delivered to the side of the tracks. It turned out that those young boys had the job of passing lunches to the passing train crews. They were nice kids and they made Paxton Junction feel like home.

The sun dropped behind the mountains but its rays continued to paint many distant peaks a vibrant red/yellow/orange splash of color. Late that night the sound of powerful locomotives woke me. I snapped from a deep sleep, quickly stowed the gear and stood ready for the approaching train. As it passed through Paxton Junction it hardly slowed and was traveling much too fast. I stoked up the fire, unpacked my gear and crawled back into my still warm bedroll. Many trains passed throughout the night but I elected to stay in the comforting warmth of my bedroll.

The sun washed over the mountain tops in an orgy of color as a can of spam was heated for breakfast. An hour or so later a young man pulled up to the tracks in an old pickup truck. I struck up a conversation with Dave and he told me he lived in the nearby city of Paradise. He said he was picking up the middle and butt ends of old railroad ties that were discarded by the railroad. He used these in his landscaping business. He worked until early afternoon and generously shared his thermos of hot coffee before he left for Paradise.

By late afternoon there had not been a single slow train. The sun was low in the sky, the fire was blazing and it looked like it would be another cool night at Paxton Junction. It was certainly a hospitable spot! As I was beginning to drift into sleep, car lights emerged from the forest and slowly moved along the tracks toward my jungle camp. I was on full alert but soon found that it was Dave and a couple of friends. They had brought a couple cases of beer and were set to have a party. We had a fantastic time talking and drinking until three in the morning. It seemed that my "circle" of people was expanding.

It was now Sunday morning, still at Paxton junction. Dave and his friends returned to the tracks and collected more old railroad ties for a couple of hours. One of them told me that I could probably catch a train in Portola, fifty miles away. My spirit and body were both ready to move, so late in the afternoon, after several more failed attempts to catch a train, I decided to try the highway. It was not long before a young couple stopped and gave me a ride to the small town of Quincy. I stopped at a quiet little bar and treated myself to a couple of beers and had many good talks with the local residents before hitting the road again. When I arrived at Portola there was a long train that looked like it was about to highball eastward. I climbed aboard an empty rock car and the train immediately began to roll.

Sullivan's Chicago Bar

The train in the Portola yard was at least a mile long and made up entirely of empty rock cars. The cars were fairly comfortable as the high sides provided shelter from the icy wind as we sped across the desert in the cold night air. The evening marked the end of another marvelous day, especially with the fresh thoughts of the many pleasant people met during the past few days. The Portola train rolled all night long with only brief stops until it reached Winnemucca in north central Nevada, where during a stop I found a water hydrant, got cleaned up and replenished my water supply to prepare for a daytime desert crossing. Then it was back on the train and the very hot trip to Elko.

In Elko I met some old hobos heating beans over a fire made from a can filled with sand that was saturated with gasoline. My Korean War buddies had told me about that trick, but I had never seen it actually work. Two of the hobos were going east so we joined ranks, found a train and were soon on the way to Salt Lake City.

In looking back at the rather long stay at the Kiddie and Paxton Junctions rail yards it gave me a feeling of satisfaction that a high level of E^2OL was maintained in spite of the many missed trains. It served as a vivid reminder that we should enjoy each moment of life regardless of our situation.

We three hobos had an easy ride to Salt Lake City. The train dropped our boxcar before we reached the main yard, so I walked about ten miles with one of the hobos and we had a pleasant conversation almost every step of the way, just two American hobos passing the time by exercising and philosophizing about a more peaceful world. We parted ways and I headed for the Roper yard

Upon reaching the Roper yard I found a hobo sitting comfortably by a campfire among some discarded railroad ties. "Burger Red" motioned for me to sit down and share his campsite. It turned out we had much to talk about as he was retired Air Force with service in both World War II and Korea. We discussed politics and the military for a couple of hours, and then I went deeper into the Roper yard to see about a Denver train, finding it with the help of a few geese. I crawled into a boxcar, secured the open door with some man traps and fell into a deep sleep. During the night my "Denver car" was bumped around numerous times as they put the train together. The light from a rising sun awakened me and the train began to "stretch" as we prepared to roll from the Roper yard. We were on the way to Denver and passing through more of the spectacular Utah countryside. I was feeling rather happy and enjoying the slow ride as it provided plenty of time to absorb the beauty of the land as it scrolled past my open boxcar door.

As we moved farther east the Rocky Mountains appeared as snow-capped giants. The magnificent peaks were illuminated by many brilliant colors from the rays of the setting sun. What a breathtaking spectacle for my thirty-sixth birthday! In Grand Junction the train stopped and my boxcar was knocked around for most of the night. When it became clear it was going nowhere, I abandoned it and went in search for another.

Some Philosophy

Good communication with the hobos appeared to stem from the fact that many shared a similar philosophy of life. Which was basically: to enjoy yourself while not infringing on anyone's right to do the same. Hobos were often willing to share what they had as long as it did not infringe on their ability to enjoy life. That attitude worked nicely on the iron trail because sometimes you had extra water or food and sometimes you didn't. Sometimes you had a nice warm campfire and other times you didn't. Such a philosophy encouraged one to be self-sufficient and very much aware of their Basic Needs. Many times, in the more "civilized" communities of society, people had no idea what their needs were, let alone their Basic Needs. In other words, they did not have an understanding about how to get along in this world with the minimum requirements for survival. It was a sense of individuality and self-sufficiency that was missing. Many, if not most, city people became way too dependent on services outside of themselves and often physically very far away.

In the world of the hobo, once you fulfilled your Basic Needs, and perhaps some small surplus that you could comfortably carry, you could then share any extras with others. Sharing would then nearly always guarantee that your personal Enjoyment and Enrichment of Life would be increased. A fellow hobo would rarely help another if such sharing would infringe on their personnel E^2OL. Just as importantly such hobos also expected the same treatment from fellow train travelers. Such behavior made for a very successful sub-culture perhaps that was one reason the hobo sub-culture had continued to thrive. Of course, there were a few track riders not adhering to this "law" of the tracks. If you stayed reasonably alert those unhappy, predator type individuals were usually easily avoided.

While waiting for an east bound in Grand Junction "Hobo Joe," introduced himself and we settled under a large tree and talked about trains, politics and food—both of us happened to be hungry. Joe told me about a small grocery store only a few miles up the tracks. My offer was to buy the bread and beans if he would hike to the store. Joe gladly took me up on the offer. While Hobo Joe made the trek, I searched for an eastbound train while also catching up on sewing projects. A couple of hours later a smiling Joe returned. He had the bread and beans – showed me the receipt and counted out the change. How about that!? Trust was a valuable asset in the hobo culture, as in all cultures. We built a small campfire and had a great breakfast of warm beans and bread. About the time we finished breakfast a hot shot pulled into the yard. We said our goodbyes, I found a spot, built a cardboard nest, and was soon rolling east.

That hot shot was definitely priority freight and it was burning up the tracks all the way, a thrilling ride. The train passed through something like thirty tunnels, during which I learned something new: when a train passed through a tunnel the black and sooty smoke from the diesel engines settled on whatever was in the tunnel. In this case, that meant me. But the thick layer of black soot in my hair and on my body was well worth the spectacular views offered from the open flatcar. I arrived in the Burlington and Northern rail yards in the early evening, found a water hydrant and quickly washed the black soot from my body.

I wanted to keep moving, but when I called my friend Ramey just to say hello he insisted I spend some time with him and his girlfriend Katie in Englewood. The next day, after they went off to do their errands, I relaxed at their comfortable house. I struggled with words to describe the wonderful feelings that were flowing throughout my body and spirit. I'm no hobo poet, but the following verse seemed to accurately describe my state of mind at that time.

Sun Streaming through large green house plants,

Soft tones of wicker, wind chimes in the Denver breeze
Brown and gold house cat lounging, solitude in the afternoon
Rockies in the distance echo of train tunnels
Oh, happy day--many more to come in this land,
America, a home for the free and the red, white and blue.

Traveling throughout our great land solidified my belief that it was not the government which made our country great, but it was the citizens--the *people*. This idea was reinforced by many of the people that I met while traveling the rails. Such a thought might seem simplistic but it was one thing to say or read it and yet another to really experience it as this hobo had.

At Peace
Ramey fixed an incredible dinner of pepper steak and rice which was his tasty specialty. It was so very lovely sitting at the large oak dinner table with the company of friends as the early evening sun streaming through the open windows. The mental high experienced was equal to any drug-induced intoxication. The only rival feeling, in terms of intensity, was shared sex, but then that was a different kind of feeling. It was as if every pore of my physical body was open and free to absorb all the pleasant sensations offered by the universe.

The eyes seem to be the major receptive center for such high-level energy. I suddenly *saw* and *felt* much more than normal, it was similar to the total relaxation following hot sexual encounter. The spirit was somehow set free via the channels of mind and sense organs. It was the feeling of Total Serenity induced by a great sense of well-being while being at peace with the universe. That feeling was often present on the tracks, but I rarely found the appropriate words or the time to describe it.

The Enjoyment and Enlightenment of Life present ninety-nine percent of the time must exist as a range of feelings. The feeling of Total Serenity is the ultimate we can experience as spirits bound in our physical bodies. Such Total Serenity has been given many names by philosophers and religious leaders. For me, the construct that represents the highest level of E^2OL is best described as Total Serenity. It represents the highest level on the Enjoyment of Life continuum. It goes beyond serenity in that physical senses actually became super sensitive, making them more receptive to incoming stimuli. Such increased sensitivity results in a flooding of the spirit with the *value* in the physical and spiritual universe.

I went to a very pleasant lake directly behind Ramey's house; it was alive with many small and brilliantly colored sail boats. I sat next to the babbling stream which feed the lake. In the distance, the regal Rockies were bathed in a sunset of contrasting colors of gold, orange, silver and blue – it was especially beautiful. Ducks and large swans glided across the lake in serenity. It was my moment; this was my universe since not a single person saw or felt those stimuli exactly as I did! People passed on the nearby foot path; but my unique observation point, my space/time was mine and mine alone. I was alone, with myself, without desire!

Later, we had another dinner on the front lawn, picnic style, under clear stars and bathed in a gentle breeze. What was the feeling that brought tears of joy to my eyes? Are joyful tears brought on by Total Serenity? The wonder of the universe, our space/time shared with others? It was the giving of energy in the form of knowledge, whether in the classroom or at the oak table with Ramey and Katie. It was all very stimulating food for my soul. It was a realization that the energy derived from pure joy and happiness could fill the spirit, overflow to be shared with other receptive individuals. It was that open honest exchange of energy which powered the engines of our reality, our space/time, our universe.

The next afternoon I said my goodbyes and walked to the bus stop with a bagful of cookies Ramey's daughter had baked for me and a cold beer tucked away in my cargo pocket. At the Denver and the Burlington Northern railroad yards I found a clean boxcar and soon thereafter was gliding along the tracks toward Lincoln, Nebraska, in the cool night air. In Lincoln I met some nice knockers and they let me wash up in one of their shanties, gave me a jug of ice water, and told me exactly where to hide while waiting for an east bound.

It wasn't long before my next train rumbled down the main tracks toward my hideout. I jumped aboard and built a comfortable cardboard nest and was soon highballing across the Iowa plains through an energetic storm. Loud thunder, brilliant lightning, violent wind and rain kept the night filled with excitement. Eventually I landed in Cicero, a suburb of Chicago, where my train was being broken up. Once my feet were on Cicero ground a gumshoe spotted me and then escorted me from the B&N yard. He was a nice guy and actually gave me directions to the Baltimore and Ohio railroad yard, where I could catch a train east.

I walked through the tough Chicago streets in full military combat gear (less the M-16) for about twelve miles on that hot, humid day, seeing some interesting characters along the way, before I found the yard. A local tavern beckoned me to stop to buy a quart of beer and I sat in the shade of some super large cottonwoods overlooking the rail yard and sipped leisurely. I was reminded of the many hot afternoons spent in Cape Girardeau, drinking a beer or two by the side of the Mississippi watching the river flow as time seemed to stand still.

Eventually I ventured into the yard and talked with several knockers only to find that the yard was the B&O's after all. I decided to go all out and buy another quart of beer at Sullivan's Tavern. One of the many rough looking characters sitting at the bar loudly asked, "Hey bud, where ya going?" We had a short conversation and as I turned to leave, he invited me to sit down and have a beer. Pretty soon my new friend Ken ordered me a big bowl of Sullivan's famous chili.

Sullivan's Bar seemed to represent the heart of America. The owner/bartender was a retired Chicago cop with most of the patrons being fellow policemen or fireman. Ken proudly described and then told several stories about his seven kids. For the next couple of hours, the talk was lively; several beers were downed and I still had the unopened quart. Somehow, I managed to make it back to the tracks in my intoxicated state, actually I was dead drunk. I settled in between two long strings of boxcars and heard the laughing of young girls. Much to my surprise two attractive high school girls came walking along the tracks taking a short cut home. We talked for several minutes before they continued on their happy way. They walked away as I sank, sort of melted, deeper into the rocks in that Chicago train yard. Somehow, I crawled into an open boxcar and after a few hours of being bumped around we finally started to move in an easterly direction. It was nice to be on the move, the cool air felt great as Chicago slowly faded away as we reached open fields and fresh smelling countryside.

Very little of that train ride was remembered but as the sun was rising, we arrived in Elkhart, Indiana. I talked with friendly yard geese who told me where to find the departure yard. It was a nice early morning walk before ending up in one of the trainmen shanties where there was a continuous supply of fresh coffee and great conversations. The knockers urged me to take a break and head into town to visit the local mission. They said that hobos spoke highly of the place and it was especially known for its great food and hospitality. Never having visited such a place, I decided to check out the "Faith Mission" in downtown Elkhart. The townspeople were nice, some smiles and no evil looks when walking down Main Street toward the mission.

At the mission I got food, a shower, did my laundry, and got a little gospel preaching and a pleasant discussion with Ray, the man in charge. He quietly told me that people are usually required to stay for three days, but he'd make an exception for me.

That morning I had noticed how easily my light-colored khaki shirt got dirty, so I'd decided to replace it with a darker olive drab military-type shirt. Turns out the Faith Mission had just one such shirt and in my size, the only one on their rack of clothing. It would now be much easier for me to present a much cleaner appearance.

Once back to the main Conrail yard conversations with the knockers indicated that the east bound would not be leaving until late that evening. They told me that earlier that morning there was a derailment in the yard and the repair crew had been lifting cars and fixing the damage at a feverish pace. They had been working non-stop all day long to get the rails cleared for traffic. The trainmaster was on the scene supervising the work. It was quite an operation and very interesting to watch the riggers hooking up the boxcars to the heavy cranes which would then lift them upright. It wasn't long before evening arrived and the railroad cook brought dinner to the hungry Gangi crew. I had been talking with various workers throughout the afternoon and one of the riggers walked over to my temporary campsite and told me to help myself to the food. I had two of the fattest, most delicious ham and cheese sandwiches that could ever be remembered. Then there was homemade fudge cake and ice-cold milk for dessert. Wow – my Basic Needs were certainly met and vastly exceeded on that pleasing evening. With a full belly and a smile on my face it was a hike toward the departure yard; once there a clean boxcar was found and settled in to wait for the signal.

We didn't leave until three in the morning but once on the roll we kept moving until we reached Toledo, Ohio, which was one hundred miles closer to D.C. It was beginning to look like I'd make it to the nation's capital for the Fourth of July celebration.

It was a comfortable ride to Conway, Pennsylvania which was just outside Pittsburgh--the train came to a smooth stop and was broken apart. I humped ALICE for a few miles to reach the departure yard. A pleasant talk with a train crew and they decided to help me get to the B&O yards which were several miles away by giving me a ride on one of the local trains. Gladly climbed on board and made myself comfortable in the second engine. Before you knew it, I was in the B&O yard. The yard seemed very quiet, no knockers and not a single moving train was to be seen and I began to wonder whether I was in the right place. After exploring that rather desolate appearing yard, an empty caboose provided a place to catch a few winks. It was not long before an approaching train was heard, it was east bound, and I caught it on the run as it slowly passed through that quiet yard.

That train continued eastward, crossed the Allegheny River and into the very heart of the steel mills. Great showers of fire and sparks seemed at times to engulf our train. While stopped at one of the many mills I asked the engineer if our train was going to a yard where a faster east bound train might be caught. He had been startled and surprised to see me climb into his engine's cab. But after the initial shock was over he was friendly. He confirmed that his train was only on a local run and that it would make several stops throughout the night. The friendly engineer told me "by morning we'll be in Connellsville where there is a major B&O rail yard, so make yourself comfortable." It was the "luck of the Irish" once again; thank you Mom.

Just as the engineer said, we arrived in the B&O yard early in the morning. The train crew invited me to their wash room to get cleaned up and scratch off the whiskers. It was a real nice bunch of guys. One worker invited me to the local YMCA to have breakfast. We soon jumped into his car for a short drive to the trainmen's hangout and had a hardy breakfast that was accompanied by constant and cheerful conversation.

Why Not More Philosophy?

The previous twenty-four-hour period had certainly been exciting and deserving of a high Space/Time Marker Value. Many good things were happening, one after another, and so fast that my spirit was soaring through the clouds. It was necessary to consciously recognize and then remind myself of the basic goodness present in so many of our fellow humans. It was often a struggle to find words to accurately describe all the wonderful things constantly being experienced. One thing for sure was that thoughts about different types of Enjoyment and Enlightenment of Life (E^2OL) and/or Total Serenity (TS) were in my mind. Already established in my vernacular was the concept of Total Serenity (TS). How did that Total Serenity differ from the many feelings experienced in the immediate twenty-four-hour period? Both those states of mind were enjoyable but there was a definite difference. When in the state of Total Serenity, one's doors of perceptions were maximized and ready to receive and process all stimuli offered by the immediate physical reality. It seemed to me that the state of TS was achieved when you were no longer required to expend energy to reach the highest level of E^2OL. It seemed to me that when in the Total

Serenity state of mind, you actually became a source of positive energy from which others might derive enjoyment. It was as if good, happy feelings bounced back and forth between individuals with little or no effort – it happened naturally.

YMCA Breakfast

Following breakfast my new trainmen buddy and I emerged from the YMCA to be greeted by a beautiful Sunday morning, clean, totally refreshed, energized, with waves of Total Serenity washing over my spirit. It was a short ride to pick up my gear which was followed by a firm handshake from my new friend. I continued to feel the waves of pleasure continued while walking lightly (almost floating) into the B&O freight yards. A huge, brilliant American flag that appeared to be brand new floated easily in the breeze high above those rail yards. That feeling of TS had been occurring more frequently and I discovered that it could be elicited at will if I tried hard enough. That is – if I devoted enough energy in the correct direction. After all it was only a different way to look at reality, a simple state of mind. That state of mind resulted when we chose to direct our personal storehouse of energy in a manner which elicited pleasurable feelings. The pleasurable feelings of Total Serenity arose mainly from our spiritual base. Our external reality could either encourage or discourage the attainment of Total Serenity – it was up to us to decide. That morning there was no doubt that the Creator intended that the universe belonged to me! Its purpose was to enhance my Enrichment and Enjoyment of Life. But please, remember that there was plenty of room in that wonderful universe for others to do the same. The observation that there was plenty of "universal energy" for everyone must be one of the basic laws of nature. It seemed to be a natural truth.

I climbed into the cab of the last locomotive of another east-bound train. It was not long before we were easily rolling alongside the beautiful Allegheny River and on into the mountains. Once again, the crew members of that train were especially nice.

Trains had mingled with my mind and spirit. We passed through many small towns and there was an abundance of American flags flying on this Fourth of July weekend. We lost one engine when going up the mountain and had to pull onto a siding while we waited for a replacement from the yard which was many miles to the east. The crew invited me forward for cold drinks and conversation. The hospitality of the many railroad men met during my travels never ceased to amaze me. Their attempts to be helpful to this vagabond hobo was boosting my spiritual side higher and higher. If this keeps going, I might just explode – turn into vapor! My home on the iron trail was more than comfortable thanks to the men and a few women I had met in the many rail yards of America.

The replacement engine was hooked up and we soon arrived in Cumberland, Maryland where the engines were separated from the boxcars. I jumped off and waited for the new crew and power units. The town's atmosphere was very relaxing and the river of life seemed to be filled with food for the spirit. A ten-minute wait and we were once again moving down those ribbons of steel toward our nation's capital.

Just thirty miles from D.C. we stopped to change crews. The new brass buttons authoritatively told me, "This train will only slow to forty miles per hour as we pass through D.C. on the way to Baltimore." He also said that it would be difficult, if not impossible, to catch a train from the yard we were in that would stop at the capital. Just as they prepared to highball he changed his mind and told me to climb aboard. He said, "I'll have the engineer slow the train as we pass through D.C. so you can get off." He even invited me to ride in the very front seat of the lead engine which provided a completely different viewpoint. The tracks flew right at me, then under my feet from that new vantage point. There was a gentle shuffle like motion as it would slowly rise and fall from one side to the other. It was astonishing to witness that 4000 horsepower monster gently gliding down the tracks in a side-to-side and up-and-down motion. It was a beautiful dance and I was a part of it!

When we reached D.C. the brass buttons wanted to know where to slow the train. I told him, " anywhere along New York Avenue would be perfect." As we approached my jump off point, the engineer began to throttle down, the train slowed and a professional jump and run exit was made. I waved to the crew; there was a loud roar as they put the hammer down and then, in a black cloud of diesel smoke, the train picked up speed and disappeared into the clear, cool night of D.C. Once again, the blessings were felt and our Creator was thanked after having safely delivered this traveler to our nation's capital.

Italo's Barber Shop

Thanks to my train friends, it was a magnificent D.C. arrival. As I crossed the tracks to reach the road to the White House I reminisced about the times Marlene and I had walked that same street, bringing a smile to my happy face. It was a beautiful Sunday evening with a comfortable temperature of around seventy degrees. After a couple hours of hiking, I arrived at the Capitol Building grounds where I spoke with a sergeant in the Capitol Police Force. He turned out to be a real friendly fellow once he determined I wasn't a threat. The gentleman cop reminded me that there was no camping anywhere in the District. I beg to differ: After we parted company, I slipped into the darkness and managed to find small plot of deep green grass under some pine trees near the National Botanical Gardens, where I spread out my bedroll and caught a few hours of welcome sleep.

I enjoyed the sunrise on one of the Mall's park benches between the Capitol Building and the Washington Monument. The power and energy of the sun's light rays seemed to fill my body. For some strange reason it felt good to be back in D.C. and watching the city come to life on that early Monday morning. I walked to the local grocery store for a can of beans and was happy to see they were only twenty-seven cents! Across from the National Archives Building I began the process of turning beans into energy and excess gas. A young woman joined me on my park bench. We began to talk and she told me she was on her way to work at the Museum of Natural History and was a little early. She was very cute jail bait at seventeen years old and with brilliant green eyes! She was a pleasant distraction for this female-deprived hobo. I fell in love almost instantly, but she only gave me a cute little smile when I asked her if she wanted to go steady. We had a spirited conversation for several minutes and then she continued on her way to work.

I found out that it took a considerable effort (large energy expenditure) to keep both my body and ALICE gear clean and fresh while traveling on the freights. It took a good two hours that morning to do all the necessary sewing, polishing, washing, and grocery shopping to get organized for the business at hand. I had much to accomplish on that D.C. visit and was having trouble deciding where to begin.

My first stop was the National Archives where I met a young bureaucrat named Steve. He was a pleasant individual and was helpful in showing me the section that contained Watergate documents. A friend had given me a copy of the original arrest report for the Watergate burglars. I wanted to see if it was in the Archives. Steve escorted me deep into the Watergate section, where we both looked for any such document; none was to be found. He asked for a copy for the National Archives. I put my initials on the arrest report and gave him the copy. He told me that he would do a more extensive investigation to determine if they had any such document, and if not, they would surely be interested in obtaining the original.

Next on my self-imposed "to do" list was a meeting at the FBI HQ to talk with someone from the Director's Office regarding the susceptibility of freight trains to terrorist attack. He appeared sympathetic to my point of view and stated that he was not aware that the FBI had officially studied that aspect of National Security. He said the FBI only had authority to investigate incidents *after* they occur. It was not part of the FBI's mission to guard against such terrorist attacks, stating, "We only have seventy-five hundred agents nationwide." He made the point that if the FBI's mission changed to include the protection of freight trains they would need a massive increase in manpower. We also discussed the current Sky Marshall program which was supposed to protect our airways from terrorist attack. I suggested that such a system might be feasible for our national railroads, but he didn't seem to think so.

With that out of the way, I decided to try to find the new love of my life, Emily, whom I had met on the park bench that morning. I headed to the Museum of Natural History, where Emily was a "tour guide." I thought of a tour guide as being a knowledgeable person who walked along with a group of people given information and responding to questions. But in D.C. it apparently entailed standing in a stationary booth and passing out automatic electronic devices which played recorded messages when the tourist stood in front of an exhibit. It was another example of how the government often manipulated language for their benefit. Surely, they received more pay as a "tour guide" than an employee that simply passed out electronic devices.

Not interested in that sort of tour, I headed out to the Mall, where I was approached by several supporters of the of the Unification Church. I must have looked like a vulnerable target as they invited me to dinner at their Washington HQ. I accepted. Dave, the leader of the group of supporters, listened intently to my philosophy which, in Dave's opinion, appeared to correspond in some ways with their Church's views. We had a great dinner prepared by a young lady named Beverly. The meal's main course was that afternoon's catch of Blue Fish from the Chesapeake Bay. Following a magnificent dinner, we retired to the sitting room of that rather impressive ex-Libyan Embassy building. We talked for some time until the latent pressure to join their religion became too much and I saddled up and hit the trail back to the Organization of American States (OAS) Building to bed down at my favorite outdoor D.C. campsite. My hideout was beginning to feel a little like home as my comfortable bedroll welcomed me aboard for a good night's sleep.

Pre-dawn darkness awakened this hobo, then a leisurely and pleasant walk to the west end of the Mall. After milling around for a good part of the day, I went to my favorite barber shop to see Italo. He spent over an hour giving me a careful haircut and shave as we both talked constantly. Italo's good friend, Angelo, was having some legal problems with the government. He wanted me to talk with her to see if I might help – perhaps some advice. We talked on the phone for over thirty minutes and agreed to meet to discuss her problem further. Then Ben, Italo's shoe shine man, took me to the laundry near his home in the Ghetto. I changed into my Navy flight suit (a gift from an ex-navy pilot) as everything else needed washing. We rode the city bus deep into a neighborhood where it seemed like I was the only white man. Ben seemed to know everyone on the crowded streets. He took me to his favorite fried chicken place and bought us a bucket filled with chicken wings, which we ate while waiting for my laundry.

Italo had offered to let me stay at his barber shop whenever I was in town, so I headed back there with my clean clothes. Chuck, a very interesting and patriotic fellow who was retired from the United States Air Force, was also staying at the shop. He flew Saber Jets in many combat missions during the Korean War and had the scars to prove it. Chuck had much to talk about and we stayed up late into the night. Early in the morning at the barber shop, Chuck made us coffee and another day began for just another two members of the human race. It was real life, right then, not the next day, not the day before – it was only the current moment that mattered! I took a deep breath and felt that all my channels of perception were wide open and absorbing all of nature's energy that our Creator had provided for our use.

Visited a couple of congressman's offices to lobby for new planes for the California Air National Guard. Brought up the subject in letters but now was the time for a follow up personal visit. In particular I wanted to help secure new "H" model C-130's for the 146th Tactical Air Wing. Congresswoman Fielder's office said they had investigated my previously stated safety concerns and found that only twelve of the new models were authorized for the entire fiscal year. They further stated that there were no plans to increase that number. I tried to make the case that the 146th TAW (Tactical Air Wing) should get these dozen aircraft and headed for Congressman Burgener's office. At both offices my treatment was respectful but there was little, if any, interest in working toward securing those planes for the 146th Air Wing. It was suspected that those types of decision are made at the Pentagon and normally not questioned at the Congressional level.

Made a trip to the Library of Congress for some research – not the tourist tour but into the working part. It was my first time in the Library and found that it was very impressive. However, it seemed a little strange to have tourist filing by while observing our work through large plate glass windows. High on the wall was a quotation that made a lot of sense, it read as follows: "Of the law there can be no less acknowledged than that her voice is in harmony with the land." I thought to myself that it was too bad that most of our lawmakers did not follow the principle annunciated in that quotation.

I returned to the barber shop after leaving the Library of Congress. Italo invited me to his house in the Virginia suburb of Annandale. It was a fantastic evening with Italo and his family. We had a good dinner and then sat on his porch and talked for hours. It became clear that he loved America very much. He told me, "I left Italy twelve years ago and have not regretted it for one minute." He was very proud to call himself an American and greatly appreciated the opportunity to build a secure life for himself and his family. It was a great night's sleep in a real bed in Italo's spare bedroom.

The next night it was back to Italo's shop for an evening with Chuck. He was on one hundred percent disability from wounds suffered when he was shot down over North Korea. Anti-aircraft fire hit his jet on a mission and tore away the muscles around his midsection. The injury had always been considered non-repairable until some recent experimental surgical techniques seemed to indicate that he might be helped. He had a large skin bag (about the size of a basketball) which protruded from his lower side. He told me that the bag contained his guts which had slipped from his normal body cavity. He hoped to get the operation soon. He gave me all the details on each of the three times he was shot down. One time he found himself 100 miles deep in enemy territory. It took him three months to reach friendly forces. It was an honor when that American hero handed me an American flag patch and then helped me sew it on my ALICE gear. He was as proud as I when we finished our little sewing project. What a great way to spend a Fourth of July weekend, sitting in an old-style barber shop with a good-natured vet, talking about our country and the freedoms we all enjoyed.

A Little More Philosophy

Since my personal E^2OL was approaching one hundred percent it was a good time to analyze any non-E^2OL experiences in detail. My observations seemed to indicate that non-E^2OL could easily result when one had unpleasant thoughts about an uncertain future. It was rare but the fact that it did happen could not be denied. It was a time when I somehow forgot to enjoy the current moment while also showing an excessive concern for my status in some future time. Such a vision of the future related directly to one's ability to enjoy each and every moment. Perhaps one way to reach one hundred percent E^2OL might be to analyze the non-E^2OL every time it occurred. Insight into the reasons for non-E^2OL, as they occurred, would provide valuable information for any effort to achieve one hundred percent E^2OL.

Two past examples of non-E^2OL experiences came to mind: 1) no money for food and 2) comparing myself with others my age and feeling I should be well established in some profession. Actually, these two situations were almost identical and most likely were derived from the same emotion—fear of the future. Related to those thoughts was a fear that the lack of a profession or even a steady income was an impairment in obtaining a permanent female relationship. Sometimes the thought would surface that my nomadic lifestyle was depriving me of a happy and long-term relationship. This assessment called for a change in my behavior. This was just a little scary. Somehow, so far in life, blessings had been showered on me in the form of very special women both prior to and during my hobo days. To sum up my thoughts on reasons for non-E^2OL: lack of money, no marketable profession and no steady relationship with family or females. Actually, those three things seemed to be very closely related. As is often said; food for thought.

Another way to further understand the three contributing factors to non-E^2OL could be to rank them from most important to least. Most important might be family and female companionship, then profession and finally money. My experience had taught me that female companionship would provide more enjoyment than any professional accomplishment or money. Money was the least important while a profession would definitely fulfill a productive instinct. Perhaps the productive instincts were being fulfilled through the introspective acquisition of New Knowledge and then sharing the knowledge with others. It was satisfying to share the true meaning of the Enjoyment and Enrichment of Life philosophy. It had very often brought joy and peace to this hobo and perhaps others as well. No matter which path chosen, money and profession seemed to take care of themselves. It looked like perhaps my recently occurring non-E^2OL hinged on lack of a steady relationship. It was the close personal communication with another human being that was missing.

It seemed like I was right back to the original Formula for Life. In other words, as each successive item in the "formula" was met there was a need for more. Hence when one's Basic Needs were fulfilled one needed more – perhaps the acquisition of New Knowledge fulfilled that new need. For myself those needs were met through travel and exposing myself to new stimuli hence, New Knowledge.

Back on the Mall
Sitting in the National Art Museum in a plushily cushioned wrought iron chair. I was absorbing the gentle energy released from the trickling sound of water coming from a nearby fountain. The vivid green colors of the indoor foliage and the brilliant splashes of gold radiating from the many flowers. I sat there in a trance-like Total Serenity state of mind, and one of the Unification Church members walked up to say hello and then re-invited me to stay at the Embassy Building. The offer was once again politely declined.

It was a sure thing that a place more conducive to E^2OL could be found but not at the embassy. All that was needed was a place to lay my head, for a place to make a bed and for a place to sew some thread.

While I was relaxing on the Mall on July 3, a rather nice lady struck up a conversation. She was having a lunch break from her duties at the Justice Department. Susan hardly ate anything being that she talked constantly.

Being rather curious about my hobo lifestyle she asked many questions. Before going back to work she invited me to her house for an early Independence Day dinner. It was great dinner with a very pleasant lady. We continued our conversations which soon morphed into gentle kisses. To make a long story short, she invited me to spend the night and it was not to sleep on her couch. There were many, many pleasant kisses throughout the night.

The next morning, I hiked several miles from Susan's house in a steady but very light rain —it was so very beautiful and memories of the night brought a broad smile to my face. The G.I. poncho that Chuck had given me kept me warm and dry. In the McPherson Square Park I spoke with some rather boisterous pigeons. I wasn't sure about my mental health, but truly felt as if the world was mine to enjoy. The sun burst through the grey clouds of the late afternoon, just in time for the Beach Boys Concert at the Washington Monument. Later that evening the fireworks show was magnificent, with many earsplitting reports and concussions felt throughout the entire body. It was a spirit moving display of beauty and power. Spent another couple of days camped at the OAS Building which was very peaceful in spite of the half million people in the capitol for the concert and fireworks.

If one lived by the philosophy that there was Value in Everything then one would always move toward visions and goals in a state of serenity. If one chose the E^2OL way of life then everything became a valuable learning experience since "everything" could be perceived as valuable. It was then up to each individual how such experiences added to one's energy base of knowledge – that was the assignment of STMVs to incoming stimuli. The New Knowledge would in turn assist one on the road to Total Serenity.

My first stop in the Senate Office Building the next day was at Alabama Senator Denton's office to meet with the staff of his Subcommittee on Security and Terrorism. Staff members appeared to be very receptive to my inquiry and permitted me to review some not-yet-public hearing reports of testimony given by CIA Director Colby. Colby had testified that there were three major aspects to combating terrorism; intelligence, security processes, and public support. I sat in the office and read transcripts since it was still restricted information and could not be copied. It made for interesting reading and it was enlightening regarding the many potential terrorist targets in this country.

I had only visited the Pentagon once before and it was obvious that security was now much less repressive. Total Serenity was very much in evidence. The physical surroundings of the building and security were familiar and thus required less of an expenditure of energy, leaving more energy for the spiritual realm.

I managed to meet with a Lieutenant Colonel from the Pentagon's White House Liaison Office regarding the new "H" model C-130's for the 146th Tactical Air Wing in California. We talked about the need for new planes and he set up an appointment for me to talk with a colonel in the Congressional Liaison's Office. That conversation went well and it was learned that the decision as to who will get the "H" models was in the hands of the Pentagon and the chairman of the congressional committee.

After another meeting I headed for my barber shop headquarters. Walking across the Roosevelt Bridge a Government Huey helicopter flew by low and parallel to my direction of travel with the side door open. A young-looking man, dressed in an olive-drab battle dress uniform stood in the wind behind what appeared to be a mini-gun. Impressive! I continued through Georgetown on "M" Street, over to Pennsylvania Avenue to the Executive Office of the President (EOP) Building. Managed to talk with some administration people and picked up some public documents. Then it was on to the barber shop.

I was well supplied and satisfied and ready for my departure from the Capital. Almost everything on my "to-do" list had been accomplished during my short stay in D.C. It was hard to leave, mainly because a certain level of fondness had grown for all the barber shop gang and especially Chuck. He wanted me to stay around until he got settled in his new home at the D.C. Veterans Home. He bought me a can of snuff, a P-38 (military style can-opener) and slipped me a five-dollar bill with a huge smile on his face. Our last discussion was about how we had both proven, in our own way, that we were willing to fight to keep the freedoms offered by these United States.

My last night was spent in the arms of sweet Sue. We drank some wonderful blended scotch whisky called "Pinch" and enjoyed good conversation and many more kisses throughout the night. Sue had to work the next morning and with a smiling face and another kiss told me to "sleep in, make yourself at home and lock up when you leave." I crawled from bed at ten in the morning. A note by the side of the bed invited me to stay, but the urge to travel overcame thoughts of more pleasant times with my new friend. I saddled up and headed for DuPont Circle to catch the subway to the train tracks. It was an exciting and fun filled visit that would be remembered for a long time. The D.C. visit had come to an end. The iron trail was calling once again!

Long Black Snake and The Silver Cadillac

Within a few minutes of my arrival at the B&O rail yard a long black snake (coal train) sped toward me. It was traveling fast but, fueled by a desire to get out of town, I sprinted alongside and grabbed a coal car ladder and held on for dear life. The fast-moving train nearly jerked my arms from their sockets, but I managed to somehow hang on and then climbed into an empty but very dirty coal car. The small hammock I always carried came in handy as I strung it across the steeply sloped sides of the car. It was a comfortable place to relax. The hammock gently swayed back and forth as we passed through and over the Catoctin Mountains just northwest of D.C. It wasn't long before we came to a stop in Brunswick, Maryland. The novelty of the swinging hammock on that "snake" train had worn off. I jumped off to find a train with a clean boxcar.

Normally that little Maryland town must be a peaceful and tranquil place; not that day. There were helicopters overhead, state police, sheriffs and local cops with blood hounds all over the streets and railroad yard. One of the knockers told me that a convicted killer had escaped from prison and had been spotted in this area. Within a couple of hours things calmed down.

Throughout that day many trains passed through that little town of Brunswick. An older man was walking along the edge of the rail yard stopped to say hello. Barney was a retired railroad engineer who was getting some exercise and told me, "Sometimes I like to come here and remember the good times while working for the railroad." We swapped railroad stories for over an hour while we sat comfortably in the shade of the trees next to that very busy yard. He pointed to a nearby building "That's where the trainmen can take a shower and get cleaned up, I'm sure no one will mind if you use it." Barney had noticed the coal dust covering me from riding the "black snake" last night. Before that pleasant man went on his way, he told me where to find the west bound Cumberland train. We wished each other good luck and said goodbye. I headed for a shower and shave. Barney was right, no one seemed to mind.

I found a clean boxcar on the Cumberland train, and while waiting to roll the brakeman came to my boxcar and said, "Why don't you ride in the caboose, its more comfortable?" I later learned that Barney had talked with Louie, the engineer on that train, and asked the brass buttons to let me ride in style. It was my first ride in the caboose and it was very comfortable, at least when compared with a boxcar. The B&O was part of the larger Chessie System which had treated this track rider very well. That night, while sleeping in the caboose's bunk, I was abruptly awakened by the sound of four powerful locomotives coming up from behind to give us a push over the mountain.

Dawn arrived in another trainmen's shanty waiting for a Cincinnati bound B&O freight train. I used the quiet time to make some adjustments on my ALICE gear in the train inspector's shanty. The inspector was a retired Navy man who had worked for the railroad ever since he left the service twenty-five years ago. He appeared to be upbeat about everything and was especially high on life. Carl made me feel at home, so much so that when he went outside for a train inspection, he would ask me take his phone messages. He pleasantly surprised me late that afternoon when he returned to the shanty with a like-new navy foul weather suit and handed it to me. It was very nice, olive drab in color and fit perfectly. I happily accepted that surprise gift and arranged my house to accommodate this latest addition to the ALICE gear. Thank you, Carl!

Back on the train we passed over the Shenandoah River and then into the Harper's Ferry area which was beautiful on this moonlit night. In the Cumberland yard I switched to a highballer heading southwest, to West Virginia then Ohio and toward Cincinnati.

We rolled into Cincinnati yard just as the sun rose and I jumped from the train as it slowly came to a stop. I cleaned up then began my hunt for the "Gateway" train.

St. Louis was one hundred seventy miles away. It looked like I would arrive in time to see my parents, who were due to visit sister Jeanie in a few days. We arrived at a railroad siding called "Cabin Junction," just outside East St Louis, right on schedule, and after a long walk and some wrong turns I managed to find the yard I needed just as a huge storm struck. I managed to quickly find an empty crummy and ducked inside, where I shaved and cleaned up while waiting for the storm to pass. More friendly knockers showed me the train going south toward Cape Girardeau. It took an hour to find a grain car and about another hour the train pulled out of the yard with the weather threatening.

Another Midwest thunder storm struck with high winds and driving rain battering my exposed outpost. It was time to test Carl's navy foul weather gear. It worked! My body remained warm and dry. I had a nice ride through the Illinois countryside, then we crossed the Mississippi River and rolled into the "show me state" of Missouri. My thoughts drifted to the idea that when we are able to find Value in Everything then present and future paths became unimportant. That was the manner which I chose to live. It did not matter that a train was missed, for there was always something valuable ahead no matter which path or train one chooses.

The train arrived in the Scott City train yard at three in the afternoon. I walked to Interstate 55 and within a few minutes three young girls, in a big Lincoln, picked me up and gave me a cold beer. Following a spirited, lively ride and wild conversation they let me off at Smitty's Bar in the Cape. I talked with some old friends and then headed for one of my favorite spots at the Cape, the banks of the Mississippi. My campsite was still there. I dropped my gear on the river bank and fell asleep to the sound of the sloshing river and crackling fire. It was so peaceful and pleasant as beautiful memories of this place filled my brain and then mingled with the current reality.

The next day was spent on the SEMO campus in the Kent Library absorbing more brain food in air-conditioned comfort. While relaxing on a high hill overlooking the Mississippi, Mike, who used to work with my sister at the hospital, started a conversation. We talked for an hour or so and he invited me to his place for a cold beer. Several beers later, this hobo was feeling no pain. I headed for the tracks that had brought me a few days ago. I had plenty of time before my parents arrived, so decided to take another train ride. I found an empty caboose hooked to a string of rock cars, climbed aboard and immediately fell into a deep sleep—more like passed out. A little before dawn a train whistle woke me from a deep sleep, and I quickly pulled on my boots, saddled up, stepped over one track and caught the St. Louis train on the run. What a great way to get up in the morning!

The tracks for the Frisco/Santa Fe railroad were on the Missouri side of the river so the terrain would be new and interesting – fresh food for the brain. The Mississippi River provided many fabulous views as the boats and barges leisurely cruised the river. About twenty miles out of town we stopped to pick up boxcars. A brakeman who was walking the train stopped at my boxcar, during our conversation he said that the Frisco Line had been purchased by the Burlington Northern Railroad. The B&N had always been a hobo friendly railroad to ride. It looked like the Cape had a good connection to all points west.

The sun rose as a brilliant red and orange disc and was slowly burning through the morning river mist. The sun painted a swath of brilliant flaming colors on the flooded and now overflowing river that reached to the rails on which we rode. We passed through the pleasant little river town of Crystal and rolled into the northwestern portion of St. Louis. It was a surprise to find that that railroad yard was close to my friend's house in University City.

I stopped at a fountain near the old Carter headquarters. The fountain was in the center of the traffic circle so many cars passed directly in front of it. It was possible to observe car passengers as they took quick glances at the musical rhythm of the water as it danced in the clean air. It occurred to me that only taking a glance at the beauty of the fountain was a metaphor for life itself. Many individuals passed the "musical fountain of life" without ever pausing to enjoy all it had to offer. Life was much like that Maryland Plaza Fountain; some people didn't slow down, others would slow a little, some circled once, some two or three times. Very few had the circumstances that would allow them to pause and experience all the beauty life had to offer. It was certainly a blessing to be in a position to simply stand back and observe the beauty of the spiritual and physical environments encountered during my travels. The fountain was only one small example of the many gifts received on that day and every day of my life.

I made it to my friend Sally's place just in time for a great dinner and a nice evening of   lively conversation. Following a long hot shower, it was time for a little kissing and a good night's sleep. Sally left for work early in the morning and told me to make myself at home. Everything was emptied from my ALICE rucksack, removed its frame and gave it a much-needed bath. After a couple of months on the tracks the olive drab color had almost changed to black. The solitude, in air-conditioned comfort, was enjoyed immensely. Did my laundry and took care of some neglected letter writing. Tried to reach my friend Duke at the Seafarer's Union, and found he was really on that proverbial "slow boat to China."

It was another pleasant evening and it was hard to believe that it was my fourth day in St. Louis. It was certainly true that time passed quickly when you were having fun. Spent much quality time with Sally but she had left me enough freedom to work on little personal projects that had been neglected.

Morning time and Sally brought me a great breakfast in bed. We said our goodbyes and my two black limousines were ready to move. It was a six-mile hike from "U City" to the B&N yard. Waited there for what the knockers called the "river train." I decided to crawl into a caboose, remove my boots, and get some shuteye. I was awakened at three in the morning by two young gumshoes who then questioned me at great length. After much discussion they told me to get in their patrol car. Visions of jail flashed through my head; gladly that was not to be the case! The two gumshoes proceeded to drive the mile or so to the head end of the "river train." Once there they let me out and told me to find a place to sleep and to "please stay out of sight." How about that? The many friendly attitudes and behaviors that were constantly encountered on the rails still amazed me.

The "river train" slowly pulled out of that St. Louis B&N yard just a little before dawn and several hours later came to a stop directly in front of the main gate of the Missouri Barge Line, on the southern edge of the Cape. I walked directly to the barge line offices to talk with the boss. The office people were very nice, they gave me an application and told me that the Port Engineer was the man who did the hiring but he was on vacation. They advised me to return in three weeks but that the chances of getting hired were very slim. That barge line was a relatively small family operation that ran three boats, all boats currently had full crews and few ever quit the river. What appealed to me about river work were the thirty days on and thirty days off--with pay! Just think, the rails could still be ridden! Walked to the Central Inn and cooled off with a couple of beers and then headed for the farm.

Thinking About Human Interactions

During my prior stays at the farm I had left a pile of materials, mostly political stuff, that were stored in the basement and taking up needed space. I ended up burning most of it, as I didn't want to carry it with me. It was an interesting experience to watch my prior campaign "work" go up in smoke. The emotional feeling was surely not as strong as it would have been one year ago when my attachment to such things was much more important. Actually, a bit of pleasure was experienced while burning and watching the papers become meaningless ashes. All those so-called "important" documents, letters and publications made one wonder how they added to my personal and/or to our nation's productivity. It is suspected that much of what was burning had only served the purpose of making printers rich.

Perhaps my interaction with various government agencies was actually a contributing factor toward waste. There was the realization that there was expense involved every time information was requested of the government. The feeling was that sometimes my actions were actually encouraging waste. But such interaction did provide me with a way of finding out what government was doing with our tax money. At what point should it be said that enough was enough and stop supporting the government's position that they were providing useful information to the public? Was this hobo part of the "unofficial" government bureaucracy? Had he reached a degree of insider status since he learned to maneuver within the system by experience and New Knowledge.

The smoke cleared from my paper burning operation and the household began to awaken. We had a delightful and happy time bringing one another up to date. We had a nice dinner, more family conversation and then a good night's sleep.

It was Sunday evening at the farm, everyone had gone to town. I was alone with Dave and Jeanne's homemade elderberry wine. At that time of solitude thoughts of disappearing came to mind. Little contact with people or maybe less time at any one stop. How about traveling faster and having fewer stops? Was that possible? Was my current traveling leading to someone, somewhere or to something? The rate of movement was irrelevant when viewed by oneself. When on the move one found many places to land, new people and horizons and of course New Knowledge. Where was that common free spirit—how many others in our great land; The tramps of Kiddie Junction, the ladies of San Jose, Tempe, St. Louis or Altadena, where was synchronicity? The question seemed to be whether a synchronous relationship was even a possibility? The question came back to the concept of time and changes in relationships with the passage of time; it could not be denied that relationships did change.

I began to understand and truly believe that *nothing* was real except change. Many people spent their lives seeking security through the maintenance of the status quo while denying the basic law of change. Perhaps the rate of change varied in a physical sense. Individuals who opened their doors of perception to physical reality would experience constant change more acutely than those having a narrower vision of the physical world. Those with the narrow vision spent time and energy denying change and in doing so they found a certain measure of security. Those that denied change had occasional times when change could not be ignored but it would be quickly suppressed. For individuals acutely aware of constant change such change become commonplace and unimportant. The question was whether changes in themselves became non-stimulating much the same as security and stability? The underlying fact was that physical reality was undergoing a process of constant change; it was up to the individual whether they chose to acknowledge or ignore the change.

Since we were all individuals living within our *personal* universe others did not see us as we saw ourselves. There was no possible way for another individual to see us as we saw ourselves! It was a physical impossibility. That was one powerful reason why synchronous relationships were difficult to locate and maintain. However, relationships based on constant change were possible. Physical separation might be an answer to those times when non-synchronous periods became prevalent. Perhaps one reason synchronism often broke down with the passage of time was that individuals greatly varied in their ability to devote energy in a manner which maintained a steady relationship. The thought was that if one underestimated their impact was the impact diminished? The actual impact really made no difference as long as the E^2OL principle was maintained.

Some people had a way of asking you to do something when actually they were not "asking" but "telling" you. Now, most adult humans did not appreciate being told what to do unless the value was easily recognized. If the "asking" or "telling" added to E^2OL then it was Enriching and Enjoyable. It would become a positive addition to one's energy base of knowledge. People who wanted you to do something for them were assuming that you owed them something or that at some time in the future you would ask for something. That *quid pro quo* assumption was often a source of confusion even when such energy trades were discussed from the start. The result was that the parties to the energy exchange were often required to expend extensive energy to maintain E^2OL. One rule that might be applied to personal interactions was: If you ask someone for assistance (that required energy expenditure) then it must be understood by both parties that it made no difference to the relationship if the wish was or was not granted. If granted then nothing was expected in return. We should, however, remember that "value begets value." So, it seemed that we should be generous with any surplus energy but never at the expense of personal E^2OL.

Ready for a Boxcar
It was another quiet afternoon on the farm as everyone had gone to town.

Decided to take a walk with Rusty, the family collie. It was actually cool that day and there was a nice breeze blowing across that Missouri farmland. The stream was running full from the recent rains and you could almost hear the soy beans grow. It was certainly pleasant at the Cape. Back from my long walk and everyone had returned, we had a delicious dinner, stayed up late talking for another pleasant evening.

I was ready to move again and return to the solitude of the iron trail. Such solitude was one sure way to control the non-E^2OL. Non-E^2OL could result when you either failed to enrich and enjoy yourself or when you were required to expend energy in a non-productive way. An example would be listening to non-E^2OL type talk as when someone was attempting to get you to do something that was inconsistent with your E^2OL. When that happened, you were required to expend energy to assign a *value* to incoming stimuli. That was the Space/Time Marker Value or STMV assignment process. Even when living according to the principle that there was Value in Everything it took varying amounts of energy to identify stimuli which enhanced our E^2OL. Some environments such as solitude required minimal energy expenditure. However, we must remember that E^2OL and Total Serenity was derived from the spirit and therefore could be reached in any environment.

Dad and Dave gave me a ride to town and let me off at the SEMO campus. I quickly got inside the library to escape a rapidly approaching thunderstorm. Stayed inside for a few hours of pleasant reading during the storm, then to Uncle Kenny's to say goodbye. Headed for the B&N tracks with a stop at the Central Inn. There were some strangers at the bar who looked like something dragged from under a rock. One of them was loudly bragging to his companion that he was collecting unemployment and getting hundreds of dollars' worth of food stamps every month. The whole conversation made me sick. Sick with them and sick with the government for making it possible for such people to survive. One of the aims of many politicians was to convince the producers in society that money and services received such as unemployment insurance and food stamps resulted from a caring state. Politicians liked to hide the fact that all money used by the government to pay for such projects were derived from the citizens of the state. Such a method of expropriating wealth from a state's citizenry had been going on for centuries. It always worked to enrich those in power at the expense of the less influential citizens. Such schemes ultimately lead to the downfall of the state since the producers eventually realize the fraud and would then refuse to feed the parasitic government. Citizens must be vigilant and oppose government programs which actually destroyed the independent spirit that had been engrained in our culture.

Silver Cadillac

The pleasant atmosphere of the banks of the Mississippi and B&N tracks was a good place to start my hunt for a train. I had several interesting conversations with long time Cape residents and filled my cargo pockets with large delicious green apples that were growing next to the tracks. Within thirty minutes I was on a slow, easygoing southbound freight. I decided to do something that was really not such a good idea when train hopping. My ride was on an auto rack loaded with new Cadillacs. A silver Cadillac was unlocked, so I climbed inside, started the motor, ran the air conditioner and listened to music in cool comfort. It was an abuse of the freedom to ride the freights, but I told myself it would only be that one time.

We rolled into Memphis right on schedule and before long I was on another train rushing through a cool, clear night. Dawn arrived as the train slowed in rolling hills dotted with trees and pastures looking much like a well-kept golf course. The sun was a yellow disc of muted light slowly burning through the morning fog. It was so serene; nothing could be heard except for the occasional morning song of some far-off bird. When the train once again pulled into a siding, I left my flatcar and found a clean boxcar complete with a large packing cushion filled with air—an air mattress! The mattress made for a very smooth ride on that southern journey.

The train stopped directly on the main line in some very beautiful, hilly countryside. There must have been a serious mechanical malfunction such as a broken air line, as freights rarely stopped on the main track without having a very good reason. As we waited to roll, I thought that it might be nice to buy a caboose, find some inexpensive real estate near the tracks and stop traveling for a while. Valentine, Texas, might be an enjoyable place to lay my head, make a bed, and to sew some thread.

The train crew quickly made repairs and we rolled into the pleasant city of Birmingham, Alabama sometimes called the "magic city." The southern people were friendly and they would frequently help this hobo in many ways. The weather was extremely hot and humid, much like you would expect under a jungle canopy. I gave myself a standard G.I. bath while standing in front of a sink in a railroad shanty. Believe it or not, the body was clean enough for a trip downtown.

It was a quick visit to Senator Denton's district office. Then I returned to the yard to look for a north bound train. The heat and humidity were oppressive on that day. It made a deep impression on my brain; thoughts of the northern coolness filled my head. While these thoughts drifted through my totally fried brain the winds arrived with great gusts of blissful cool air, thunder, lightning and rain. In one instant the environment completely changed and my over-heated body was rapidly cooling down. I thanked my creator once again – thank you God!

I had a wonderful trip north to Memphis; the numerous thunder storms provided many stimuli for my tired body and soul. Arrived in Memphis, did my morning chores and jumped off since the knockers were breaking the train apart. The cool air of the night was gone; the hot humid southern air once again began its oppressive work. A new north bound train was found and just waiting for it to head down the tracks. Several hours passed before we headed north. Just outside Memphis another thunderstorm struck again--one of the most powerful and wildest ever seen. Thunder, lightning, rain and high winds had knocked many large trees and their limbs to the ground. The boxcar rocked and rolled from the constant buffeting of the violent wind. The rain came not in drops but more like buckets or curtains of water which rhythmically assaulted the open doors of my boxcar.

The trip south from St. Louis on the B&N tracks gave one a spectacular view since the tracks ran along the Mississippi river. The many thunderstorms had caused the river to flood in several places; it often lapped at the roadbed of our tracks. The vantage point from the top of my auto rack offered a panoramic view that would be hard to match. Towering cliffs of brilliant white Missouri shale, dark green pine trees, a carpet of morning glories, and the fast-moving water of the river overwhelmed my senses. Icing on the cake was the rising orange sun burning through the early morning mist that left a sparkling trail of golden light on the water extending from one side of the great Mississippi right to edge of the tracks. It was a wonderful blessing to be able to observe and absorb the magnificent beauty present in that time and space.

As the train passed through the Cape it didn't stop, meaning I'd have to jump. That dangerous maneuver was accomplished by hanging on to the side of the railroad car, getting your feet moving as fast as possible, then letting go as you hit the ground, sort of like running for your life. You see the ground was moving by at whatever speed the train was going and you were sitting still on the train. Part of the problem for the hobo was that you must quickly judge when the train had slowed as much as it would.

I climbed down to the last step on the ladder and when my feet hit the ground they were kicked high into the air. Not to be discouraged I tried again. The second time I let go of the train, ran, and somehow managed not to fall, which was much preferred to tumbling in the rocks.

I noticed a measuring device at the edge of the water and it indicated that the river level was at thirty-one feet. The local residents said that thirty-two feet was the official flood stage; they were watching it closely. The river was filled with floating and partially submerged debris which made navigation extremely difficult for the river boat captains. The slight breeze and the sound from the lapping river somehow seemed to take the edge off the humid southern heat. While I relaxed on the green grass at the rivers' side, two old timers walked up and started a conversation about the river and riding the rails. One of them had spent a couple of years riding the rails as a much younger man – he had the stories to prove it.

I had a restful few hours beside the mighty, and flooded, Mississippi and then went to the local ice cream parlor for a special treat – a real hobo's dream. Then to Kent Library on the SEMO campus for a little reading in air-conditioned comfort. The sky looked wild; the forecast was for more thunderstorms and especially high winds. The shelter offered by the library would be appreciated when the storm struck. I found a beautiful and secluded corner room with large windows that were filled with lush emerald green ferns – an excellent place for the absorption of brain food. I stayed until closing time, saddled up and headed for the tracks to find a quiet place to rest for the evening. I sacked out in a caboose which looked like it hadn't moved in years. I managed to get some welcome sleep but was rudely awakened a few hours later when my caboose jolted to a start and began to roll down the tracks. Very quickly pulled on my boots, grabbed ALICE and jumped from the moving train. Found another crummy and managed to sleep until just before dawn. While walking down the tracks I met a local fellow who invited me to a "greasy spoon" for breakfast. Following breakfast and some good conversation it was back to the tracks where Gene, a railroad detective, struck up a conversation. He said, "Some of the trainmen told me there was a hobo in my yard." I told him I was just in town trying to get a job on the river. He wished me luck and told me, "Be careful and don't get caught hopping the freights."

Unfortunately, the barge line folks didn't have a job for me. Although disappointed it was possible for me to head down the tracks in high spirits. I hiked to the campus and relaxed in the shade of a 100-year-old giant oak tree. I spent a couple of hours absorbing all the beauty of that place and then returned to the library for more reading. I let my mind race from one topic to the next. I wondered how such brain activity was related to the Total

Serenity (TS) state of mind. Once you attained TS you found that you had a sense of well-being regardless of physical surroundings. It seemed that the TS state of mind reduced one's sensitivity to external stimuli and left more energy to concentrate on pure mental activity. What a wild thought!

I called cousin Russell, Uncle Kenny's son, who picked me up at the library for a ride to the Central Inn. We had a couple of beers at the bar, picked up a six pack and then drove to the B&N yard. We talked about married versus single life as Russ was having difficulties with his very attractive wife, Judy. We talked, drank beer and it was soon time for me to hit the cinder trail.

Back to the yards where I heard that old train whistle from a northbound and caught it on the run. Where was I headed next? Immediately my new St. Louis friend, Sally, came to mind.

The train was smooth as it glided along the rushing river's edge. We stopped in the rustic river front town of Wittenberg. In less than a minute, those flying dive bombers, mosquitoes, almost carried me off – they were relentless in their repeated attacks. It was a pleasant light rain as my hike through Forest Park began. The streets were deserted in those early morning hours. The city was silent. I walked for three hours to University City and then called Sally who once again invited me to stay at her house for a few days. It wasn't long before I was at Sally's making ALICE gear changes and doing some minor sewing projects. We had a great time bringing each other up-to-date. It was just fun to spend time with her. I had a feeling that she felt the same way about me. Sally's sister came over for an early morning breakfast and we watched a two-hour Star Trek special. Soon more friends arrived and the house was filled with lively female conversation (and one male – me) on that nice Saturday morning

One beautiful afternoon at Sally's was spent reading my old hobo journal notes; had all those good times actually happened? Almost all the notes revealed a constant stream of enjoyable experiences – that was what filled my memory banks. Those few days with friends in St. Louis would certainly add to my stream of pleasant times. Later that evening Sally and new friend Shelia gave me a fun-filled ride to the B&N railroad terminal on the Missouri side of the Mississippi River. Hugs and sweet, juicy kisses goodbye and off to find a train.

Pre-employment Vacation

The long, humid hike from St. Louis to the Chicago and Northwestern (C&NW) freight yard in Madison, Illinois, was physically and mentally challenging. I was saturated with sweat and constantly under attack by bugs hungry for blood. The "value" in that hike resided in the challenge it presented, overcoming the adversity and then getting on with my life. The reward was also in the intense feeling of satisfaction upon reaching the C&NW yards at two o'clock in the morning. Within minutes of entering that yard a brass button leisurely approached me. For several minutes we discussed politics and freight trains and he soon invited me into his wonderfully air-conditioned train shanty to share his lunch. We relaxed in cool comfort as he handed me a huge and delicious hot and spicy polish sausage sandwich – my eyes lit up! My new friend told me that a north bound train would leave in a couple of hours and then walked with me to show me exactly where it was.

Soon I was in a clean boxcar, comfortably sitting in a cardboard nest, lazily rolling down the tracks in yet another thunderstorm. Nearby streams were overflowing their banks; it looked like a flood to me. We made it into Iowa and it was still raining. I lay back, using ALICE as a backrest and totally enjoyed the scenic rolling hills of eastern Iowa and the intense sensations generated by that loud and powerful thunderstorm. Many streams were flooded and water was often flowing along both sides of the tracks. Very little land could be seen and the water extended for miles in all directions. It was beginning to feel more than a little creepy! Would this train get be able to get through all the water?

That westbound train slowed to a crawl, most likely because of the flooding, and it took several hours before we arrived in Neilson, Iowa. I became impatient with that slow freight. Was there an expected destination?

My thoughts were unclear. We stopped on the outskirts of Des Moines where the brass buttons casually told me where to catch a westbound. I sat in the relative cool shade of an old boxcar and waited and ate a can of beans with a few slices of bread. It was really good to be back on the tracks; the cinders felt great under the strength of my tough combat boots.

I hopped on the westbound and right back off again in the Bell yard, a real "bo park." I used the yard master's telephone to call Iowa friends, Big Al and Sandra, but they were on vacation, so we wouldn't get together that time. A westbound grain train was found and while looking for a place to ride a I spotted a bad air leak. I told the brass buttons and then took a seat in the last of the four engines that were pulling that very heavy grain train. The crew knew they had a passenger on board which seemed to be no problem —actually they appeared happy. It had been a long time since riding in the engine, the upgrade was enjoyable. That particular engine had an unusual and rather large outside area, sort of a porch. It would be easy to go out and gaze at the beautiful star filled sky and listen to the roar of the diesels as we highballed across the Iowa and Kansas plains.

We arrived in Kansas City just as the great shining disk of the morning sun rose above the horizon. Since that grain train ended in Kansas City one of the crew came to my engine and told me exactly where to jump off to make a connection for another westbound. I jumped from the moving train and walked through the city, mostly on the tracks but sometimes on the streets. I felt refreshed following the comfortable all-night ride in the engine. While walking along the tracks a pig train (these were usually high priority trains loaded with truck trailers) sped toward me. I failed to catch it as it was traveling just a little too fast.

After several miles of walking the tracks I stopped to talk with a group of workers. They warned me that their yard was hot with many gumshoes. They advised me to take to the street and circle around to the departure yard.

Cool Ice Water

There was a row of small modest homes near the tracks. In front of one was a Latino-looking man washing a truck with a garden hose. I made a motion toward the hose and asked him for a drink--he refused. He did call out to his wife, in Spanish, to get me a glass of ice water from his house. He then motioned for me to join them on his porch. Ended up staying for a couple of hours. While relaxing on the porch, they served me; three sandwiches, a coke, many glasses of milk and Cuban coffee. They spoke little, if any,

English and their eight-year-old son acted as a translator. Less than one year ago the family had come to our country in order to escape the communist regime of Castro. They were very big fans of the USA and President Carter was their most honored hero! They were able to enter this country as a result of Carter's policies.

Excitement seemed to permeate the air when they found out about me working for President Carter. They watched my every move, with more than a little fascination, as my ALICE gear was searched and Carter memorabilia removed and handed to them. They became very emotional and more animated after they were told that they that they could keep the campaign buttons and letterhead as a gift from me. They thanked me profusely through their young son who had been acting as a translator. They were truly excited! We had a great time eating, drinking, talking and just relaxing on that pleasant porch overlooking the Kansas City freight yards. It was time to saddle up and head for the tracks while waving goodbye as ALICE and I headed down that quiet city street.

I ventured into the Santa Fe departure yard to see about catching a west bound and the only thing that got caught was me! Two Santa Fe railroad detectives nabbed me and took me to their office for a little friendly question and answer period. Mike and Paul were both professional and when they realized I posed no threat the discussion turned to politics and train security. However, in the end, Mike strongly advised me to head for the highway and not "his" train yard."

I hoisted my gear and took off in the direction of Interstate 70. Several miles later three rough looking characters saw me humping the ALICE gear and offered me a lift in their New Jersey van; I accepted and jumped into the back. They were going to California to find work and the bikini clad beach girls of Malibu. The van was comfortable, the conversation lively and I was getting closer to the mile-high city of Denver. The three guys told me that they had to make a side trip north, so I got out at WaKeeney, Kansas, and camped at a quiet roadside park.

The next morning, an active-duty Air Force Officer stopped to give me a ride. We were on the way to Colorado Springs, where he was currently stationed. We had much to talk about regarding the military and especially the vulnerability of the minuteman missile launching sites. He confided in me that the communication systems for the Launch Control Facilities (LCF's) were extremely susceptible to sabotage. We discussed possible solutions during our three-hundred-mile trip. David had combat experience in Vietnam where he flew B-52 missions. He had also taken part in the

Pueblo incident and the Middle East war. David was definitely a good American and spoke highly of our country and the Air Force. It was a pleasure riding and talking with him and learning about his service to our country. He told me about his brother-in-law's interesting work in the oil fields of northern Utah. He told me, "Check out the small town of Vernal, Utah, look up my brother-in-law at Dowell, and see about a job." He thought work for this errant hobo might be waiting in the oil fields.

David dropped me on the outskirts of Colorado Springs where he turned off the highway and then it was a pleasant ten-mile hike into and through Colorado Springs. I sat at the edge of the Denver Rio Grande and Western Railroad (D&RGW) yard and relaxed in the cool shade of some large cottonwood trees. Following my pleasant ride with David and recent gumshoe encounter, I decided to continue on the highway.

E^2OL Becomes E^3OL

I made it to Englewood to visit my friend Ramey. He wasn't at home so I relaxed by the lake. I spent the time recalling all the interesting conversations with the many people that gave this vagabond the rides which took me from Kansas City to Denver. My highway experience had been pleasant but there was something special about the magic of the rails – the rails were calling. There was a stiff, cool breeze, cloudy sky and the serenity by the lakeside was evident, my spirit was at rest. The philosophy which had guided my life for the past couple of years rewarded me with such moments of Total Serenity. That personal philosophy had developed from Enjoyment of Life (EOL) to include Enrichment of Life (E^2OL). Therefore, up to that point in time, my philosophy embodied the concept of both Enjoyment and Enrichment of Life. Another term which very often slipped into my thoughts regarding my personal philosophy was "Enlightenment." It was time to add Enlightenment to Enjoyment and Enrichment therefore E^2OL would be modified to read E^3OL- it became "E-cubed OL."

Katie, Ramey and Jennette came home and we brought each other up to date. They wondered how it was possible to pursue my unusual lifestyle and yet pursue Enjoyment, Enrichment and Enlightenment of Life (E^3OL). I explained that I surely didn't have all the answers but my philosophy of life was working for me. They wanted to know about my plans for the future, where would life's path take me. How could a person such as myself live with such a flexible view of direction and no apparent goals? At the time my personal vision for my future would be kept to myself. I wished to be thought of and accepted only as a good-natured happy hobo – there was no more! I didn't wish for my friends or the people met while traveling to think of me in any other way. Knowledge of my future vision would only have the potential to introduce static into our conversations. If the personal vision for my future was pleasant there was no reason to speak about it – that vision is a personal matter.

I stayed with my Englewood friends for three days. Then headed for downtown Denver to see, Don and Mike, a couple of friends from my days with President Carter. They were now working for a congresswoman. I found them both at the congresswoman's office, in high spirits and anxious to reminisce about the campaign work we did for Carter. A few hours later Don and I headed for the tracks, but first stopped at a local bar and drank way too many beers. By the time we were ready to leave we were both well lubricated. We both walked (staggered) to the D&RGW railroad yard in downtown Denver. He was fascinated with the whole idea of an "invisible hobo culture" and just had to experience a "touch" of it for himself. He was thoroughly impressed when I gave him a guided tour of the rail yard. The tour included a "walk through" of a string of running locomotives that were waiting to be moved to a train. Don soon headed for his warm bed, it was time for me to hike the tracks to find a place to get some rest (and perhaps sober up a little) before catching a west bound freight. I was able to snatch a couple hours sleep before the sun rose to start another day on the tracks.

It was time to move out and see about a westbound train. In less than an hour I climbed on board a very unusual short train consisting of only thirteen cars. Found a flatcar and in a few minutes, we were on the roll toward Grand Junction on a beautiful sunny morning in scenic Colorado.

Hobo Gets a Job

I had decided to make my way to Vernal and check out David's suggestion about a job in the "oil patch." Since there were no railroad tracks to Vernal, I hopped off the train at Grand Junction and hit the highway. A few minutes on the road and a friendly young oil rig welder gave me a ride and insisted on buying breakfast. Following a great breakfast and conversation he dropped me at the only highway leading through the mountains to Vernal. Another beautiful sunshine filled morning, standing in front of a picturesque little country store on the road to Utah. It was another extremely happy day! It was approaching that Total Serenity feeling that was rarely experienced.

Following a short fifteen-minute wait, Gary and his young son stopped and offered me a ride all the way to Vernal. Turns out Gary was not only from Vernal, where he managed the Circle K, but was also good friends with David's brother Garth. We had much to talk about during the three hour trip. The ride through the mountains and over Douglas Pass gave me a good introduction to the special beauty of the area. It would be nice to spend some time in that magnificent part of the world and perhaps earn a little money. Everything was falling into place, especially when one lived by the philosophy that *value* could be found on whichever path we chose to take.

Gary let me off a couple of blocks from the Dowell Company facility. I walked, with my ALICE gear on my back, directly to the office and completed the application for an oil field worker/truck driver position that was now open. The young lady took my application and told me to wait. Several minutes later Garth invited me to his office for an interview. We had a productive thirty-minute talk and he tentatively hired me contingent on a clean driving record. Problem was, it could take two weeks to get my record. I hoofed it into town to try to figure out how to speed up the process, first to the Utah Motor Vehicle Department, then the Utah Highway Patrol, and finally the Uintah County Sheriffs' Department office. Nobody could help.

As I sat in front of the sheriff's office pondering my plight, a deputy sheriff walked toward the office. I got his attention and told him of my troubles. He cheerfully told me to come inside, he entered my info into his computer, and within a minute or so he had confirmed that I had a perfect driving record. He then called Garth at Dowell (they were good friends) and told him my driving record was clean with no violations. Garth told me to call him on Friday for the final word. The company really looked like a nice place to work. I decided to find a place to camp for a couple of days. A little used, if not totally abandoned city park on the west side of town looked like a good campsite. It was equipped with a couple of picnic tables, deep green grass, fire pit and lots of shade trees.

The Main Street of Vernal was alive with oil equipment rigs and new pickup trucks decked out with roll bars, wide tires and fancy paint jobs. The trucks must be a mark of the affluent young oil rig workers bountiful in that area of Utah. You could actually "feel" the excitement in the air. With the coming of the cool evening that little town seemed to come alive with the energy of youth. As I wrote the words "excitement in the air" there was a loud crash, the screeching of tires and breaking glass. I was the first to arrive at the accident scene, where I saw a motorcycle smashed against the side of one of those fancy pickups. The driver of the cycle was spread-eagled in the street. The young man looked up at me through pain filled eyes and asked me to call his friend, Gary, the guy who had given me a ride into town that morning – wow! It was definitely a small world--especially in Vernal. I made the phone call and Gary was very surprised to hear from me. Meanwhile the paramedics had arrived and took the injured motorcycle driver to the hospital.

After that brief excitement it was a pleasant and relaxing evening at my new campsite. There was a large unused metal culvert near the park – there would be shelter if it decided to rain. That evening the culvert provided shelter as a heavy thunderstorm struck at two in the morning. It was a short run to the culvert and totally avoided getting wet. Got up at dawn, organized ALICE and then hiked to the center of town. There was another park behind the Dinosaur Museum, a tourist attraction, and it provided a place to relax in the cool shade of the early morning. Gary's son, Eric, approached me and wanted to know if I was working yet. In town less than twenty-four hours and I was already bumping into people who recognized me. Small towns were conducive to that sort of thing. There was definitely a good feeling about town. I spent a nice afternoon in the public library adjacent to the park reading and learning about oil wells and the geology of the area.

Friday morning arrived; got cleaned up and walked to a phone to see if this hobo would soon be going to work. Garth would not be able to tell me for sure until later that afternoon. It was a good feeling to be looking for work while also not being overly concerned about the outcome even though very short of money. Of course, my relaxed attitude was attributed to my belief that every path had some value. It was the principle that there was Value in Everything (VIE). In my mind was the thought that living by the principles of E^3OL would be possible whether or not working for Dowell became a reality. Enjoyment of Life would always be possible if the correct attitude was maintained. If one chose to live according to the E^3OL philosophy then material rewards such as dollars became independent of the energy expended required for work. The dollars became a bonus rather than an end onto themselves. The rewards offered by Enjoyment, Enrichment and Enlightenment were much greater than money. They always resulted in an expansion of our energy base of knowledge which was a growth of the spiritual self.

While relaxing in the park I realized that a point in my life had been reached where I honestly recognized that money had ceased to be my principle motivator. The opportunity for personal growth via the accumulation of New Knowledge was more important than any possible financial reward. I had managed to briefly experience some luxury had been briefly experienced in my lifetime and it was discovered that such rewards didn't last long. The money and the things purchased somehow had little meaning – the excitement was always short-lived and lacked real substance. Out of such past experiences had grown the Enjoyment, Enrichment and Enlightenment of Life philosophy. It was nice to be free!

I called Garth in the late afternoon, and he told me "you have the job, you can start Monday or take two weeks to take care of any business you might have." I elected to wait to take care of a few things in California. I walked down Main Street feeling light footed, and decided to catch a bus to Salt Lake City for the west coast rail connection. The maintenance of E^3OL required very little energy expenditure on that wonderful afternoon. I treated myself to a couple of cold beers at a local beer joint next to the bus depot. I would soon have plenty of money for beans and the status as a soon to be taxpayer was cause for at least a little celebration.

Pre-employment Vacation

I caught the Trailways Bus and sat next to a Dallas, Texas, policeman who had been visiting friends in Vernal. By the time we reached Salt Lake City the policeman said he was tired of bus riding and told me, "I am going to the airport, fuck this bus, you can have my Eagle Pass." The "Eagle Pass" that he gave me was good for unlimited bus riding for the next two weeks. How about that – just when I had to report for work! It looked like those steel ribbons would have to wait for another time and place. The relative comfort of the bus was very much appreciated it was time to just sit back and relax.

In Salt Lake a conversation was started with a nice young lady by the name of Lucy, from Delaware. While waiting for our buses we talked for hours. We soon found we were waiting for the same bus—happy day indeed. At one of the later bus stops we gently drifted beyond talk and begin to get closer, you know, touchy, almost kissing, but not quite yet. When we returned to the bus we moved to the very last row at the back of the bus. That was when that sweet young thing turned into a hot, passion filled woman! We parted company in Los Angeles after a most stimulating sixteen-hour make-out session. We did just about everything that a man and woman could do together.

From downtown Los Angeles it was a city bus for the San Fernando Valley, where I checked in with friends and family and put a shine on the combat boots and the brass buckle before meeting with the commander of the 146th Tactical Air Wing regarding my recent Pentagon visit. It would turn out that the commander's appointment after seeing me was with none other than President Ronald Reagan. While the base commander and I were talking, the president's helicopter, "Marine One," landed on the tarmac just outside. I left by one door and the president entered through another.

I headed back to Altadena to check in at the hardware store, library and, of course, the BBH, the cop bar, to see my "old timer" buddies. After a couple drinks I stopped at the liquor store for a pint of brandy and headed for that good old cinder trail.

While walking down Altadena's Lake Street it was time to let my spirit soar. My body was physically in that place but my mind was moving elsewhere and I soon found myself in Glendale's Southern Pacific yard, in a clean boxcar headed for the Colton yards. From the Colton yard I hiked a few miles to John's neighborhood and my "Colton Command Post," where I visited with John, Linda, and their young son, J.D. There always seemed to be "peaceful shelter" at John's.

After a great night's rest, I was up at dawn and headed for the "Rana" yard to see about a train south to San Diego. On the way there was a little stream and I decided to relax for a couple of hours and reflect on the many people and the good times I had been blessed with while traveling around these United States. The water in the stream seemed to be a metaphor for life. An individual could choose to sit by the stream's edge or one could jump in and experience all that the stream of life had to offer. Long ago this hobo made the decision to jump into the stream of life. It was a little scary at first, but it certainly did have its rewards. My next move was to search for a slow-moving freight train.

A I hiked along the tracks I heard someone call out: "Hey sarge, where do you think you're going?" It was a gumshoe and he wanted me out of his railroad yard. We had a civilized, but short, conversation, and then I was on my way again. A few minutes later a pig train easily rolled south along the tracks. I jumped aboard and was on my way, not sure where the train was headed. The pig train was really moving and threw up huge clouds of dust as it blasted through many small towns. It passed through the Bandini yard and then pulled into the familiar AT&SF yards on the outskirts of Los Angeles. A pleasant knocker told me that the "night coaster" would leave early that evening. It was time to find a shade tree and perhaps meet some railroad workers.

The trip south on the "night coaster" was always energizing as it rolled through many busy industrial areas, passed the California Angels baseball field, and then along miles of oceanfront beach. It would only slow as it passed through Oceanside; another jump and run exit. I managed to stay on the feet and felt happy to be in "Marine Corps City" on the beautiful Pacific Coast. I caught the local bus to the parent's house, let myself in and spent time getting cleaned up and rearranging my ALICE gear. Mom and dad came home and were extremely happy to hear about my status as an employed person. Sometimes it was hard for them to relate to my E^3OL philosophy.

I had a very pleasant stay and decided to use the "Eagle Pass" and travel to Vernal in the relative luxury of the air-conditioned bus. It would be a life without the freight trains for a while but certain advantages offered by bus travel would soon become apparent.

Oil Patch in the U.S.A.

My bus left the Oceanside depot late in the afternoon at the height of rush hour traffic. I got off the bus for a short walk at the Riverside station, and when I got back on there were a pair of bright pink panties lying on my bus seat – really! I held them up and waved them in the air. Their owner, Katy, soon came forward to claim them and shyly apologized for having dropped them. I invited her to sit with me. We became very well acquainted during our ride north toward Las Vegas.

Katy was a very attractive (in a showgirl kind of way) blonde from Las Vegas. We kissed for most of the trip from Riverside to Vegas. It was a stimulating and fun filled night. When we stopped kissing long enough to talk, she coyly told me, "I was just released from a mental hospital where I spent time for shooting my boyfriend and brother." I was shocked, naturally, but not enough to stop me from continuing our make-out session. As we got close to Las Vegas she casually asked me, "Why don't you come to my house for some breakfast and more fun?" As my body protested, my survival instinct declined. I said a sad goodbye to Katy and proceeded to hang out in the Las Vegas bus depot to wait for the bus to Salt Lake City.

A few hours later an exotic looking woman smoothly strolled across some open space in the bus depot and into my field of vision. When we boarded the same bus, I decided it was time for action and to make contact with this mysterious lady. My spirits lifted when I saw she was sitting by herself toward the middle of the bus.

"Would you like some company?" I asked.

She responded with an indecipherable facial expression followed by a shrug. "It's fine with me," she said in a Caribbean accent. The conversation was great and the afternoon passed quickly. We actually kissed and held one another tightly for much of the time on the road. We arrived in Salt Lake City, somewhat in heat from all the making out. Lyn was a singer from Jamaica and was in the United States for several singing engagements. We talked it over and decided that we should get a room together in a nearby motel. We would spend at least one night together before she traveled on to Edmonton, Canada, where she was to perform at a night club.

Upon entering the hotel room we immediately fell on the floor, passionately entwined as if one. Looking up from the floor I noticed we hadn't even closed the door – I kicked it shut with my foot. From that moment on it was hot and furious love-making until just before dawn. I expressed admiration for her love-making and awe with her high level of passion. She told me "all the girls from my island are sexually hot and are quite free with sex."

I awoke with the sun but my new friend, Lyn, was fast asleep. I watched her sleep while also gazing out the window to see the city awaken. What wonderful events would that peaceful day bring? Everything felt so good – explosions of fulfillment overwhelmed my spirit. We spent the morning together and the pleasure of her company continued until she had to catch a bus north to Edmonton. We passionately kissed goodbye and off she went, her bright smile beaming through the bus window. I figured that I might never see her again.

My Vernal bound bus did not leave until that evening, so I spent the rest of the day as a tourist. While having lunch in the park that afternoon that wonderful feeling of Total Serenity descended on my body and spirit. The park was next to the Mormon Temple and those pleasant train yard sounds drifted on the air as soothing music for my brain. My lunch, of beans and crackers, had never tasted so delicious. I entered the Temple and listened to a practice session of the famous Mormon Temple Tabernacle Choir. The music of those beautiful voices brought to mind my new Jamaican friend and our wonderful night together. She had made a huge impact on my brain.

The ride to Vernal passed through many deep canyons and high peaks of the Wasatch Mountain Range. As we dropped into the Green River Valley it felt like arriving at "home." I strolled slowly to my campsite in the Westside Park. Relaxed on that cool night and thought about the high level of synchronicity with my new lady friend.

In the dim light of dawn, the sound of a far-off bugle playing reveille caused me to open my eyes. I did my morning chores, then some reading, and headed to the local Chamber of Commerce to see about the housing situation. I needed something a little more stable than the metal culvert in the city park.

Life as a River

It was early evening and the cool breezes were blowing over the valley, it felt refreshing. Many thoughts were flashing through the brain. Why was I in that small town? Where would my next stop be and what would the future bring? It was fully understood that every path taken in the past had brought me to this particular place and time. Once again, life could be compared to a river where you safely sat on the shore or actually jumped in and took a chance.

Expanding that idea, we might consider one's entire lifetime of experiences as a river. It continuously moved as a single unit but at the same moment it consisted of separate parts each dependent on the other. The banks of the "river of life" could be seen as time while the flow of the water was the energy which made up individual life experiences. All events in the future would be connected with the continuous flow of life's energy and the shoreline of time. Being there in Vernal resulted in a feeling of "strangeness." It seemed as if I was holding fast on the shore while life's river flowed past. During that particular time thoughts of the future tended to make me long for the freedom of physical movement. Such visions tended to diminish the importance of the moment and served to generate feelings *less* than enjoyable. One must keep in mind that by holding fast in one place one could increase the storehouse of knowledge just as if one moved from one place to another. You could easily increase New Knowledge while also maintaining freedom of spirit. However, it was understood that it might require more energy to maintain the balance between the mind racing forward and the physical body being in one place. We could plan for a future while not letting those visions of the future interfere with the acquisition of New Knowledge. That strategy seemed to be the best way to proceed. It would be an interesting experience to maintain freedom of spirit while remaining physically stationary in Utah.

Perhaps that entire line of inward aimed thought was a result of an impatience for the Dowell adventure to begin. Was it the anxiousness for the acquisition of the New Knowledge that would surely be associated with my new job that was making me uneasy? One of the positive aspects of my introspective thought was that personal growth resulted with an increase in one's energy base of knowledge. That line of thought lead to further questions as to whether non-E^3OL could result in valuable outcomes by creating an imbalance which would then be balanced. In other words, could non-E^{3}OL provide introspective thought and thus result in New Knowledge? Such a method of learning might be rather expensive in terms of energy expenditure but valuable just the same. Such a method of turning non-E^{3}OL into E^{3}OL via the "Enlightenment" component seemed to be a practical way of dealing with such a situation. The key was to identify the imbalance immediately and then act to restore equilibrium.

I found an old abandoned house trailer on the east side of town. This new bivouac was within sight of Dowell and it looked like the perfect interim spot until a real place to live was located. For now, the old trailer provided a roof over my head, I had beans in my rucksack, and E^{3}OL in the spirit. All the while luscious thoughts of Lyn danced merrily in my brain. The sun seemed to explode as it burst through the pitch-black clouds that hung just above the horizon; it then silently slid behind the mountains.

It was a cloudy, cool Saturday morning and after doing morning duties it was off to the library for a leisurely day of reading. During my years as a college student, I would often yearn to be able to read for pure pleasure rather than at the direction of a professor. Just put me on a desert island, give me plenty of books and happiness would result. That may be stretching it somewhat but quiet time in a library always rated high as one of my pleasures in life.

It was another Saturday night in Vernal, an American city with the customary parade of cruisers on Main Street, tape decks blasting, and everyone enjoying life. I walked along the street, humping the ALICE gear toward my new home on the east side of town. I stopped at the store, picked up a quart of beer, dropped ALICE in the trailer, found a comfortable place to relax outside and began to totally enjoy that pleasantly cool evening. It was twilight time and large masses of dark black clouds were stacked along the distant mountain peaks. In my "backyard" there were all kinds of oil drilling equipment piled in various heaps which made for a strange foreground for the living canvas of mountains and sky. The black clouds accelerated the oncoming darkness. The boiling black masses of storm clouds suddenly came alive with brilliant flashes of lightning. The clouds and lighting covered the entire western horizon. It made for a spectacular light show and the coolness of the breeze hinted of a possible rainstorm. It was a powerful yet peaceful feeling at that new campsite.

Finding Value in Everything

The dawn broke on a very peaceful Sunday morning. I hiked to Naples, an even smaller town about five miles east of Vernal. It was a pleasant place along the Green River. A comfortable spot was found in the shade of a huge cottonwood tree next to the emerald green colored river. A couple of kittens came by and started to play in the tall green grass, stalking one another, springing into the air, and having what appeared to be an enjoyable time. It brought to mind how in years gone by I had often yearned for such a worry free, easy lifestyle. Why was it that we humans chose to burden ourselves with so many problems in our day to day lives? Why was it so difficult to live in our world with so many problems lurking around every corner? Perhaps the answer was that we humans created our own problems. Life's difficulties were brought about by our thoughts and actions. One might ask: How about the victim of a crime? How does the crime victim create the problem? My answer is there is Value in Everything, even being attacked by a criminal. Sometimes such *value* could be difficult to identify, but with the correct state of mind you would eventually see it. Thus, the crime victim could transform the criminal act into a valuable experience; it would however require an expenditure of energy.

In looking closer at my firm belief that there was Value in Everything, it was understood that it was a way of living one's total life. This was especially true when we found ourselves in situations where E^3OL appeared to be minimal or perhaps non-existent. Let us consider the extreme case of dying. Death was another form of expansion if we recognized our being to be part of all the matter of the universe. When we die, we ultimately become more synchronous with the universe. Our storehouse of thoughts (in the form of energy and mass) does not cease to exist for we know that energy cannot be created or destroyed. At death our mass, which was congealed energy, simply takes another form and is distributed throughout the universe perhaps as radiation and/or cosmic dust. Following that line of reasoning the *value* in dying is that our lifetime of accumulated energy is then distributed throughout the universe. You might say that it is recycled and we become part of everything. In death we truly expand to our greatest capacity. Whether we would be aware of such expansion is yet another question. Perhaps there is a kernel of awareness (perhaps the soul) which allows us to become keenly aware of other planes of existence. Is that new existence *heaven?* And is it there that we directly communicated with our Creator?

In less extreme cases, such as living day to day, we often find ourselves in various situations where it is difficult to identify *value*. In such situations we are required to "think extra hard" when processing energy (thinking) in an attempt to identify the value. At times we might feel (and rightly so) that the expenditure of energy is not balancing out. In other words, it requires too much of an effort (energy expenditure) to identify the value in something which could then result in E^3OL. Such energy processing is the assignment of a Space/Time Marker Value (STMV) to incoming stimuli. That assignment of STVMs requires us to expend energy, thus we must be protective of how we assign such values – we are the master of our energy use. When we find ourselves in a situation where value is difficult to identify it becomes our responsibility to move (mentally and/or physically) to a less energy consuming environment. That is the major reason that freedom of the body and spirit is such a sought-out condition of humankind.

Once we understand that what we perceive as a "problem" is only a creation within our own consciousness, we can then direct our energies to change the situation. So called "problems" are only a state of mind. We have the power within us to effect change. Our actions can ultimately bring us to a state of consciousness of Total Serenity (TS). The mental state of TS will free the spirit and permit us to become at one with the energies of the universe. Total Serenity enables us to communicate with the universe and to be at peace with every particle of energy in God's creation.

A Working Man

Monday morning brought another beautiful sunrise with golden rays piercing the morning mist. I was anxious to get started working in the "oil patch" of America. There was no doubt in my mind that working for greenbacks would be well worth the expenditure of energy.

The first day at Dowell consisted of ten hours in the classroom. Safety was the most emphasized topic since our work environment was extremely dangerous. As I prepared to hump ALICE to my old trailer at the end of the day, Garth intervened. When he found out I was homeless, he said the company would put me up in a hotel until I found something and that they'd give me three hundred dollars to help me with living expenses until my first paycheck arrived. The wisdom of my decision to take David's advice and come to Vernal was being constantly reinforced on that great first day on the job.

I checked into a motel, took a nice long hot shower, flopped down on a king size water bed and watched a movie on cable television while drinking a cold beer! I had cash in my pocket, a roof over my head, plenty of food and memories of sweet Lyn. That new life situation offered a great opportunity to analyze and compare the E^3OL experienced last night in the cold trailer on the east side of town. It required less of an energy expenditure to maintain enjoyment this night and to study and complete piles of paperwork for the job. Once again, it was a personal observation of solid evidence that every path was indeed valuable. Coming to Utah with only a few dollars, no place to stay and yet feeling something valuable would result provided additional evidence that my philosophy of life had merit. Relaxing in the luxury of that hotel room, the old adage "boxcar to mansion" seemed to accurately describe my current status.

That experience was a graphic illustration of how our life situation could change in a blink of the eye. If that was the case then why should we spend valuable energy on a greater concern for the future than was required? It made no difference whether one went from "rags to riches" or "riches to rags" as long as E^3OL was part of our mental outlook on life. Once it was understood that material comfort, beyond our Basic Needs, had little bearing on whether you could enjoy life, you could move free as the wind through the timeless universe and romp (as those Green river kittens) in the tall green grass of life.

It was an eventful first week at Dowell, leaving little energy to think about the many new experiences. It seemed like an all-out assault on my physical and mental receptors. During the training exercise for the self-contained breathing apparatus, they rudely ripped the gas mask from your face in a dark gas and smoke-filled room. I also drove an eighteen-wheeler for the first time. It was great fun as a new and exciting experience. The instructor took me to the outskirts of Vernal where he pulled the big truck to the side of the road and told me, "Get in the driver's seat and take me up that mountain over there." We headed for the mountain with him given instructions on shifting and staying on the road as we traveled down that little-used back road. I shifted through the *thirteen* gears fairly well as the International Diesel wound its way up the mountain.

My first actual job came after several days of training, it was in Rangely, Colorado. It turned to be an unusual and exciting job as the oil well suffered a "blowout." It was out of control and everyone ran for cover as heavy metal pipe and other debris were blasted into the air and began falling back toward us fragile humans. Drill pipe weighing thousands of pounds was flying out of the well and into the air in a gush of water, oil and mud. It certainly got my adrenaline flowing. Several minutes later the engineers got the well under control and repair work was started immediately. For the more seasoned oil patch workers it was just another job – no big deal. The men were very professional and proud of their work, which was reassuring because the work required a team effort and one man's mistake or carelessness became everyone's problem. Your health and welfare almost always depended on fellow workers.

Sunday morning started at 2 am for a ten hour well job then it was back to my new home. Just lounging under the backyard apple tree with a nice cool breeze coming from the west and feeling so blessed. My new home was a big four-bedroom house which I shared with three young men who either worked directly in the oil patch or in something closely related. It had been an interesting and exciting two weeks. There was no doubt that vast stores of New Knowledge had been accumulated. The acquisition of knowledge was one of the key parts of the E^3OL philosophy. For when you were learning, you were actually growing and enriching your spiritual self. As long as one learned something, the path became a valuable one. If you lived for New Knowledge and the E^3OL principle then every moment of life would be enjoyable. The difficult part of reaching such a state was answering the question as to what it was you wanted to do at any particular moment. That question became much easier if you believed that all paths could result in a feeling of well-being. All one had to do was to make sure that the chosen path provided opportunities to enrich our mind through New Knowledge. One must also believe that there was Value in Everything (VIE)! It was each individual's responsibility to identify that *value* and then benefit from whatever it had to offer. If we found value in our personal universe, we would receive value in return. Value was everywhere; we must open our minds and absorb the energy it had for our soul. When one believed in the concept of VIE then choices became less energy consuming. If you lived according to the VIE concept you would be at peace. You would look upon your own death with a smile on your face for your spirit would then be free.

At Dowell we were on call twenty-four hours a day and seven days a week. During the third week on the job, I got a call at three in the morning instructing me to be prepared to move out in one hour. There was an emergency job in Steamboat Springs, Colorado, about an eight-hour drive from Vernal. Our equipment convoy started to roll a little before dawn. For me it was service as an observer/trainee since Dowell's two-week safety school was still in my future. The morning and early afternoon were spent, as a passenger, driving through beautiful countryside that was covered with aspen trees just now beginning to display their beautiful autumn colors. Deer could be seen grazing among the trees which made the natural beauty of that place even more spectacular. We completed the emergency repairs on the oil well and spent the night at a first-class motel in Steamboat Springs. Another policy that we workers appreciated was that we all had private rooms—no double bunking for Dowell employees. It was a pleasant drive home to Vernal in the morning. My return was just in time for two days off which was followed by a trip to Tulsa, Oklahoma, for a two-week safety school.

The time spent learning about the operation of the heavy machinery used in the oil patch was proving to be an enjoyable experience. E^3OL was in evidence and the value in the school was very easily identified. My plan for spending time in the oil patch was moving along very nicely and New Knowledge was coming as quickly as could be absorbed. The second week at the safety school started with me getting behind the wheel of a Dowell eighteen-wheel equipment truck. The driving instructor, myself, and two students headed down Historic U.S. Route 66 for my first highway truck driving experience. It was a beautiful day with a brilliant blue sky, broken clouds, gentle breezes and temperatures in the low seventies. What a perfectly wonderful day! Total Serenity was very much in evidence. The friendly driving instructor and we three students spent the entire day trucking down the highway and learning how to handle that rather large oil field equipment rig.

The two weeks at safety school passed very quickly. It was a productive fourteen days and my brain had been considerably expanded. The 727-jetliner climbed into the early morning sun through scattered clouds on a beautiful Saturday morning. On the way home to Vernal. It was definitely a Total Serenity morning. My mind seemed to mix with the clouds as the powerful jet soared toward those invisible daytime stars high in the sky. My energy mingled with the atoms of the jet and the space/time through which we traveled; we were as one. How many others on the flight were experiencing Total Serenity? It really didn't matter because we were all part of everyone, sharing the universe and moving through this phantom world in ethereal space and time. It was a great feeling to be at peace with all of God's creation. One of the interesting things concerning the feeling of Total Serenity was that the physical environment had no effect on whether one might experience it or not. TS could occur while walking down a country road, riding in a boxcar, in a modern jet aircraft at twenty-thousand feet, or perhaps while in the midst of a group of individuals who cared less about any such feeling. It was a feeling independent of environmental surroundings. It was a spiritual state dealing with non-physical reality and represented the highest level of the human mind.

After a few months on the job, I returned from a three-day assignment at an isolated oil and gas field in southern Wyoming and was surprised and delighted to find out Lyn was coming for a visit. Lyn arrived on the late afternoon bus right on time. We had a wonderfully stimulating eight days before she had to return to Canada for another singing engagement. The time passed much too quickly, and once again I waved to her as she left Vernal on the Trailways Bus going north. We soon discovered that we had much in common despite our very different backgrounds. Her colorful stories about her culture were so very enjoyable. She talked about the island people and experiences while growing up in Jamaica. Lyn told me about her cabin in the Blue Mountains of Jamaica and invited me for an extended visit.

I spent an interesting two weeks working on a big job in Los Alamos, New Mexico, at a United States Department of Energy drilling site. The well was an experimental project and dealt with geo-thermal power and the generation of electricity from the earth's internal heat. The well itself was five miles deep, most of which had been drilled through solid granite. There were many problems, which gave us plenty of standby time. It was exciting to work on that project and taxed our crew's skills to the limit. Operating the high-pressure jet turbine during pumping experiments proved to be heart stopping on more than one occasion. Our job was to pump activated chemicals into that five miles deep well under the extremely high pressure of 15,000 pounds per square inch (home water pipes have about eighty pounds per square inch). While doing that we had to make sure things didn't blow sky high. The pumping process required that all operators pay very close attention to all instruments on the control panel as well as instructions coming over the headset from the main control center. Sometimes pressure would unexpectedly shoot up and you'd hear a screaming, terror filled voice yelling, "SHUT IT DOWN – SHUT IT DOWN!" You certainly didn't want to fall asleep while performing that work. We lost a man to just such an unanticipated pressure spike when an incorrectly positioned heavy steel pipe unexpectedly twisted and hit a man's head.

There were many interesting and exciting times working in the oil patch. I could get quite defensive with those who unfairly criticized the oil industry as a whole. The environmental lobby often went way over board on their anti-drilling stance. That was how they made their income, so you could be sure they sometimes became loud and obnoxious when defending their activities. In my experience in the oil and gas fields, there was no observable damage to the environment. The wells were so spread out and so many miles into the mountains that there was little evidence of anything offensive about their operations. The wildlife appeared to actually like all the activity. In fact, the places visited, while working, were some of the most beautiful and pristine ever seen. The scattered oil well development appeared to have a positive impact. Our convoy of many heavy trucks would go to a drilling site and maybe stay for a couple of days and then pack up and leave, usually on a very difficult mountain road. I spent many wonderful early mornings at such beautiful sites getting set-up to "frac" a well. Such stimulated wells would then produce more oil or gas. For myself, the time spent in the oil patch was looked at in a positive light. It was a feeling of pride to have had the opportunity to learn about and then participate in that American industry.

Over a period of several months the well servicing jobs for Dowell were beginning to dry up due to a world-wide oil glut. Rumors of layoffs had become a reality and fifty percent of the work force was sent walking. The geo-thermal job in New Mexico was to be my last Dowell job. I had enjoyed the work and built up a nice nest egg with which I could maybe buy some land.

By then Lyn had been staying with me for a couple of months. She agreed to watch the Vernal HQ while this hobo made some trips. We lived together in a duplex which offered more privacy than in the prior rooming house. The rent was low, so Vernal could be used as a base for a few months.

One night I stayed up until three in the morning reading a book about a search and rescue mission in the Vietnam war. It was a factual story about a mission that used carpet bombing by B-52s to cover Jolly Green helicopters which then attempted to extract a downed Air Force pilot. The descriptions of the bombing runs were especially graphic and exciting. Three hours after falling asleep I was awakened by what I thought were explosions. I, stumbled to the living room to see a brilliant red and orange sky rising from the mountain range into a very black and boiling morning sky. The great booms continued as if they were moving in my direction. For a moment it was hard for my mind to distinguish whether that was a dream or perhaps several errant B-52s making a bombing run on Vernal. Soon the morning haze was cleared from my brain and I realized that we were not under attack. I settled down to enjoy one of the most vivid storms I had ever witnessed. Within minutes the inky black clouds had totally extinguished the sunrise. The thunder increased dramatically followed with great flashes of lightning going in all directions. The show ended and I crawled into bed with my warm and responsive Jamaican friend. Living according to E^3OL continued to pay excellent dividends!

Boxcars and the General

With autumn in the air, I decided it was time to take to the boxcars and just go someplace--anyplace. I walked to the tiny Vernal depot and caught the bus for Salt Lake City. The driver ended up giving me a free ride, beyond Salt Lake and to the Ogden Union Pacific freight yards and pulled the big bus to the side of the busy road right next to the tracks. With a firm handshake and smiles all around we said our goodbyes, good luck wishes and he dropped a sometime vagabond hobo at the freight yard.

Saddled up and headed into the dark yard with a slight sense of apprehension as my absence from the iron trail had been many months. What if my warnings to the D.C. crowd about terrorism on the trains might have been taken seriously? What if a government SWAT team swooped down on me and took me to jail as a suspected terrorist? The apprehension quickly disappeared as I walked deeper into the yard and reached a crummy with the crew standing around talking. The brass buttons immediately said, "If you're going west you better find a place fast as we are just about to leave for California." I only found an open gondola car loaded with steel "I" beams. Any experienced hobo would tell you never to ride steel as it would sometimes unexpectedly shift and could easily cause serious injury or even death. Standing next to the gondola car, trying to decide whether to continue my run forward in search of a better spot, the train began to roll. Decision made. I climbed onto the car and carefully positioned myself amongst the tons of steel and settled in for the ride.

Crossing the Great Salt Lake was absolutely beautiful--nothing short of spectacular. The stars were so very bright they reflected streamers of gold across the dark waters of the salt lake. The train pulled onto a siding to let a fast moving Amtrak passenger train pass. The passenger train's distinctive whistle brought back many pleasant memories of hobo jungles and past rides. The following day we crossed a very hot desert. I carefully rationed my water and still used just under a gallon as the open car provided little shade from the desert sun. It seemed as if the sun would never fall. That westbound rolled all the way to Sparks, Nevada, before it was broken apart. It was a good feeling to be across the vast expanse of the Northern Nevada Desert. The brakeman and a couple of hobos had told me that the Sparks yard was "hot" so I abandoned my steel-laden car and jumped from the moving train before it pulled into the main yard.

I replenished my water supply and rested for a couple of hours before walking into the main yard, while keeping alert for gumshoes. I spotted a westbound and ended up on the same sort of gondola car as before. We started rolling, but soon stopped. Not knowing what was going on, I carefully looked about and saw two gumshoes walking the train. I crawled deeper into the steel and pulled some packing paper around me. The footsteps of the gumshoes crunched on the rocks as they came closer and climbed up the side of my steel ladened car. A stab of light flashed across my hiding place. Then silence as the gumshoe climbed down and walked away. A few minutes later, the sound of sharp voices and scuffling rang out as they took some unlucky riders from the car just ahead of mine. I stayed hidden and actually fell asleep in my cramped little hideout among the giant steel girders. Much later that night we once again bumped to a start on a beautiful star filled night. The Sparks yard had lived up to its reputation as being hot--it was a good feeling to be highballing down the open tracks putting miles between myself and Sparks.

I drifted in and out of sleep and awoke in the pitch blackness of some unknown railroad yard. My perception of time and distance was completely wacky. I had no idea how far we had traveled or where I was. I was totally surprised to find that I was in Roseville, California.

A quick look around the yard revealed another train that was pulling out. I jumped aboard and rode to Elvis Junction at the State Capitol. Hiked to a small city park, washed, shaved, changed into clean clothes, and was now ready for the Capitol Building. I managed to find a wide smile on a California State Policeman who stopped to talk and then *invited* me inside to check out the Capitol Building.

I Reached the State Assembly Chambers and sat down and began to recognize political faces of both friends and foes alike. It was an interesting session in a surreal way, as an outsider there was little chance of understanding what was going on. Boredom soon set in as I tried to digest what I thought to be bullshit – it seemed to be somewhat like a fictional movie.

I spent most of the day in Sacramento and then caught a slow freight out of Elvis Junction for the short ride back to the Roseville yard. I spent the night in a jungle near the "rock pile" section of the yard. It was the first good, non-moving night's sleep in a long time. Early in the morning my train rumbled toward my jungle and I saddled up and jumped aboard as it passed.

Relaxing in a San Jose hobo jungle and talking with a World War II veteran about war heroes and the great USA. He told me about his time spent on the Pacific Island of Iwo Jima and how he carried ammo for Ira Hayes. You might remember Hayes as one of the U.S. Marines who gained fame as one of the "grunts" that raised the American flag on Iwo Jima. That pleasant veteran had many interesting stories about jungle patrols as they struggled to take the Island from the Japanese. I had a few bucks and my new hobo friend offered to make a "run" to a nearby liquor store to get a quart of beer for me and a bottle of wine for him. Upon his return, we two hobos chilled in the cool shade of the majestic eucalyptus trees. All afternoon we drank, talked and watched the trains go by without a care in the world! Late in the afternoon my Marine friend moved on and it was time to organize some new "light fight" gear acquired in Vernal. The additional suspender style web gear supported pouches, butt pack and more canteens. It was working fine and made life as a hobo a little easier-- things were closer at hand. Shaving and washing could now be accomplished without dropping ALICE to the ground; mobility had been increased.

Train riding could be much like combat training and served a real purpose by keeping one alert, quick to react and in good physical condition. Not afraid to carry a load, ready to move in an instant and always keeping eyes and ears wide open. It was the philosophy that told one to--eat, sleep, wash and relax when you could for there may be no tomorrow. When riding the freight trains, I learned to treat every move as a reconnaissance mission so as to be fully aware of my surroundings. Some referred to it as "situational awareness" or just "SA." All of the required mental and physical practices on the trains were not dissimilar to combat training. Perhaps there were other ways to look at train riding but for me it was as real as any combat mission. The "enemies" for my combat simulation were the railroad detectives and an occasional sociopath. The successful hobo must always stay alert so as to avoid capture and any chance encounters with those wishing to do you harm. Train riding was sometimes like an adrenaline pumping combat training exercise.

The night was spent in the carpeted hobo jungle and I decided to stay in San Jose for a while. The urge to call Ann was suppressed – not sure why but perhaps something to do with Lyn. The solitude of that pleasant camping spot would simply be enjoyed. It was a real "bo park" with knockers being extra friendly. Conversation with the knockers was always a short walk away and when silence was cherished it was back to the jungle. During the day one of the knockers, trying to be helpful, pointed to a string of boxcars and said "those boxcars should be going south sometime during the night." I moved my camp into a clean car and slept while waiting to move out. An hour before dawn it was still in the San Jose yard and it didn't look like it would be moving anytime soon. Jumped from the boxcar and headed for some nearby trees as the sun began to burn through the heavy bay area fog.

It was a pleasant day in the new jungle as it was much closer to the main yard, making it easier to catch a train – my spirit was ready for change. Was awakened by the sound of powerful locomotives at about two in the morning. Quickly, gear was stowed and I jumped on board as it rolled toward Watsonville, about seventy-five miles to the south. After that short trip, it was a hike to the local grocery store for some bread and beans – another healthy breakfast. After breakfast it was back to the tracks but I really didn't care if I caught a ride. The yard had a nice friendly feel about it. I got cleaned up, set up camp under some nearby trees and let a few trains pass as the constant cool breeze made that little corner of the earth rather comfortable. Watsonville was a small farming town and both sides of the tracks were lined with fields of big juicy strawberries. It was a good place to camp for a few hours or perhaps days. Brandon's market was close by, so if a thirst developed, cold beer was always nearby. A mid-afternoon lunch of strawberries and beer, not that bad! By late afternoon the Los Angeles train came rolling down the tracks and stopped near my camp. It was time to move out.

A boxcar with both doors wide open (meaning good views) was soon found and within a few minutes we were rolling south on the coast route. The tracks ran along the ocean for many miles. A fantastic sunset was a special treat as we rhythmically and smoothly moved along those hardened steel ribbons. The trip from Watsonville to Los Angeles took twenty-four hours, an easy ride for this old long-distance hobo. Landed in the Southern Pacific Glendale yard and caught a bus to the corner of Victory and Van Nuys Boulevards. Called my friend Bob who said "come camp out at my house for a couple of days." His offer was accepted and camp was set up in his spare room. It was nice to once again sleep in a non-moving bed, but for some reason, at three in the morning, the urge to move overcame my spirit. I left the house and walked several miles to an all-night coffee shop at the corner of Victory and Laurel Boulevards. It was good to be back in the old 40th California Assembly District. This area was very familiar as it was here that I first ran for public office years ago. Pleasant memories filled my head, it was so very peaceful drinking coffee and watching the rays of early dawn gradually turn darkness into light.

Spent the day on the road with Bob as he serviced his vending machines. The evening was filled with pleasant conversation with Bob's sister and her male friend. Next morning, saddled up and made the ten-mile hike to the 146th Tactical. The base commander, Colonel Allen was on a mission in Alaska so it was a long, and very pleasant, conversation with Wendy, his longtime assistant. My friend Frank, who now ran the Aerial Port, was doing fine and seemed to be very busy as always. The Aerial Port looked to be military "spic and span" as Sergeant Frank was a big believer in small details, especially when it came to equipment for "his" C-130s. Frank had to leave the base, but told me, "Make yourself at home and use the showers if you want." Took him up on the offer and generally had free run of the base. Colonel Russell Allen had the entire base looking very impressive. Managed to collect a wealth of information for my next visit with Pentagon people regarding their need to replace their aging fleet of "Herky Birds" as their beloved C-130s were nicknamed.

Frank returned from his meetings and gave me a ride to Norm's place. Norm wasn't at home so reading and relaxing in the shade by his swimming pool was the first order of business. Norm soon arrived and was surprised and appeared to be happy to see me. As usual he was in high spirits and looked healthy as a race horse. We talked about the world political situation and how some elements in our government were trying to disarm law abiding citizens through restrictive gun laws. We talked about security issues and generally had a great couple of days. It was good to see my old buddy but it was time to saddle up and move out. Headed for Altadena to visit friends and the San Gabriel Mountains.

Caught the Hollywood bus, talked with my Korean friend (the wig shop owner at Hollywood and Vine) and jumped on the Lake Street bus. Within an hour it was time to relax at the BBH bar and make small talk with bartender Linda on this peaceful afternoon. Made a trip to the Altadena library for a visit with Mary Ann and Verdell who were surprised to see me. Stopped to see Paul at the hardware store and then back to BBH where the evening crowd was beginning to arrive. The bar had taken on a new motif as it was now decorated with peace officer patches and other police memorabilia. It had always been a hangout for off duty police and sheriffs, but now it was advertised. It was a nice atmosphere. It was a feeling much like "being home." My ALICE gear, stacked in the corner, was a topic of conversation for those who didn't know me. The many stately pine trees on the beautiful grounds of the Altadena library became my camping spot for the evening. After a night of a beautiful full moon, I caught the bus to the San Fernando Valley via Hollywood and, after a good visit, it was on to Oceanside to see my parents. They wanted to travel to the Mojave Desert to see my Brother Tom's new homesite, so we piled into the car and headed north to a place called Llano. It was a small unincorporated area with a population of about 2,000 souls. It was in the extreme northeast corner of Los Angeles County and about 150 miles north of Oceanside.

The "General" in the Mojave Desert

Tom and his wife, Doreen, were looking healthy and happy at their new home site in the high desert. Their 2 ½ acre piece of land was looking good as they were now living in a mobile home and not the apartment in Northridge. According to Tom, the first major improvement project that was immediately needed was to bring a water line to the property. No problem – this could be done!

I purchased the flight operations office trailer from the adjacent small airport and moved it to one corner of Tom and Doreen's land. The old trailer was called the "General" as it was manufactured by the General Coach Company in Indiana. It was sure to provide peaceful shelter for this wandering hobo. My new campsite in California's Mojave Desert was the source of many happy thoughts and plans. It had wonderful views of the snow-capped mountains of the San Gabriel Range. There were frequent magnificent sunsets and brilliant full moons showing in the crisp, clean desert air. The beautiful sights and the howling of the wild coyotes all combined to give that place a potential as a more permanent place of rest and relaxation — perhaps even to plant some trees.

The General was secured with concrete anchors deep in the desert sand-- high winds had been known to actually turn over small trailers such as mine. A little work on the General's inside and it was transformed into a cozy home in the desert. I stayed in the Mojave for a couple of weeks working on the property and putting in a temporary water system that was supplied by a four-hundred-gallon tank. I also began to fence in the one-quarter mile that made up the perimeter of the property. Things around the General were beginning to take shape so it was time to hit the cinder trail. Time to get back to Vernal and spend some quality time with Lyn.

Tom dropped me at the Santa Fe rail yards located in San Bernardino. Within two hours a train rumbled down the tracks toward my hiding place. It was caught on the run and we were soon winding our way through the "Blue Cut" of El Cajon Pass, which separated the San Bernardino and the San Gabriel Mountain Ranges. It was a wonderfully cool, crisp California evening in a clear star filled night. I disembarked in the Yermo yard, a real "bo park", to wait for a Los Angeles to Vegas hot shot. I made it to Vegas, and from there it wasn't long before we were highballing through some very scenic parts of Utah on that pleasant Sunday morning.

In Salt Lake I headed for the Trailways bus depot to catch a ride over the scenic Wasatch Mountains and into the Green River Valley and the pleasant town of Vernal. It was late September and it was a happy feeling to be back. Lyn was looking very beautiful. After we said "hello" and "kissed" for a couple of hours it was time for some letter writing and then I visited some of my old Vernal friends. The town looked good and the leaves were just beginning to turn to their brilliant autumn colors from the coolness of the coming winter. My first evening back a thunder storm struck, complete with many loud booms of thunder and flashes of lightning. It was a nice welcome back.

For the past few months serious thought had been given as to how to get hired working on the boats and barges that travel our inland waterways such as the Mississippi River. From what had been learned it seemed that chances of getting hired would be vastly improved if a two-week naval course, only offered in Arkansas, was completed. So, after a couple of weeks of enjoying rest and relaxation in Vernal, a bus was caught that was headed for the National River Academy in Helena, Arkansas. I told Lyn we would have to give up the place in Vernal. She didn't appear to be terribly upset about losing her place in Vernal and we went our separate ways and would remain good friends and occasional lovers.

The River Academy

The bus stopped for a short break in some small town in Kansas and as I stood on a street corner a very attractive, conservatively dressed lady and her friend walked up behind me. As they passed the good looking one reached out and grabbed my butt with a couple of firm squeezes. As I turned to face her, she smiled and told her friend, "Don't worry the Marines have landed." Before I could react, they both quickly continued down the street leaving me standing there with a big smile on my face. In a small Kansas town!

The bus passed through Kansas City, Kansas, as it followed railroad the tracks that I had walked many times. It felt good to be in an air- conditioned bus. Once in Helena a local businessman met us at the bus station and gave us a ride twelve miles south to the Academy in his new gold Cadillac.

Within the next few hours the rest of the class arrived and we were assigned bunkmates and cabins just as if we were working on a real riverboat. I got the top bunk and Mac from Baton Rouge, Louisiana settled in below. We were treated to a hearty meal and Commanding Officer (CO) Tooker delivered an after-dinner introduction/welcome speech. We then headed for our bunks at ten o'clock (2200 HRS) with the advice to be prepared for a five in the morning (0500 HRS) wake up call. Mac and I were restless and couldn't sleep, so about midnight we went to the galley for coffee and snacks. He had spent his military service time in the U.S. Navy and called such time "Midrats" short for midnight rations. He was a nice young man and we talked until two in the morning.

The next morning we got our unit assignments as well as when we had to pull security/fire watch duty. My assignment was the 0400 to 0600 security watch. There was definitely a good atmosphere around the River Academy —it was beginning to feel as if it would be a good investment. Almost ninety percent of the current students had already been promised jobs on the river. A few of us were still looking.

During my time at the Academy Mark, a fellow classmate, offered to give me a ride north to St. Louis. After two weeks of confinement at the Academy we decided to party a little so we picked up some beer. By the time we reached Scott City, Missouri, the beer had numbed most of my brain cells. Decided to have Mark drop me at the tracks. Had a couple of days before being due at the river boat offices in St. Louis so riding the rails would be a good way pass some time.

Gangster Threat in East St. Louis

It wasn't long before this drunken track rider was once again on the familiar tracks which led to St. Louis. A fast freight train was caught on the run and several hours later it came to a stop in Dupo, Illinois. Humped ALICE through the roughest and meanest sections of East St. Louis. At that time, East St. Louis was also known as the murder capital of the world. It was late at night and while walking the tracks about a half-dozen, of what appeared to be "gang members", gave me an evil look and some shouts along the lines of, "What the fuck are you doing in our neighborhood." The feeling was that they would just as soon see me dead or at least severely injured and then separated from my very interesting ALICE gear. It was decided that some defensive action was needed and I immediately began a rather hair-raising climb up a vertical support beam of a railroad trestle to reach the tracks sixty feet above. They continued their shouting as they thought their prey was on the run. However, they did not choose to follow the crazy white hobo up that support leg. I laboriously climbed to within ten feet of the tracks; exhausted and with my arms and legs shaking with fatigue and adrenaline all the result of my current predicament. I was about to climb the last few feet to reach the "safety" of the tracks when a very long, slow train approached. No place to go with gang members below and a train above, so I hung on to the steel beam with one hand and my Air Force survival knife in the other. The dumb bastards below thought my only plan was escape when actually I was just going for high ground. Silently, I screamed, "Come on up and get me you scum bags." In reality their taunts were never once answered in a hope that by keeping quiet, they would not be as anxious to fire any guns they might have. Ten or fifteen minutes passed (it seemed like forever) before the train passed overhead. I climbed the last few feet and threw myself up and onto the still warm train tracks. I tried to catch my breath for a short couple of minutes and then scrambled along the rails to find someplace to get off the tracks if another train approached. A small platform, used for train equipment, was found, it would provide a safe place if another train came rolling down the tracks. I collapsed as a heap of tired flesh and drank a full canteen of water. It felt good to be alive and unharmed. After letting my muscles recover and then relaxing for several minutes the trek along the trestle continued to where it turned onto the familiar General MacArthur Bridge over the Mississippi River. I crossed the bridge into St. Louis, found a place to catch my breath and a couple hours of much needed sleep. The next morning, the barge company was contacted and they still didn't have a place on one of their boats. Discouraged, I caught a westbound bus.

In Lawrence, Kansas, a young woman got on the bus and took the empty seat next to me. Teresa introduced herself with the qualifier that she preferred to be called by her nickname "Calamity Jane," which was also the name of her clothing store. We had a good time talking all the way to Beloit, about one hundred and fifty miles away, where she was going to "get away for a couple of weeks." She was attractive, wearing army battle fatigues, carried a loaded thirty-eight special pistol and a German officer's dagger for backup. She proudly showed me both weapons. We talked for the entire trip, making the hours pleasantly pass very quickly. It would be nice to meet her again someday as she was an intriguing female.

I reached Vernal and told Lyn that rent would be paid for one more month and then she would be on her own. The news didn't seem to surprise her since the possibility had been discussed on my last visit. It was a productive time in Vernal. Many friends were contacted and also used the post office to ship books and small household items to my new place in the desert so that I'd be free to take the cinder trail if I so desired. Freedom to choose was still an important part of part of my decision making. My stay in Vernal lasted for a couple of weeks. Then I said good-bye to my Jamaican friend and left my nice little "line shack" for the last time.

Arriving in California, brother Tom met me at the Palmdale bus station and gave me a ride to the General. The property looked good as they had been working on several projects. The first night in the General was cold since it had no working heater. The next day was spent working on a small heater as the snow was now down to 4,000 feet, not far from the General. In spite of the cold, it was great to be back at my peaceful shelter in the Mojave Desert. On that first night back, it was journal writing late into the night by the light of a candle. The pitter patter of light rain (not yet snow), the crash of thunder and flashes of lightning made for a nice backdrop for my thoughts. It was fully recognized and appreciated that a very pleasant corner of the world had been found.

A week passed quickly and my stuff from Vernal arrived. It was fun unpacking and finding places for everything in my new place. All the stuff from Utah made the General feel much more like a home. During the winter months in the desert, it got dark early so my days were spent organizing and working in the trailer in order to make use of the daylight. The hours of darkness were saved for reading and writing by the light of the just acquired kerosene lantern. There was no water, electrical power nor natural gas supply anywhere near that desert property.

It was five in the afternoon and the sky was already an inky black dotted with the early evening stars. The mountains were lit to a soft glow from behind by the lights of the Metropolitan area of Los Angeles. If you could fly directly from my place in the desert across the mountain range it would only be about 15 miles to reach Los Angeles. The normal land route was on Highway 14 and was a 65-mile trip around the mountain range. There was a shorter way through the mountains, perhaps forty-five miles, which was on winding and steep roads.

As the night descended the light from the moon and stars made the snow-covered mountains appear to be very close. A train whistle could be heard drifting across the desert floor followed by the throaty pounding sound of powerful diesel engines as they slowly crawled up the gradual incline of the desert floor. All those sights and sounds competed for brain space in that very special time and place.

The many pending projects on the land and in the General destroyed any chance of getting bored. The Post Office was only a two-mile hike through the desert and it was my sole contact with the outside world.

I continued to keep in touch with river barge companies and it was beginning to look like an on-target shot at a job might be possible. Relaxed in the soft glow of the kerosene lantern on the eve of my departure and realized how that place and the General represented something very valuable in my life. That small trailer on the desert floor was a place to continue the seemingly never-ending search for the meaning of my life. It seemed to me that the time spent in such enjoyable places was most appreciated when first arriving and just prior to leaving. Perhaps it was because we became accustomed to our surroundings and eventually took them for granted. Expressed in a more spiritual fashion we could say that we fail to acknowledge the gifts God has given us to help us along our path. My self-directed advice was to expend energy every day in a way that reminded your spirit of the value of the current moment. Thank God for the Creation. For me that area of thought was very stimulating. There were many unanswered questions concerning constant change and how the spirit sought movement and growth via the absorption of New Knowledge.

Tom and Doreen gave me a ride to Palmdale and we had breakfast at their favorite German restaurant. It was another beautiful sunny California morning. It was time to check out the St. Louis Boat companies one more time. The first leg of the bus trip to look for boat work took me to downtown Los Angeles for a five-hour layover. After the prior weeks of solitude in the desert the busy bus terminal, filled with people of all kinds, was a shock but somehow, I survived that short visit to the "City of Angels." The first bus out was caught but it only reached the city of Riverside before it broke down. They gave us a replacement bus and we all shuffled our bags and ourselves into the new bus. I found myself sitting next to an attractive lady – how did that happen? She said she was a Canadian from the city of Toronto. We gradually became more and more friendly with each other. "Friendly" rapidly progressed to the point where we warmed up – then it was a hot and heavy make-out session lasting many blissful hours. Many, many sweet kisses under the spell of a Gibbous moon as we shared the California white wine which filled my canteen. Jean told me "I would someday like to ride the freights with you." She had a very competitive outlook on life and an athletic body. She was a Sports Instructor for the University of Illinois at Carbondale. We reached Phoenix and sat together in the bus depot. Jean had some homemade bread and pear blossom honey--we had a snack while we waited for our separate buses. Her bus was called out first and as we were kissing goodbye she reached around with both hands, grabbed and then tightly squeezed my butt, smiled broadly and then disappeared forever. Reinforced once again was my belief that women were fascinating and complex creatures and were the number one reason for man to get up in the morning. For sure, life would be pretty boring without them--our Creator had the right approach.

With Lyn in Dallas

Lyn had kept in touch via mail and an occasional relayed telephone call. She had delayed her trip home to Jamaica and was now staying in Dallas, Texas and after a brief telephone conversation she invited me to stay with her until my employment on the river happened. Arrived in Dallas at five in the morning and then took the city bus to the large house in an up-scale part of Dallas. Lyn was staying with some friends that owned a restaurant in downtown Dallas.

My early morning bus driver was a colorful and very talkative ex-Marine. Being the only passenger on that outward-bound morning bus made a lively conversation about politics, freight trains and the meaning of life possible. It wasn't long before it was time to get off the bus and say goodbye to my new friend. It was time to find Lyn's new landing spot. Once I found her house she welcomed me with a hot shower, shave and many luscious kisses that lasted for a long, long time. Her two friends with whom she was staying were out of town for two weeks so we could run around naked – more fun.

One week in Dallas and it was time to head for St. Louis. Sitting in the bus and just thinking about the concept of "humor." Perhaps the motivation for these thoughts had been recent conversations with Lyn and how she disliked my mobile lifestyle. She just wanted me to "settle down" was the way she expressed her most recent attitude. Her rather harsh criticism of my chosen life-style had been taken to heart. It was requiring way too much energy and pushing my Enjoyment of Life to the sidelines. The conclusion was that more humor was needed in my life! Could "humor" represent one dimension of the E³OL philosophy. If you tended to take life less seriously (relax about which path you chose to follow) you opened yourself up to Enlightenment, Enrichment and Enjoyment. More time would be spent trying to find humor in various life situations. My thoughts led to the conclusion that it did not take much energy to put a smile on one's face. You would expect that such behavior might actually result in a net gain of energy. It simply involved looking at the world with a less serious perspective. Screw it, her negative feelings about my behavior shouldn't impact my ability to Enjoy my Life--drive on!

Departed Dallas at nine in the evening and had a layover in Tulsa at two in the morning. It was late but decided to call, Melissa, a friend from the oil patch days. We talked for some time and she seemed to be enjoying her work and life. Back on the bus and rode to St. Louis where it was a hike of about twelve miles to University City to hopefully visit Sally and Shelia. The hike was good exercise on that hot Missouri afternoon. It was a couple of miles from their house when this very tired puppy gave them a call to see if they were open for a visitor. It was more than fine. It was a nice place to hang out while waiting to ship out on a river boat. The latest word was that a job may be available soon with a ship-out date in a few weeks. Beginning to wonder if getting hired on the river was nothing but a pipe dream.

It was another beautiful morning when Sally and her friend Kathy gave me a ride to the bus depot for another trip west. It was good that a high level of E³OL was maintained in spite of still being unemployed. It had been possible to remain in an enjoyable state of mind partly because humor could be found in the situation.

On journey west we arrived in Denver at five in the morning and made the change to Trailways bus line. With Trailways it was possible to reach Vernal, where I could pick up some money at the bank. At the bus depot a delightful older gentleman from Sussex, England, struck up a conversation. He was a traveling musician and had many tales of his world travels and especially his time spent in Australia. We exchanged stories of our travels for hours. He invited me to visit his English cottage that had recently been turned into a music museum. Cyril Phillips was his name and he was billed as "The Traveling Troubadour--Ballads, Songs and Yarns of an English Farmer Born in Devon 1911." It was rewarding to experience his willingness, actually eagerness to share many yarns with this "sometimes hobo." Cyril was a very special fellow!

I was able to hop off the bus in Vernal, take care of my business, and hop back on the same bus. I stayed with friends for a night in Salt Lake City and still made it to Oceanside in time to spend Christmas with my parents, Tom, Doreen and sister Renee. Lyn called my parents' house and wanted me to visit her while she was in Los Angeles for a singing gig at some Hollywood nightclub. She was staying with a friend in Corona Del Mar which was just north about fifty miles. It appeared that she had pushed aside her unhappiness with my chosen free and easy lifestyle. Soon I had landed on Dolphin Terrace overlooking Balboa Island. I had good memories of spending long-ago vacations on the Island with my then-girlfriend Barbie, her two children, and my Jimmy and Wendy. Lyn looked stunning and was full of energy; we had a great time in the mirrored earth-shine bedroom. The great company and physical surroundings made the Total Serenity state of mind easy to maintain. After a couple of days, I headed for Llano and the peace and quiet offered by the General.

Desert Challenger Landing

The bus trip from L.A. to Palmdale was four solid hours of non-E^3OL experience for me. "Ouch – it was horrible!" Perhaps I was having too many thoughts of the future. I arrived in Palmdale late in the evening, then set out on foot for Llano and the General, hiking the final several miles through the open desert. Beautiful ice crystals covered the dark sandy ground sparkling like diamonds in the light of a brilliant full moon. At the General I built a campfire and relaxed in its circle of warming energy. The moon over the Joshua trees, dogs resting in the firelight, cat scampering about in the dark night and a brisk wind made it a special time. It was very serene! E^3OL was slowly returning and it sure felt lovely!

Analysis

Could the recent non-E^3OL be related to thoughts that my future held no purpose? Could the simple answer be that the current state of mind resulted from too much of a concern for the future? Dwelling on what might or might not happen often results in non-E^3OL and smothers one's adventurous spirit. The effect of the non-E^3OL type communications over the previous days likely had built up within my soul. Perhaps my spirit was hit by a tremendous amount of non-E^3OL and reacted with the excessive energy drain in an effort to ward off its effects. My ability to assign Space/Time Marker Values (STMVs) was overtaxed; this then drained energy to a point which caused non-E^3OL. Thus, the energy consuming process of assigning the value (the STMV process) simply surpassed my available energy; the result was a net loss and unhappy feelings. Maybe it was time to enjoy the solitude offered by the desert and play the hermit card.

I spent a sunny, cool New Year's Day in the Mojave Desert reading and collecting firewood. What a perfectly wonderful way to pass the first day of the year. The solitude was greater than usual as Tom, Doreen and son Jade were away for a few weeks in Los Angeles.

A large, portable and disassembled airplane hangar sat at the front of the property. It was being stored there by a bankrupted flight school that at one time had offices at the adjacent airport. I had tried to get the owner to remove it, but they had ignored my pleas. After a few weeks passed with no action, I told the owner that the hanger was now for sale to the highest bidder. They responded immediately and a construction crew came and trucked it away. The view of the desert from the General was dramatically improved. The move generated new work. A row of trees could be planted and a driveway constructed where the hanger had been stored. Also, I found some scrap lumber and within a few hours had built a nice bed. That evening there was a beautiful sunset with bright red, orange and blue fading into a purple sky. Meandering through the multi-colors of the sunset was a magnificent silver thread of a rocket trail that was launched from Vandenberg Missile Base. Combined in that sunset was a mixture of both man's and nature's work – it seemed to reach deep into my body and soul.

Reason for My Life

In my attempt to further define a reason for my life, I began to question the possibility of the de-emphasis of relativistic terms such as "good" and "bad" from my everyday existence. Part of the effort required that "good" and "bad" be carefully defined since they resulted from our cultural education; they were based on a reality that was learned. Understanding that, could we actually say there was "good" and "bad" in other than learned reality?

Over the past several years much of my energy had been devoted to an attempt to determine the purpose of my life by building a Formula for Life equation. Perhaps part of the process might involve the question as to why the Creator had given me the ability to think about such things. Thus far, my efforts to develop a formula which accurately described the purpose of my life, or simply to provide insight as to why I was on this earth, had led to the unfinished equation given below.

$$E^3OL + VIE = POL \rightarrow TS$$

E^3OL represents: Enlightenment, Enrichment and Enjoyment of Life

VIE represents: Value in Everything
POL represents: Purpose of Life
TS represents: Total Serenity

The second element of the equation (VIE) was closely related to my effort to minimize or eliminate the conceptualizations of "good" and "bad" from my Formula for Life. The use of the term "value" in "Value in Everything" was a direct effort to eliminate the need to identify "good" and "bad" in our everyday experiences. Using value, other than good and bad, was a more accurate way of describing my reality. My reality was that all my life experiences existed on a continuum composed of levels of valuable stimuli. This was contrasted with a good/bad continuum.

The concept of what was "good" and "bad" resulted from culturally learned values that were attached to events occurring in our lives. How could matter and/or energy be assigned a condition of "good" or "bad?" It seemed that valuable experiences resulted in the expansion of one's consciousness (adding to one's individual and universal store of energy) and provided a certain measure of synchronicity with creation. The value of experiences might vary greatly among individuals depending on how they had learned to react to the world illusion--which of course was their reality. Value was something we learned (just as good and bad) thus the identification of the value in environmental stimuli became a personal and societal matter. My immediate tendency was to rely more on personal rather than societal definitions of value whenever it became necessary to assign value to incoming stimuli. It was a collective society which defined experiences which were considered "valuable" therefore those that choose to live in any organized society should strive to live according to the adopted "values." That did not mean that an individual member of that society could not expend energy to identify the value in any human experience. It must also be recognized that in every society there were individuals who may assign value to experiences that were the exact opposite to the success of that society. In the extreme case, a criminal may take the life of another and then offer reasons, which in their mind justified the murder. Such individuals must be removed from society. This does not negate the belief that there was some value in everyone and everything. However, sometimes it just took a tremendous amount of energy to identify the value. That's why those humans having easy to identify value are such a pleasure to be around. Others, not possessing this quality make it difficult to form any type of close relationship.

In thinking more about the concept of Value in Everything and good and bad it might be useful to apply that element of my philosophy to daily experiences. Hopefully such looking inward would then provide additional evidence that there was indeed Value in Everything. One example that came to mind was a World War II antique German bayonet that my father had given me years ago. Someone had once used it as a pry bar and broke a quarter inch from the point. When first seeing the broken blade, no value in the broken blade was recognized. The broken blade was labeled as "bad." If the idea that there was Value in Everything was applied what would happen? A small sharpening stone was found and many, many relaxing hours were spent putting a sharp point on the fine steel blade. The value in the broken blade was in the enjoyment and satisfaction of a job well done. It was *Enlightening* through my realization that it could even be repaired. And in learning how to correctly use a sharpening stone to put a point on that fine blade made from quality German steel. It was *Enriching* via the learning experience and my energy base of knowledge was expanded. The repair also represented an *Enjoyable* accomplishment and prideful event in that it was once again almost good as new – although a little shorter. The antique souvenir bayonet had actually increased in value since more personal energy had been invested in the blade. The value in the broken blade resided in that it had increased my energy base of knowledge via E^3OL.

Looking for the Value in Everything sometimes requires much mental work. However, if one truly believed that there was Value in Everything, then nothing became an obstacle to one's personal growth. Every human experience had some value that would be realized sooner or later. It must be understood that various amounts of energy were required to identify the E^3OL elements of events that occurred in our reality. It is also a fact that we were often called upon to expend an excessive amount of energy in an attempt to identify the value in some situations. However, if we believed in the basic concept of Value in Everything all events in our life had the potential to become an *Enlightening, Enriching* and *Enjoyable* experiences but it was up to us to make that happen.

Working in the Desert

Work at my new desert home site continued. I built a sturdy outhouse — my old style slit latrine became a thing of the past. I set up a solar powered shower using my old diving compressor to pressurize the water system. With colder weather on the horizon, I needed to improve on the small propane heater in the leaky and poorly insulated trailer.

Also, on the agenda was bringing running water to the property. The water company didn't want to pay for the line, so I went about trying to convince the other property owners to pitch and support the waterline project. After months of correspondence, we finally had a meeting with the representatives of 10 of the 16 parcels that were directly affected and managed to agree on a route for the water line which satisfied everyone. That one meeting was the end product of months of preparatory work. But the work itself, as much as the meeting itself or whether the water line would be built, brought me much satisfaction. It was easy to identify the Value in the project.

Early morning brought a very unusual mass of low swirling clouds, patches of blue sky and the golden rays of sunlight moved together as if in a fast-paced ballet. The sun appeared briefly, filling the sky with the luminosity of many moisture laden rays which sweep down from the snowcapped mountains to the desert floor. The display was all viewed from a warm bed with the background of shifting winds accompanied by the gentle pitter patter of raindrops on the windows. Nature was very busy in deciding which way to go on that stunning early morning. The beauty of God's creation that was on display that morning was beyond my ability to describe in written words – it was definitely mind expanding.

Impeccable Work

I found myself needing to clarify the notion that all work should be done in an impeccable manner, by which I mean performing to one's best ability. When work was done in an impeccable manner then one would be free from fault or blame for the outcome or non-outcome. Each individual should be the only judge of the impeccability of one's behavior or performance of work. However, we as individuals or as collective society could observe behavior and determine whether it lived up to our standards of impeccability. The question became whether the efforts at work fulfilled the needs of the society or of the person employing the "worker." If someone was performing work to their best ability and falling short of the goal, then replacement with another would be justified.

When one performed with impeccability it could easily result in a valuable balance between the body and spirit. Our physical actions occurred in conjunction with activities of the mind, which in turn were based on learned standards of behavior. Therefore, we learned to judge our own performance on past associations, hence the only standard of impeccability must come from the self. Those who do not meet one's personal standards must not be judged. The only judge as to whether another human was going about their business in an impeccable manner would be that person's conscience. That inner voice could be summoned when we directed thoughts (energy) inward while at the same time being aware of our outward actions. In other words, we might ask our self, "To what degree of impeccability was I performing?" Self-improvement by degrees was certainly possible and perhaps that was an important aspect of living within our bodies. We were continually changing both in outward earthly actions and by the growth of our spirit. Thus, one purpose of life was to seek such expansion yet maintain a degree of synchronicity between the body and spirit. Constant change or growth was a natural part of all life. Perhaps the only "constant" in our realm of understanding was that everything was constantly changing. When energy was on the move, as in constant change, whatever we decided to absorb from space/time could be exciting and rewarding for our spirit.

If an individual was wise enough to accept the responsibility for being the sole judge of one's own work standard it followed that they might be living close to a philosophy of life similar to E^3OL. If a chosen path led to non-E^3OL then the prudent thing to be done, by a being of impeccable character, would be to cease the activity--immediately. That happened when the energy expenditure required to identify the *value* in any human experience exceeded the amount available. When that happened, you were certainly not enjoying the situation. Once this situation was identified your direction should change to a less energy consuming activity. Be aware that others would often be quick to judge such a change in direction as something less than impeccable. Such a judgment made no difference as long as you were at ease with your inner voice and convinced of your impeccable behavior.

The Mojave high desert turned icy cold and the mountains were magically transformed into towering masses of brilliant white snow: sparkling pyramids of ice. It was a rare visual feast. Night arrived and the full moon rose as the wind rocked the General. Between gusts there was nothing but the silence of the desert. My thought was about how blessed I was at being able to be there, and in having the time available to participate in the seasonal changes of nature.

It was Friday afternoon and Tom loaned me his car so I could visit my children. They had moved to Tehachapi, a small community about seventy miles to the northwest. That lovely town site was located in a mountain range that could be seen from the General. It had been a long time since seeing Jimmy and Wendy. They both looked and sounded fantastic and seemed to be happy and doing fine without their errant father. They had a nice home in a private gated community nestled in the mountains. Hanna and her husband went out for the evening and left me alone with the kids — it was a very nice gesture. We had much to talk about and stayed up late into the night telling one another about various happenings in our lives. The three of us had a great time and in spite of my wanderings around the country they still seemed to know and love their father — it was an amazing feeling!

Lost in a Desert Snowstorm

Lyn arrived for a three-day visit, two of which were very pleasant. On the third day, however, I took her to the Palmdale bus station and we parted on very strained relations. I awoke early the next morning to do some rock work and at noon it suddenly turned very cold and started to snow. The white stuff continued to fall all afternoon, turning the land of sun and sand into a blizzard. The desert took on a completely different look and it seemed that my body had been transported to some unknown land. I couldn't resist the urge to saddle up and venture into the swirling snowstorm. Very soon I became, wandering around blindly through the whiteout, it was time to fight back a touch of panic. After about an hour of wandering around I came across a barbed wire fence, giving me some idea as to where I was. I followed the fence for a half-mile and discovered my whereabouts. It was strange to be totally lost within a mile of the General. I made it back and relaxed in the General's warmth while the fury of the storm swirled all around. I awoke to more than a foot of powder melting in the early morning sun. Just two days later it was gone, and there were patches of vibrant green grass springing to life in the desert sand.

I was getting restless and yearned for a challenge, so I decided to sign up for a two-week jungle-type warfare course with the Mercenary Association in Dolomite, Alabama.

Before moving out, I spent time on work projects around the property; built cabinets, re-worked the solar shower, painted the General, repaired the wind damage from the last windstorm, and spent three days working on expanding the property water system. The nights were beginning to warm and you could comfortably relax in the cool night air. It was difficult to re-arrange ALICE in preparation for the training at the Alabama Mercenary School, as ALICE's configuration had become quite comfortable with my soul.

Just when things started to look good on the property Tom and Doreen brought the news, they were thinking about selling out and moving back to the city. I had no standing to protest and could only offer advice that my experience in life had taught me that a piece of land was about the only possession worthy of having beyond Basic Needs. If the property was sold it would be easy to identify the value in the time spent working to improve our home site. It had always been consistent with E^3OL. However, the thought of all these newly planted trees shriveling and dying was kind of strange. The world would continue to turn whether the trees lived or died. As it turned out their idea of returning to the city didn't last but a few weeks.

A couple of months passed and nothing happened on the water line project. Some of the property owners decided that they didn't want to spend the money. The decision to put in a personal temporary water line from the closest connection was made. It would be built a little shy of fire department specifications but would certainly meet our needs. It took three days to dig the trench for the line with pick and shovel. The hookup point at the nearby airport was over half mile away. The water flowed and it looked like my efforts were rewarded. Also installed were many hundreds of feet of water line for the trees.

Another major project was putting up a 45 foot flagpole. Howard, the owner of the nearby Pearblossom hardware store, had some heavy-duty steel utility poles that he donated for the worthy cause. Being a survivor of the Pearl Harbor attack he was very supportive of this rather patriotic project. We started with the utility pole and with the help of Allen, a retired U.S. Navy welder, we added another 15 feet of two-inch pipe. The hole had been dug but no way to move the pole to the property. Within a couple of days Howard found someone with a long trailer and we moved it to the hole for twenty bucks. It was a real operation getting it to stand upright without any heavy equipment. We raised it by making an "A" frame contraption and then using the Datsun truck to pull it upright. It looked great with my souvenir Victory Drive-in copper ball high on top. That evening, flag-pole music drifted to the general; it sounded delightful.

Mojave Green

The Mojave Green is a particularly deadly type of rattlesnake that lives in this part of the high desert. The Mojave Green kills its victim with venom that destroys the ability of the blood to carry oxygen while also attacking the nervous system. There is some evidence the dangerous viper has the most powerful venom of all snakes in North America as well as an aggressive nature. Most other poisonous snakes would quickly retreat from an oncoming human – not so with the Mojave Green. It stands its ground and refuses to yield. I found this out the scary way when I stepped from the General one morning to find a coiled, rattling and hissing angry "Green." The snake considered me as the trespasser and just wanted me to go away. Its wide-open mouth and long fangs sent shivers of fear up my spine. Luckily there was a long-handled shovel next to the door and the threat was quickly disposed by separating its head from its body. The snake was a beautiful olive color, hence the name Mojave Green; its skin looked good hanging on the General's wall.

Edwards Air Force Base

On April 9, 1983 I watched the first landing of the Challenger Space Shuttle at Edwards Air Force Base, only about 20 miles from the General. It was a beautiful day and many thousands of people filled the on-base observation area to witness the landing. It was a magnificent experience to watch the shuttle silently glide through a crystal-clear desert sky as over a hundred thousand people loudly cheered as it approached the sand and concrete landing strip. Shouts of "made in America" filled the air. It looked like a great boxcar smoothly gliding through the sky; a crescendo of cheers culminated at touchdown and then continued on for several minutes. It was an exciting, proud and emotional time--tears were choked back as the Challenger rolled to a safe landing.

   I prepared for my own upcoming mission at the Alabama Mercenary School by humping ALICE through the desert heat. It felt great as my extra pounds started to melt away and muscles tightened. Lyn visited a couple of times, usually dropping in with no notice. The trains were looking more enticing by the day; perhaps it was the nice weather which stirred my wanderlust. Those steel ribbons were once again calling out to my soul.

Living in the Present

One fine day as I was sitting in the outhouse, the door ajar, looking at the flagpole and the red white and blue floating in the breeze, I felt as if the flag and pole were different. That day, I really saw, heard and felt the sheer beauty of that particular aspect of my physical world. Once we understood that physical reality, such as the flagpole, was not immortal we were reminded to fully enjoy such stimuli on a moment-to-moment basis. Once we stopped looking at the past and into the future, we could really enjoy the current moment. We could then let such Enjoyment, Enlightenment and Enrichment fill our spirit. Perhaps we, as people, did this to varying degrees; the trick was to do it *all* the time. It sometimes seemed that societal pressures discouraged this attitude because of the demands of time sensitive activities.

I dispatched another rattlesnake that morning while on desert patrol. Rice and roasted snake for breakfast; it was excellent preparation for my upcoming attendance at the mercenary training camp.

I made a trip "down below," which was what locals called Los Angeles, to pick up supplies and visit friends. While walking toward Palmdale an attractive woman, Peggy, pulled up next to me in an olive-colored Blazer and cheerfully asked if I needed a ride. It seemed she had seen me around the neighborhood and decided that she would like to meet this "new" face. We connected very well during our pleasant ride into Palmdale and she invited me to her home for dinner on my return to Llano on Sunday night. It was a lovely example of the value found in my lack of transportation.

Peggy was a long-time resident of Llano who had been selling property in the desert until her husband recently died. She was full of energy and had three young boys; she lived in a large house on the banks of Big Rock Creek, complete with running water and electricity. It was only a mile and half from the General. The dinner was great and it seemed strange sitting down to a table with dishes and silver ware after the many months of eating from my military canteen cup. Next thing I knew, she was inviting me to stay the night. During the next few weeks, we had many enjoyable times together. We took the boys camping a couple of times, once traveling to Big Sur where my old friend Don was found diving for jade.

Peggy had her house up for sale as she was moving to San Antonio, Texas, to be closer to family. I decided I'd go along to help her with the move.

Just before we left for Texas something rather interesting took place. Lyn made one of her unannounced visits to the General. I was enjoying a pleasant evening meal at Peggy's when there was a loud knock on the door and in swept a fiery, hot Jamaican woman. The people at the Outpost Café had told her where to find me. She convinced someone at the café to bring her to my quiet dinner date.

A very cordial Peggy invited her to sit down and eat while I bit my lip and wondered what would happen in that highly charged atmosphere. My ALICE gear, which sat in the corner, was being eyeballed for a possible quick getaway to the safety of the desolate desert. At one point in the "discussion," ALICE was actually hoisted to my back and made ready for an escape. Better sense prevailed and Peggy offered me the use of her Blazer to drive Lyn to stay with her friends in the Hollywood Hills. With Lyn safely deposited in Hollywood, Peggy launched into a face-to-face, heart-to-heart talk on the way back. She seemed to understand the situation with Lyn and didn't let it interrupt our plans for the Texas trip to help her move.

The day of our departure arrived--we hooked up the travel trailer and we headed for Texas on a gorgeous early desert morning. It was a great feeling to be on the road with Peggy and the boys; E^3OL was extremely easy to experience! We decided to make the trip leisurely, take back roads and camp along the way. Our first camp site was near Emory Pass in the Gila National Forest of New Mexico. It was a beautiful night in the stunning Black Mountain range that seemed to magically rise to almost 11,000 feet from the desert flatlands. It was an undeveloped site so we had the private spot just off the road all to ourselves. We next camped in the Davis Mountains near Fort Davis, Texas and then it was off to San Antonio. It was a fun trip but also nice to arrive at Peggy's first stop; her mother's house. I stayed with Peggy for a few days (sleeping on the couch) and then it was back to iron trail.

Ribbons of Steel

Late one evening Peggy gave me a ride to the Southern Pacific railroad yard near her new Texas home. Within five minutes a crummy was located at the end of a west bound that was headed for Mexico and would leave the United States near Eagle Pass. I wanted to catch a train but the possibility of being stranded at the Mexican border did not sound like fun. The train bumped to a start and I decided to jump on. As we slowed down to pass through the San Antonio yards a long train was pulling out in the opposite direction. I jumped off the west bound Mexican train and onto the rear locomotive of an east bound black snake (a coal train), destination unknown!

The black snake was extremely slow as it stopped and pulled onto sidings for every train coming from both directions. It took all night and most of the following day to reach Ennis, Texas, which was about thirty miles from Dallas. While in Ennis the crew was changed and the new engineer came to my spot in the rear engine and told me to get off his train. The only comfortable place to ride was in the engine, but rather than risk trouble I decided to take a break and let the snake leave without me. It had been a hot, uncomfortable and time-consuming trip from the Kirby yards to this point. I cleaned up, bought a couple of ice-cold beers and just relaxed by the side of the tracks. The townspeople of Ennis were friendly and a couple of guys sitting on a nearby porch of a Victorian style house invited me to join them – while holding a beer high in the air. Juan and Jerry wanted to know all there was to know about riding the freights. A little "story telling" about some of my amusing and satisfying times spent on the tracks was enjoyed by all. Several beers later a train slowly pulled into the main line looking very much like it was just waiting for the signal to roll. Goodbyes to my new beer drinking buddies, saddled up and caught it on the run for an easy ride to the Miller yard in Dallas.

I arrived a little before midnight and a knocker immediately warned me that the yard was "hot." He told me a hobo had fallen under the wheels of a freight train a few days prior and the detectives were doing everything possible to keep track riders out of the yard and off the trains. I hit the trail and left the yard miles behind me; not sure what was ahead but didn't feel like pushing my luck. There was nothing but tracks, no yard, no siding, just as I was about to turn around and get back to the Miller yard a knocker appeared and told me where there was a north bound train even though he couldn't tell me when it might leave. It didn't take me long to find it, climbed aboard and immediately fell into a deep sleep on that very hot Texas night. Managed to sleep until mid-morning when the heat of the day made it unbearable in my steel oven-like boxcar. A freight train leisurely slid into the yard from the north and the crummy came to a stop near my very hot boxcar. An experienced hobo (such as me) knew that there were often large bags of ice in the caboose during hot weather. When the crew left, the caboose was checked; sure enough, there were two large bags of ice cubes. Soon those ice bags were cooling down this very hot hobo in a very hot boxcar.

Late afternoon and the brakeman appeared and told me that the conductor would like to meet me. I jumped from my boxcar and we walked and talked all the way to the crummy which serves as a rolling office for the brass buttons. Conductor Don told me the Dallas Police had spotted me earlier but one of his brakemen told them not to bother me because I had already "paid my way." It was a very pleasant talk with Don, who then walked with me to my "Saint Mary's boxcar." Then Don invited me to a nearby ice cream parlor for a cold treat. We finished our ice cream and Don said I could ride in the caboose through Plano and on to Commerce. Heck yeah! When we arrived in Commerce Don spoke with the new brass buttons who said it was alright for me to stay aboard and ride to the Texarkana rail yard. I respectfully declined the offer to continue in the caboose and returned to my less comfortable boxcar. It seemed that both my mouth and brain were getting tired from all the recent discussions with some very talkative railroad men.

We eventually passed through Texarkana and then it was a slow ride to the, now familiar, Pine Bluff, Arkansas Southern Pacific rail yards. For some unexplained reason the slow hot ride required me to repeatedly remind myself to enjoy each moment. Non-E^3OL was attempting a comeback. When we finally reached the Pine Bluff yard it felt especially good to get my feet on the ground. One of the friendly train inspectors showed me the next north bound train and at about two in the morning it was rolling toward the "Show Me State" of Missouri. We crossed over the river and reached Scott City at about two the next afternoon.

It was a hot, humid Missouri day. I decided to test my stamina and hump the ALICE gear to the Cape by hiking along on what remained of the old highway before the Interstate was built. After several miles of hot humping my way was blocked by a river and a dilapidated, closed bridge. There were some single steel girders spanning the water which then disappeared into trees on the other side. I had little choice but to make the perilous crossing. I started out over the river while being very careful to keep my balance on the narrow steel girder. Several minutes and hundreds of feet later the bridge girder came to an abrupt stop at least fifty feet in the air. There were trees growing up and into where the roadway used to be many years ago. It was not attractive to re-trace the difficult trip to reach that point so it was decided to jump into one of the rather skinny trees next to my perch. I somehow managed to hang onto a wildly swinging tree. Once it stopped swinging from side-to-side it was a careful climb down to the safety of the rocky and very muddy riverbank. I reached the Cape a couple of hours later.

I hiked through town and relaxed in the coolness of the early evening on the bank of the Mississippi, then found an empty caboose and settled in for a long night. The next day I saddled up and headed down the tracks in the hot afternoon sun. After a very long few miles I reached the town of Chafee, where a city policeman approached me in a friendly way. It was the town's Police Chief, Ivan who seemed to be very interested in me and the ALICE gear. He offered me a place to shower and shave as well as a place to sleep (an empty jail cell) if a night in Chaffee sounded good to me. I took him up on the offer and soon after arriving the editor of the local newspaper showed up and asked for an interview. For some reason I declined.

I made my way back to the Scott City yards and caught a north bound "MOPS" train which would take me into East St Louis. The ride north was leisurely; got off at the Illinois Central tracks and hiked to the trestle which crossed the Mississippi river. Rested for several minutes before climbing up to the elevated trestle on a support beam and then onto the tracks. It was an enjoyable walk to the middle of the bridge and I found a nice place to relax and watched the boat traffic on the Mississippi far below. For some strange reason thoughts of another trip to D.C. entered my mind – quickly that notion was put aside. Congress was in recess and besides, it had been learned that the western part of the United States required much less energy to maintain my day-to-day hobo existence. There could certainly be some value in a D.C. visit but it would have to wait until I was willing to expend the required energy.

For a couple of hours, the beauty of my surroundings and vistas from my perch on the MacArthur Bridge were simply absorbed. Next, I headed for the B&N yards and had a great talk with Joe, a pleasant knocker who went out of his way to be extra helpful. He made sure that he got me on the correct train and later brought me a 5-gallon plastic bucket of ice filled with water bottles and a tuna salad sandwich! Together we sat at the edge of the tracks and talked about politics and the current state of the military. Joe had spent his service time in the Air Force and was now in the Missouri Army National Guard. He was a good American by any measure, and had many good things to say about his job, his time in the military and our country.

The west bound train out of St Louis truly had wooden axles and we did not arrive in the next major yard of Springfield, Missouri, until late in the night. It was especially nice that Joe was thoughtful enough to have brought me that wonderful bucket of ice on this very hot day. The Springfield yard was rather strange as none of the knockers seemed to know when there would be a west bound; they were not very talkative. I headed for the outskirts of the yard, as such unfriendly behavior usually meant gumshoes were close at hand. It was a ten-hour wait before catching a hot shot as it was highballing from the yard.

Early the next morning the hot shot arrived in Tulsa. I jumped off as it rolled into the main yard and then walked to a nearby small food store for some breakfast supplies. The owners, Kay and Jim were writing a song about riding the freights, and wanted help with hobo slang words. I shared with them some of the more common hobo slang that came to mind as they attended to store customers. We talked for a couple of hours and then it was off to the tracks to find a shady spot for my breakfast of beans and hot dogs.

A friendly knocker showed me that a west bound that was due to "shine" in about five hours. It left right on time and I rode it to Belen, New Mexico, where a northbound could be caught for Denver. Before getting situated on a north bound the local gumshoe politely told me, "Get the hell out of my yard and if I see you again it will be jail time for sure." The harsh language was actually said in a nice way but it was clear that he meant every word so it was no mystery that his orders should be followed – the yard was quickly existed. The thought of a northbound train was put aside.

When walking the streets of Belen loud music was heard coming from a bar, but the front door was locked. The side door was open so stuck my head in the door. The middle-aged man behind the bar told me, "We won't open for a few hours at noon." I said okay and turned to walk away, but he hollered to come on in anyway. He then poured me a cold beer and said, "I can't open until noon so I'll have to lock the door, otherwise I'll be breaking the law." The sociable bartender then brought me a plate containing two very large nicely spiced burritos. What more could a track rider want? Stayed for a couple of hours, drank plenty of beer (he kept filling my glass) and we talked continuously as he went about his business of getting the bar ready to open. By eleven o'clock it was time for me to hit the cinder trail. A firm handshake, big smiles all around and I was gone from that very agreeable place--forever.

It was decided not to take a chance on the small yard gumshoe's sincerity about the jail time so a ride was hitched to Albuquerque, where I waited by the tracks with hopes of catching a Denver bound train. That didn't work so it was back to the highway and hitching. It was short wait and attractive blonde female school teacher stopped and offered me a ride to Denver. She was from Lubbock, Texas and was going to a teacher's convention in Denver. We reached her motel and it was a shock when she asked, "Would you like to come in and take a shower before you go on your way?" The shower was indeed refreshing and with all my heart I tried to convince her that I should spend the night. She resisted my attempts at "charming" behavior and simply told me, "No way, but you can sleep in my car." Perhaps she saw the lust in the eyes and didn't want to have any part of it. It was a restless night in the front seat of her car. In the pre-dawn darkness, it was time to saddle up and quietly leave – no hello or goodbye kisses from this woman.

Barrio "Gangster" Encounter

In Denver I met up with some friendly track riders that were sitting under a bridge so it was time to take a break for lunch and conversation. The guys were rather young, late teens or early twenties, and they picked my brain about how best to ride the freight trains. They were trying to get to Washington State to find work; at least that was what they said. I stayed with them for a couple of hours and then headed for the Denver, Rio Grande & Western yard about six miles up the tracks. After an hour or so of walking it was time to get a couple of bottles of beer. The neighborhood by the tracks looked pretty rough and turned out to be the "Mexican Barrio" of Denver. I found a liquor store and was a bit relieved to see the man behind the store counter (enclosed in bullet proof glass) was white like me. He looked very surprised and asked, "What the hell are you doing in this neighborhood?" Not exactly music to my ears. I got a couple of beers and when I walked outside found a half-dozen young goons waiting, all shaved heads and many prison type cheap tattoos. One angrily asked about my military gear and uniform. He spit, "What the fuck is the government doing in our neighborhood?" I straightened my back, threw my shoulders back and told them that in this country I would go wherever I wanted. Their circle tightened around me! One tough guy that seemed to be the leader said, "We're revolutionaries and this is our neighborhood." My chest was puffed a little more and told the "tough guy" once again, that this was still America and I'll go wherever I choose. With that comment I took a step forward and thankfully the circle opened. I quickly walked away while covering my ass with quick glances over my shoulder. They walked behind for several yards and then stopped while not saying anything. After that rather threatening experience it was especially good to get back to the relative safety of the tracks.

Back in the Friendly Rail Yard

My hike continued toward the D&RGW yards and soon found a place along the tracks called Prospect Junction. It was an easy matter to catch the Salt Lake freight for a fifteen-hour ride. My experience had taught me that some cars rode smoothly, some rough, but this one seemed to be out of control, it was the roughest ride ever experienced on a freight train. Many times, during the ride it seemed to be on the verge of flying off the tracks. In fact, there were two other hobos riding with me for a couple of hours until the train came to a stop on a siding. At the moment the train came to a stop, they were gone. They looked at me as if I was crazy to stay aboard that wild riding boxcar. I stuck it out and got a thrilling ride as it sometimes bounced me two feet into the air. The two hobos who had bailed out earlier were in the next car and looked amazed when they saw me jump from the moving train as we entered Salt Lake's Roper yard.

It was a nice ten-mile uphill hike to reach Cherise's Sugarland house. Her boyfriend Paul was in town and we stayed up late into the night, drinking beer and having a great party. After a fine breakfast, a firm handshake and nice little hug from Cherise and it was time to saddle up and head for downtown Salt Lake City and the Union Pacific tracks.

There was an older gentleman sitting in a railroad shack where several tracks crossed a very busy street. Stopped to talk with this pleasant man and he explained that his job was to make sure students from nearby Westside

School got across safely as a couple children had been killed several years ago. When he learned that California was my destination, he excitedly told me, "The California train will be coming through very soon."

A shady spot was found and settled in for the wait. It wasn't long before the California bound train was caught and found myself once again happily rolling west.

It was an easy ride to Las Vegas on some smooth riding tracks and a flatcar. Just outside the Las Vegas city limits we stopped, and I saw an old car seat laying in the ballast. I threw it onto my grain car and was soon riding in style and comfort. It was a slow train, but gave me time to relax and enjoy the desert scenery. We rolled deeper into the desert and were soon skirting the Providence Mountains, which rose 7,000 feet into the desert sky. At a small outpost called Cima my train rolled to a stop. I jumped off and ran to the little store for some provisions. I asked Bob, the storeowner, if there were any small pieces of land for sale. Bob said most of the land was government land. So much for the Cima dream. Back at the tracks it was time to relax, drink a beer, eat beans and listen to the cheerful singing of the desert birds.

From Cima it was down a long grade of about ten miles, and through another railroad town called Kelso on the outskirts of an area known as the "Devils Playground." That area was marked with miles of sand dunes rising hundreds of feet above the desert floor. The train only briefly stopped in Kelso but the view of the nearby Providence Mountains was stunning and they somehow seemed to beckon me. As we rolled slowly from the Kelso depot the view was of many miles of graceful sand dunes on the south side of the tracks – they were spectacular.

My next stop was in the town of Yermo, which was the crew change point for the Los Angeles to Las Vegas trains. It was here that the crew de-trained, would sleep over and usually returned to their point of origin on the next day. While walking through the city, along old U. S. Route 66, I noticed that a cute young woman appeared to be watching me. Just had to stop to say hello and we ended up talking for an hour or so. Janet was not shy and as we were ending our conversation she casually said, "Would you teach me how to French Kiss?" Was that what she really said?! We immediately moved to a more private place in some trees by the side of the tracks and proceeded with the lesson – needless to say, it was a great fun! Following the kissing lesson Janet left but not before we exchanged our addresses. The next kissing lesson was greatly anticipated.

There was a small bar and grill next to the Yermo rail yard. The trainmen liked to go there for coffee before duty and beer after ending their shift. ALICE and I slide up to the bar and ordered a cold beer from a friendly female bartender who introduced herself as Janice. We had a nice conversation. Bartender Janice was very proud of her little town and gave me an extensive history lesson on Yermo. Yermo would be a pleasant stop for future train trips. Kissing lessons for Janet and a friendly female bartender—what more could a hobo desire?

At about midnight I embarked on a leisurely walk to the peaceful rail yard. After a couple of hours wait, a fast freight, with me aboard, was heading for the Union Pacific's Los Angeles rail yards.

I visited friends in the Valley and also checked in at the 146th TAW. Then I took the Greyhound down to Oceanside and spent a very restful three days with Mom and Dad. They wanted to visit the desert so it was a car ride back to the General. Back at the home site Tom and Doreen had planted trees and a vegetable garden in my absence. It was late August and the air was cool throughout the days even with a brightly shinning sun. The nights had been getting very cold – often close to freezing.

I spent a couple of nights at Peggy's now-vacant house. While there, a young man by the name of Jim and his wife Angie stopped by to see about renting the house. They had just moved to Los Angeles County from New York and needed a place to live. I showed them the house and they ended up leasing it with an option to buy. In another example of "it's a small world" Jim was really surprised to see me as he had spotted me about a week ago jumping off a freight in Palmdale. He certainly had a good memory for faces; I told him he should get into police work.

The quiet little Crystalaire Airport that sat adjacent to the General had never been very busy; there might be one or two flights a day. That changed when a sail plane school leased the land and air strip and started making numerous flights. One day, I got dressed in my battle dress uniform, light fight gear and started a patrol along the airport perimeter. One of the new school people watched me--he gave me the "thumbs up" and said, "I have the same gear and also like to patrol the desert." I figured he was bullshitting, but we later got to know one another and have since walked many miles in the desert together, fired off many rounds and drank more than a few beers. Bob was the senior pilot for the glider school, flying the olive drab L-19 Army recon plane, known as the "Bird Dog." When on desert patrol I would often signal Bob's L-19 with a mirror and down he came for a low altitude, and I mean low, "buzz."

After a couple of weeks back in the desert it was time to move out and head for the Mercenary School in Dolomite, Alabama. Tom, Doreen, and Bird Dog put on a beer and roasted rabbit party on the eve of the departure, and at four in the morning I headed into L.A. to catch a train from the Glendale yard.

Shortly thereafter I was on a train streaking across the desert floor. We arrived in San Antonio in 48 hours with no major stops. Peggy came to the yard and picked me up and we headed out to a piece of land she had bought near the small town of La Vernia. She also bought a travel trailer and had placed it deep in the trees; it was my kind of place.

Alabama Mercenary School

It was already August and hard to believe that training at the Mercenary School was only 4 days away. Peggy gave me a ride to San Antonio's downtown Southern Pacific yards and within half an hour I was on a train and rolling towards Dallas. We highballed for a couple of hundred miles until we reach the Fatula railroad siding where we stopped at a track crossing to let a long black snake cross.

We reached the Miller yard a little after midnight, and I jumped from my boxcar and set off to find the MOPS train. Several miles of difficult humping brought me to a very long railroad bridge spanning a river with no place to walk except on the tracks themselves. After several minutes of deep contemplation, I decided to directly challenge the bridge obstacle and attempt a crossing. About 50 yards in, I heard a train's whistle up ahead. Without a moment's hesitation it was an about face and running as fast as possible toward the safety of solid ground. After that train passed it was back on the tracks thinking that another would not be coming soon. That was a mistake; this time I had reached the middle of the bridge before a train whistle shook my now reeling brain. Since it was too far to reach either end before the rapidly approaching train turned me into ground beef, I scurried about for an escape. I was able to climb down a support column, get under the tracks, and hold on to some steel braces as the train passed directly over me. It was a heart pounding experience. The train roared overhead as the bridge shook my precarious perch. It passed and I ran, on the ties and in the dark, as fast as possible to the other side. Actually, it was a feeling of deep satisfaction that the challenge of the bridge had been accepted and this track walker was still alive but breathing heavily.

It was another five or six miles to reach the MOPS yard. It was three in the morning; fatigue was upon me and perhaps some post trauma effects from my bridge crossing experience. Luckily a train soon rolled into view and one very tired hobo crawled onto the first car, right behind the locomotives. An experienced track rider would tell you that catching this car was a bad idea, since the front cars are the most likely to be "set out", or taken off the train. I didn't care. All I wanted was a place on that Memphis bound train to lie down, close my heavy eyes and fall asleep.

I fell into a deep sleep and the next thing I knew, the train had stopped, and then started to move backwards at a speed that was rapidly increasing, which continued for a few miles. As we sped backwards, I saw our caboose sitting on the adjacent track. My car was being set out! The train was traveling much too fast to jump off. As we got closer it was clear that there was trouble up ahead as it was not an ordinary train yard, it was of the high security variety. Large gates opened into the yard while hundreds of large brilliant lights illuminated the entire yard as if it were high noon on a sunny day. Paved roads between the tracks were busy with container trucks and people coming and going. Uniformed guards stood in glass enclosures, watching where the tracks entered this formidable freight yard. The fortress like gates slammed shut as the train completed its entrance. Deeper and deeper we backed into this citadel, before finally we came to a stop. I looked about carefully to survey the situation. Not good. My first objective would be to reach a row of parked trucks about 100 yards away that would provide hiding places in their shadows. I crouched low and ran across the open space to breathlessly reach the dark shadows. From that point it was necessary to cross another 100 yards of open concrete leading into knee high grass. The grass was reached and then I crawled on my elbows and belly through the deep grass to the perimeter. There I found an extra heavy-duty chain-link fence 12 feet high and topped with razor wire and electronic movement detection devices. Those devices would send a signal to the security team if anyone tried to cut through or climb over the fence. For over an hour I slowly crawled through the deep grass following the fence toward the main gate — the only way to escape. From my new hiding place security personnel could be seen watching as they opened the gate to permit trains to enter or leave. I inched forward, waited until they were looking away and made a dash for freedom. Once through the gate a fifty-yard open area had to be crossed and then a barbed wire fence. I made it over the obstacle in a flash and disappeared into the shadows of some old warehouses and collapsed, gasping for air and soaked in sweat. It was great to be free! It was good conditioning for the Escape and Evasion portion of the upcoming mercenary school.

Between escaping possible death on the bridge in Dallas and the escape from the high security train yard it was enough of the freights – at least for a while. In the morning I caught a ride to Shreveport, Louisiana and ended up walking many miles through the city on that very hot humid day. On the outskirts of town, the leader of a twenty truck Army National Guard convoy pulled to the roadside and gave me a lift. I rode with them for about five hours--all the way to Jackson, Mississippi. We had plenty of good discussions as they were very interested in the Recondo School. That brought me to within 200 miles of the school in Alabama. It was only Wednesday night and I was not due to report until Saturday morning. Barring some disaster, like getting arrested, there was plenty of time to reach the school.

I caught a ride to the Bienville National Forest about fifty miles east of Jackson, then hiked several miles to a nice roadside picnic area and spent the night in the pines. It was a good place to freshen up, relax and get ready for the final push to the bunker on Warrior River road. As I saddled up to head for the highway, Beverly and Dan, who were also camped there, offered me a ride to Birmingham. Without any hesitation I accepted her offer and several hours later it was time to set up a campsite on Possum Creek only one mile from the Bunker.

There was a small railroad yard near my campsite with a string of boxcars quietly sitting on the tracks. A clean boxcar with plenty of cardboard was soon found and it was time to relax for the rest of the day and night. That evening several trains passed by making my boxcar campsite feel like home. It cooled off at night which made the hot humid days easier to endure. It was an easy, restful Friday at the tracks. I washed in the creek, got beer and beans at a nearby store and then spent a peaceful evening at my campsite.

Early Saturday morning I walked to the Bunker. There was no one around, so I sat down in the deep, uncut grass and leaned my back against a well-used chain link fence topped with razor wire. An hour passed and Pablo, the school's executive officer (EO), drove up with a couple of other students he had just picked up at the Birmingham airport. We checked our valuables at the Bunker and were transported to a staging area two miles away. Throughout the day students arrived and were processed for the trip to the field. There were several foreign students who spoke little English. Late in the afternoon we were ordered to put on camouflage paint and get ready to depart for the field. The training area was about twenty miles away in the hills and deep valleys near the Warrior River. The EO sternly warned us, "Once you're inserted into the area of operations you are in 'Indian

Country' and anything can happen — including being taking prisoner. From that moment forward the watchword was *alertness* — the military called it situational awareness.

The dozen or so of us loaded ourselves and gear into waiting trucks and headed for the unknown. We arrived, formed a double column and prepared for the two-mile hike to the base camp which cadre called "Little Switzerland." It was supposed to be a neutral zone, but we soon learned this was not always true. Being a gung-ho sort of guy, I volunteered for the point position of one column and an ex-Navy man took the other. We saddled up and cautiously moved along the logging road toward base camp. I detected a land mine simulator (it would result in an explosion if tripped) and made sure everyone behind knew its location. Just before we reached "Little Switzerland" we were ambushed by the School's advance team, consisting of instructors and students that had arrived earlier. The noise was deafening, as explosions and fireworks engulfed our young and innocent recon team. I was one of the first to be "killed" when a lead pellet slammed into my chest, leaving a nasty black bruise the size of a quarter. Explosions continued with flash bang grenades and fireworks streaking over our now prone bodies. As I clutched my chest in pain, there was an eerie silence, followed by numerous camouflaged figures emerging from the brush with guns at the ready. One especially ugly camo-face eerily shouted, "Welcome to the Mercenary School." Even in that hot and humid place a cold chill involuntarily crawled up my spine. What the hell had I gotten myself into?

About that time, it was clear that my suspicions were correct: this was definitely not going to be a Boy Scout camp out. As dusk arrived it was time for another "welcome," in what the cadre euphemistically called "gas indoctrination class." Simply put, it meant that each student/recruit got sprayed directly in the face with military strength C.S. gas. C.S. gas was the military's version of MACE which was the gas made available for civilian use. It was said to be more powerful than the civilian gas and brought you rapidly to your knees in pain. As each of us got splattered in the face we blindly stumbled to the murky waters of Mud Creek to wash the stinging chemical from our faces. Less than three hours had passed since school began, and I had been on the ground twice writhing in pain – this school was going to be fun!

Immediately following the gas "class" we were separated into four teams. The Team Leaders (TLs), who were all experienced graduates and Recondo patch holders, picked their team's members. Allen, a tough looking Cajun kickboxer from Louisiana picked me. We were designated as Team One and would work together for the entire combat week. It was obvious that Allen took the training very, very seriously and had extensive experience. I was happy to be on his team and have him as our Team Leader. As it turned out he was the most aggressive of all Team Leaders at that class.

It was getting dark and all teams began to silently slip into the bush after secretively receiving instructions from the Training Officer (TO). Our first mission was to set up an ambush for anyone coming into the training area. We were told new students might be coming in later that night. We reached our ambush position and I once again took the point position carrying a decommissioned CAR-15 machine gun at the lead end of the kill zone. We had to be quiet and alert at all times, since we were also fair game for the other three teams. We waited in our camouflaged position until after midnight with no incoming enemy sighted. Team Leader Allen then cautiously moved us away from the road and we set up a small patrol camp. We took turns pulling security duty, allowing each or us about one hour of sleep. At four in the morning TL Allen wanted a recon and fire mission on "Little Switzerland." Like I said before, Allen was aggressive. I volunteered and three of us (including Allen) crawled up the creek to within twenty-five yards of the base camp, lobbed flash-bang and smoke grenades into the camp and slipped away amid many angry curses from base camp personnel. It was amazing that we were able to find our way back to our patrol camp on that black Alabama night.

The Merc School operated on a schedule which allowed for very little rest. Every day, just before dawn, the teams were summoned from the field to come to base camp by three shots at which time hostilities in the field were supposed to stop. As soon as all teams assembled a two-hour hand-to-hand combat training session began. What a great way to start off another wonderful day. Full contact was the rule and many injuries resulted from that early morning activity. By the end of the first day, we had three dropouts, some with minor injuries looking for an excuse to call it quits.

We spent our nights patrolling, ambushing, being ambushed and generally just trying not to get gassed, clubbed on the head and, most importantly, captured, which was the second worst thing that could happen — after getting killed. If captured you were stripped naked, blindfolded, gassed and tied in some very uncomfortable positions for many hours, sometimes for a day or longer depending on how sadistic your captors might feel. There were *no* rules! After witnessing a prisoner interrogation "class", where a grown, naked man groveled in the dirt, begged and cried real tears for mercy, while calling out, "mommy help me" you tended to stay alert and avoid capture.

After only two days and nights in the bush my mind was saying it had been a week in the field and combat class was just about over. It was difficult to believe that only forty-eight hours had passed. Frank Camper, the School's founder and Commanding Officer (CO), explained to the class that, the first two days were the roughest and in one more day we would be over a major psychological hump. In spite of the CO's explanation, two more students dropped out, leaving us at sixteen students. The rest of the week we learned about machine guns and many weapons from around the world. We did pugil stick fighting drills—one guy was actually knocked unconscious—slack rope bridge fighting, rappelling over a forty-foot cliff into the creek under the pressure of live pellet gun fire. An ex-Marine friend was hit in the back during a rappelling drill and a lead pellet was dug from his flesh. The sniper was told not to pump up his air rifle as much after that happened. Almost everyone had ugly bruises two inches in diameter on various parts of their bodies following that rather nasty exercise. One young man suffered a dislocated shoulder during our morning hand-to-hand combat drill. The Training Officer (TO) pulled it back in place while two of us held him down. The gutsy victim continued the training and when it happened a second time, we were unable to get it back in place. He was *not* evacuated from the field but was used for base camp security during the last two days of combat week. He did *not* receive the coveted Recondo Patch since his injury prevented him from taking part in the culminating exercise, the compass run. There was no slack for the grunts at Mercenary School – you had to complete all the requirements. Our first real break came on Thursday morning when we were allowed time to bathe in Mud Creek without fear of attack and capture.

Friday was the compass run, the final test for combat week. If we passed that final trial we would receive the sought-after black and olive drab Recondo patch. For that final test the more experienced Team Leaders would not be with us, we were on our own. The training officer selected me as a Team Leader and gave me a set of compass readings. We had to reach some vaguely described point, conduct a reconnaissance of the area, and then return with all men and report to the TO before dawn on the following day. The mission began with a night time rappel into Mud Creek, loaded with all our gear that we had brought into the camp. Four teams were sent out at half hour intervals. My team departed last and therefore at the darkest hour and had the least amount of time to complete the mission. As we waited our turn we could hear the explosions and gun fire as the preceding teams tripped booby traps and ran into ambushes. We mentally plotted their progress by using the sound of explosions and gunfire as they moved toward the objective in the moonless, inky blackness of that Alabama night.

We moved to the jump off point at the top of the cliff and then rappelled into the chest-deep Mud Creek. Once everyone was safely off the cliff, we formed a column and started to slowly work our way upstream through the murky water toward a point where the cliffs fell away. We moved about one hundred yards before we were caught in a blazing ambush from the cliffs above. Fireworks and explosive devices of all kinds showered down on us as we tried to keep moving through the muddy water. The point man screamed out in pain as a grenade simulator went off much too close to his head; so close he thought that his ear had been blown away. I turned in real anger and fired my flare pistol at the hidden attackers, quickly examined his face and head, and assured him he was okay. We continued our aggressive movement into the gantlet of fire. Once out of range we found ourselves in mud well over our knees which made our forward progress extremely challenging. We plodded through the mud and water for 30 minutes and finally reached an equally muddy creek bank and threw ourselves down, gasping for air. We had only just begun! The men were all checked for wounds, giving encouragement, and we moved deeper into the sinister pitch-black woods. After many hours of struggling through several swamps and over a small mountain we reached the objective at three in the morning. We had little time to get back to camp by dawn. The entire team was dead tired as we had been beating the bush for six hours, under the stress of possible ambush, with only a few short breaks. Marine Frank took the point and we crashed into the bush, just wanting to reach base camp before the dawn deadline. One of the men, a National Guardsman from Hong Kong, wanted to give up. He was a frail man with lots of guts but was totally worn out from the all night forced march. Other team members took turns carrying his pack and encouraged him onward, for we all had to return as a unit if we were to pass the combat course. Our unit reached base camp just minutes before dawn. The reconnaissance report was given and we all earned our Recondo patches!

As the day progressed, I noticed that many of the men were packing their gear and preparing to leave the field, bailing halfway through the two-week course. Only four of us remained for Escape & Evasion week! I teamed up with Frank and we decided to limit our team to the two of us. There would be at least a dozen aggressors hunting our asses and we wanted to preserve our ability to move fast quietly.

School cadre told us that E&E wouldn't start until six that evening and that we should relax and spend the day getting prepared for the week ahead. That story was total bullshit! At noon they ordered the four of us to remove our battle jackets so they could count and record earlier pellet wounds (getting hit by sniper fire during E&E would be grounds for automatic disqualification. We were next told to put our jackets on and ordered to remove our combat boots for foot inspection. The four of us dutifully removed boots and socks and draped our feet over a log in a very awkward position. As we sat, actually more like laying on the ground, the Training Officer pretended to check our feet. Meanwhile, the armed school cadre was moving toward us from behind. A few seconds later, loud, angry screaming: "E&E has started--get the fuck out of our camp." Gunfire and explosions rang through the air as we were chased from camp like four scared rabbits—without any gear or boots! The only things we had were what we had in our battle fatigue pockets. With live bullets striking all around we headed for the creek at full speed completely forgetting we had no boots to protect our feet. My buddy Frank was close behind and pursuers not far behind him. After getting across the creek, I grabbed a fighting stick and made ready to "kill" anyone who might try to capture this scared rabbit!

We continued to run to the top of the hill and into the next valley with explosions and gunfire all around. The valley was covered with very thorny bramble bushes and short squat trees. We ran through the brambles sometimes ripping them between our naked toes. Finally, exhausted we burrowed into the bramble bushes thinking no one would dare follow us "rabbits." After carefully picking our way deep into the bush we began to clear a spot around us so we could at least turn over and face the sky. We were breathing hard and were wild eyed after the vulgar beginning of E&E. Our feet were swollen, bruised and bleeding from the barefoot escape. Young Frank looked at me with eyes wide open and said, "I can't believe this is happening, we never did anything like this in the Marines."

We stayed in our covered hideout for the rest of the first day of E&E trying to regain some semblance of good judgment. We took inventory and immediately realized we had no water, just two pieces of candy for food, a pocket knife, hat, bandana, small mosquito net, notebook, parachute cord, plastic bag and C.S. gas. I used the hat, bandana and mosquito net to fashion foot protection. I filled them with leaves and tied them to my feet with the parachute cord. Frank had a pair of socks so we stuffed them with leaves and he had a decent pair of moccasins. We spent the day in pretty good spirits in spite of our predicament. We dug deeper into the bush when we heard the stirring of twigs and imagined the enemy slipping up on our position. The buzzing of insects was often unnerving as it sometimes sounded much like human conversation. As the day wore on, we became more relaxed as we realized no one had discovered our hiding place. The sun went down and it began to cool rapidly while those hungry southern mosquitoes started to feast on our blood. Before long it turned cold and we huddled together as the insects continued to attack. It would be a very long first night on E&E. We took turns pulling camp security throughout the night which further added to our misery.

The morning sun was a welcome sight. We decided to stay put and Frank slept until late in the afternoon as I silently looked on in envy. My time was spent silently digging a tunnel deeper into the bramble bushes. The thorn covered branches were carefully woven into an alternate hideout. In the afternoon we made a tic tac toe game in the dirt and passed a couple of hours until Frank once again went to sleep.

Throughout the day gunfire and explosions could be heard as we huddled in the underbrush. The deadly noise worked on the nerves and served as a constant reminder that danger was always nearby. Large amounts of energy were expended trying to find the "value" in the exercise. It wasn't easy; the E^3OL philosophy was getting an extreme test.

The sun was out all day and the thirst overwhelming. We had gone 24 hours without water. We waited until nine that evening and started the belly crawl through the bush, up the hill towards the creek. Water was a powerful motivator. The moon was bright that night as we slowly emerged from our bramble bush camp. The going was slow as we moved from shadow to shadow in an effort to avoid detection. It was a difficult and tedious journey but it felt good to be on the move. When we reached the crest of the hill a couple of hours later we heard the Training Officer calling our names and telling us to come and get our gear. We talked it over and decided not to trust him, especially after the way E&E was sprung on us. It was surely a trap! We would survive with the little we escaped with.

It took us most of the night to reach the creek. The muddy creek water was refreshing and we made a patrol camp nearby and managed to get a couple hours sleep between guard duty. Startled by sounds in the night I awoke in the darkness thinking it was continuation of a horrific nightmare, only to discover that it wasn't a dream – this was really happening.

Morning brought an unreal looking foggy mist along that dirty, muddy, creek bank. I decided to go on a recon mission to see if the flag was up. The rules of E&E specified that sometime during the week an international orange colored flag would be raised at base camp. If the flag was up the students would then infiltrate base camp, avoiding capture, in order to pass the course. My mission was to go in, check for the flag and return to meet Frank at an old helicopter landing zone. One last large drink from the muddy creek, filled a plastic sandwich baggy with muddy water and cautiously headed toward base camp. It was very quiet when approaching "Little Switzerland," perhaps too quiet. The flag was not up but after observing the camp for several minutes' movement was noticed; three people in camp were counted. Thoughts of attempting to recover my ALICE gear were set aside and it was time to quietly slip back into the bush. I waited for Frank at the helipad for three hours, got inpatient, and then went to see if there was a food stash somewhere along the road. The Training Officer had said there would be a stash – but it could be a trap. I cautiously moved along the road for a stressful hour before an ambush was sprung by Pablo and other Mercs. They jumped from the bush with guns leveled and ordered me to drop the fighting stick and freeze. Fuck that! I turned and ran with gunfire kicking dirt around my feet, dove into the bushes, struggled to my feet and ran with the sound of gunfire impinging on the brain. My feet were bloodied once again but I managed to find a hiding place under a huge fallen tree. I caught my breath and gathered my wits. I soon realized that they had not followed me into the thorny brambles. I decided to move to another valley to the east and therefore be in a position for another recon mission from the opposite direction. I needed to find water soon as there were only a couple of mouthfuls in the baggy following the latest escape. It took many hours to slowly work my way into the new valley, where I found a stream bed with several pools of rusty colored water--it tasted good. A patrol camp was set up near one of the more camouflaged pools of rusty water. A frog jumped into the brown water; visions of the delicious frog legs danced in the head. Many hours were spent trying to find that frog but it escaped – hunger would remain.

It looked like the balance of E&E would be completed alone as there was no desire to go looking for Frank, especially after the last ambush. With his Marine training he would surely do fine on his own. Being by myself was fine and making decisions was much easier--poor judgments would only affect me. There was an old fire road adjacent to my patrol camp which headed toward base camp. Just before sunset I hiked away from the base camp to see what might be found. It turned out to be a successful mission as an old couch was found. Foam rubber was stripped from the couch and tied to some broken shower slippers and my feet with the parachute cord. Now my feet were protected – it was a happy day. Found pop bottles were used as canteens – no more baggies. There was even enough foam rubber to make a crude bedroll. The illegal dump site was next to Warrior Road and the way to freedom. That road resulted in the sudden and powerful temptation to head for town. Why was I putting myself through the torture? But no, I would stay.

As I slowly made my way along the fire road toward base camp, gunfire erupted from high above on the hills. Dirt kicked up a few yards ahead. I dived for cover and once again burrowed into the bramble bushes. Shouts from above: "Food has been stashed on the road." This rabbit was very hungry but not willing to risk capture. After waiting for several hours, I headed in the direction of base camp under cover of darkness.

I spent the next day avoiding patrols in the vicinity of base camp and waiting for the flag to be raised. Late in the afternoon of the fourth day the flag went up; its international orange color looked like a beacon of safety among the green pines. E&E was coming to an end! All that remained for me was to get under the flag without being captured. A cold rainy night was spent slowly working through base camp's security. At dawn I was in position and emerged from the bush, fighting stick in hand, once again determined to "kill" anyone who might try to stop me from victory. With a loud yell I rushed across the final twenty five yards and threw myself under the safety of the flag. It was over. I had made it! What a grand feeling! I was now a full-fledged member of the Mercenary Association and Recondo patch holder. Frank was already in base camp as he had reached the flag about two hours earlier. The other two E&E students made it to the flag late in the afternoon. Later we were all transported to the Bunker for three days of additional training in foreign weapons and explosives. It was great to be out of the field.

The Mercenary Association held graduation exercises at a local pizza restaurant where our class took the name, "Copperhead II." Then to my surprise they voted me the outstanding student for the class. It was time to sew on the Recondo patch, reflect on the past fourteen days, say goodbye to new friends, and catch a slow freight to California.

The Devil's Playground

After several weeks back in the Llano desert, I decided to return to Alabama for more Mercenary School action. Once a student earned a full membership in the Mercenary Association, they could participate in all future Association training exercises, mostly in team leadership positions. They became valuable assets for the cadre of mercenaries. I packed my ALICE gear and headed east once again.

At the second school, as a Team Leader (TL) and Instructor, I had the responsibility for the success and welfare of a team of approximately eight men. The additional responsibility felt comfortable and I managed to get some seriously good men; we called ourselves KAT II (Kick Ass Team II). The name was not very original, but team members seemed to like it. Our team's number one directive was that no one from KAT II was to be captured. However, if that happened, we would not rest until they were free. We made the whole week without losing anyone.

I headed back to Llano, where there was plenty of shooting and drinking with Bird Dog, and various projects at the property and the General to keep me busy. On my previous cinder trail trips I had become interested in the area between Yermo and Las Vegas, so I decided to go investigate it more closely. I saddled up and hitched a ride to Yermo where I hoped to catch a train for Kelso and Cima. I will also admit that part of my motivation was the possibility of more French kissing lessons. We had already exchanged several letters, so prospects were good.

I arrived in Yermo early in the morning and made a ten-mile hike into the Calico Mountains on my way to Calico Ghost Town. Calico was a tourist attraction where Janet worked during school breaks — she was now a student at UCLA. I crossed the last ridge and saw Calico's "old mule trolley," which gave ghost town visitors a ride to the higher levels of the mountain-side town. I got closer and noticed that Janet was its operator; what a stroke of luck. Up to that point I was unsure whether she could be found. When the park closed, Janet gave me a ride down the mountain and we stopped in the desert for more kissing lessons – what nice, clean fun! The next morning, Janet brought me a couple of delicious sandwiches in my campsite, teased me a little by showing me her butt and then quickly disappeared. Janet definitely stimulated enjoyable thoughts that continued as I waited for a freight train north.

I jumped on a Union Pacific hot shot late that afternoon and headed deeper into the desert. The train seemed to fly across the sandscape and didn't stop until it reached Cima about a hundred miles into the desert. My ride had been in the last engine unit and one of the crew had spent an hour talking with me during the trip. Don was an interesting fellow, very military and looked sharp in his clean olive drab M65 U.S. Army issue field jacket. When we arrived in Cima he went forward and returned with the engineer, John, who was very interested in my efforts to increase train security. Both wanted to know more about my work with the Mercenary Association. We talked for thirty minutes about my training and counter terrorism efforts then they had to continue on to Las Vegas. I decided to go back south, down the mountain, to the small desert hamlet of Kelso. I spent the night in the Cima pump house and caught the early morning freight into Kelso. It was a nice ride down the grade as the sun gradually pushed the darkness aside in the eastern sky.

In Kelso, there was an impressive railroad station building dating from the late thirties which served as a lunch room for desert travelers and railroad workers. It had a large well-kept yard with green grass and many shade trees. It looked out of place here at the edge of the "Devil's Playground" in the Mojave Desert. At the lunch counter there was one customer, an older man drinking coffee at its far end. A train crewman I had encountered had told me to look up a local hard-rock miner by the name of "OB", short for O'Brien. Don had described OB as a "colorful miner who knows that part of the desert better than anyone." I figured that the man at the end of the lunch counter just had to be O'Brien--and it was! I struck up a conversation and we hit it off from the start. OB invited me to his place where he excitedly showed me maps of the surrounding desert and locations of his "secret" diggings. As we sat in his small sand colored travel trailer, he lowered his voice and whispered in my ear "if you want, I'll show you my secret diggings in the lava fields." He also introduced me to his "partner," a large white German shepherd by the name of Whitedog.

Whitedog and I got along fine as he, like OB, had a very pleasant disposition. We talked for hours, checking his maps of the New York and Providence Mountains and it was time for me to go on a little recon mission. OB gave me a ride to the old Vulcan Mine Road south of Fountain Peak and near the old Kaiser open pit iron mine. My new pal Whitedog followed me for a couple of miles then turned back to be with his master. I could see OB watching us climb the mountain from far below. I hoped to follow a canyon to Fountain Peak and then return down the other side of the mountain, across several miles of the desert floor and then back to Kelso in a couple of days.

    I camped on the rim of the deep iron ore pit which was one quarter full of cool clear water. It was a strange and beautiful sight in the middle of some of the hottest desert land in the world. There was a fantastic sunset as the sun slowly sank behind the glittering sand dunes of the Devil's Playground. The pleasing silence was intense and seemed to encourage peace within my very soul. It was my first time being so isolated and far from any sign of civilization. An occasional plane passed far overhead or the distant throbbing of a train engine, climbing the Kelso grade, would sometimes penetrate the stillness of the night. A poncho shelter was built and made a small campfire. It would be hot beans on that magnificent evening in the Mojave Desert. It had been a long hike to reach my current campsite and it was not long before a restful sleep engulfed my body. Drifting toward sleep sweet thoughts of my new Yermo friend, Janet, floated through my brain.

    I awoke at dawn, rekindled the fire, re-heated and finished the beans and headed northeast into the canyon. Old mining claims were soon found marked with steel tags bearing the names of "Burro 8, Burro 16 & Burro 17." It felt like being a real live witness to the history of that little corner of the world. It was early in the morning, about six o'clock, and after five hours of hard, steady climbing a ridge was reached which looked like it might lead to the main peak. What a spectacular feeling as that cliff of that ridge was conquered. Further up the canyon a small plateau was found along that rugged and rocky ridge. The plateau was bathed in the cool sunshine of mid-day as a gentle breeze stirred the deep green grass which carpeted that part of the ridge. That beautiful spot seemed to demand my attention. It required a stop to absorb some small part of its magnificence. There were several trees, some as high as ten feet, all had been wonderfully shaped by the wind; they were pinion pines. I had a delicious Spam sandwich and relaxed while taking in the pleasantness of that little piece of paradise. The view beyond the plateau was nothing short of spectacular as you could see nothing but miles and miles of multi-colored desert floor and the rugged mountains that surrounded my restful spot.

The soft throbbing sound of a far off east bound train could be heard as it started up the long ten-mile climb from Kelso to Cima. Its mile long length could hardly be distinguished as it inched up the mountain grade and across the valley far below. It was an eerie feeling to realize I still had to climb that ridge, down the other side and then walk across several miles of desert to reach Kelso. I silently hoped that I had brought enough water. I moved toward the next visible high point of Fountain Peak. There was a Signal Corps station containing a register of name of prior climbers, about half a dozen since 1969, and I entered my name with the others. Some of the prior climbers had written comments indicating confusion as to whether that place was actually Fountain Peak or what one climber called False Peak. One of the notations stated that the true Fountain Peak was a quarter mile to the north. My water supply was rapidly diminishing and reaching that peak would require crossing another deep canyon. I elected not to explore in that direction and save it for another time.

It was shocking to see tall green grass and stubby pines covering that portion of the Providence Mountains. From Kelso far below they appeared to be nothing but huge jumbled masses of rusty colored dry rock. The landscape which surrounded that mountain range was some of the most desolate and hostile territory on planet earth. Those Providence Mountains were like a stunning desert oasis as a gentle breeze whispered through the pines bringing the coolness of the coming evening air — serenity was very much in evidence. After two hours of carefully climbing into Arrastra Canyon, a level spot was located under a cliff-side ledge just big enough to stretch out. A little spade work with the tri-fold military issue "E" tool and there was a nice place for a small campfire under the ledge. It was like sitting in front of a cozy fireplace. At six o'clock an inky black darkness descended on my little campsite and it was a relief to be safely at rest on the side of those beautiful mountains. That spot was so very peaceful. Deep within my spirit the realization that there was no place in the world that was better--my perch on the slopes of the Providence Mountains was, at that moment, heaven! I slept very well and then continued my downward journey just after dawn. During one point in the descent a one-hundred-foot impassable drop off stood in my way. Without rappelling equipment, it was impossible. I backtracked up the mountain canyon to find a way to bypass the cliff. Finally, I reached the relative safety of the flatlands with no broken bones after six hours of difficult climbing. It felt fantastic and rewarding to be down. All that remained was to hump ALICE across several miles of desert and into Kelso by the train tracks.

I reached town and it was straight to OB's place. OB was glad to see me and asked me to accompany him to Baker to get some beer. It sounded like great fun so we jumped in his old pickup, with Whitedog, and began the forty-mile trip to that small town on Interstate 40. Just about everyone in Baker knew OB as he happily introduced me to his many friends. We went to a local watering hole, had a few beers and headed back to Kelso. It was New Year's Eve and the entire town, maybe 20 people, was having one big party. We had a great time at the home of one of the railroad workers. It seemed like everyone wanted to talk with the stranger in town (me). It was a fantastic time.

It was a beautiful first day of the year with the Providence Mountains sparkling in the crystal clear desert air. What a great way to begin another year! The day was spent with OB and Whitedog. Much was learned about the people, geology and history of that desert area. The sun had set; we retired to his trailer and sat at the kitchen table where we would be able to see the Los Angeles bound freight grinding down the Kelso grade. At about nine in the evening, we saw the far-off engine lights, I began to gather my gear and OB said, "Relax, have another beer, the train won't be at the Kelso station for another half hour." Later we stood together, in front of the old train station, as the long freight train pulled into the yard and slowly came to a stop. We shook hands, said goodbye, and I climbed into the last engine where two other track riders were met. One of them was pretty spaced out and didn't make much sense, perhaps he was just another "burned out" wino. The other rider was well dressed, spoke very well, and carried on a conversation most of the way to Yermo. He told me, "I had a stretch of bad luck in Vegas, lost all my money, and just want to get to my home in Los Angeles." He was in good spirits in spite of his predicament. At about two in the morning, it was a jump and run exit from the moving train just on the outskirts of the Yermo yard. The jump put me closer to my Yermo jungle campsite. I got some sleep and before dawn walked to the highway and hitched the last seventy-five miles to Llano.

It felt good to be back at the General, drinking and shooting up the desert with Bird Dog. We also did a two-week security job for "The Aviator," which was being partially filmed at the Crystalaire airport. We met many nice people including the movie's star, Christopher Reeve. The catering service provided plenty of good meals for the entire two weeks. Bob and I were responsible for security twenty-four hours every day, so we established a "command post" in one of the movie set's army tents. When the movie ended, Bob surprised me early one morning by landing the L-19 in front of the General to pick me up for a flight over the desert. We landed at his place and spent the day loading forty-fives and drinking large quantities of beer. It was just another typical day in the Mojave!

I decided to head east and participate in some upcoming winter exercises at the Merc School. The trip started with a trip to Los Angeles, where I caught the east bound Greyhound. I soon met a nice, attractive woman named Jackie. She told me, "I am going to Tucson to get away from a motorcycle gang member who threatened to kill me." Later in the trip she asked me to guard her body — just for one night! I accepted the challenge, staying very close to her body throughout the long night. Someone had to do it!

It was late March and the weather turned out to be very cold when I arrived at Mercenary School. This was fine with CO Frank as part of the training included fighting and surviving in hostile weather environments. I was assigned to coach the "live fire" and rope bridge fighting exercises. When we got out of the field, Pablo's girlfriend, Debbie, set me up with a blind date. For some reason I resisted at first, but later gave in to Debbie's wishes. We went dancing at a local nightclub, a rarity for this vagabond track rider, and actually had a lot of fun. Late that night Janice gave me a ride to my campsite at the Bunker. She came inside and we sat on my bedroll for a nice make out session. So many feelings had been stirred that I escaped early the next morning and headed back West for a week.

But I just couldn't sit still. Before I knew it, I was on my way back East. Once in Alabama, I found myself calling Janice, the blind date, and she told me, "I would love to see you, come to Birmingham." A few moments later, while getting my gear organized, I noticed a good-looking lady sitting by herself at a picnic table. We started a conversation. Her name was Mary and she told me she was headed north to Michigan. We talked for several minutes, said our goodbyes, and as she was walking toward her car she turned and said, "Would you like a ride?" A broad and very bright smile erupted from my soul and spilled onto my face. We made many unscheduled stops throughout the night for both front and back seat activities. In the morning she dropped me along the Interstate at the Bessemer exit and continued on her way to Michigan. She became a pleasurable memory and hopefully the same held true for her. The experience added a tremendous amount of value to my energy base of knowledge.

I reached the staging area, the Bunker, and we all prepared for the trip to the Louisiana Calvary Base. I talked with Janice and told her that if she wanted, we could get together following Jump School. Six of us loaded our gear and ourselves into the old camouflage painted van and headed out of town. We only drove seventy miles, to the small hamlet of Cuba, before the van broke down. My idea was that we should hit the highway but Pablo won the discussion and called his girlfriend Debbie for help. In less than two hours Debbie and Janice arrived to rescue the stranded Recondo mercenaries. They had two cars and would have plenty of room for a bunch of mercenaries and their gear. I had to admit that it was good to see Janice and Debbie's smiling faces; we all piled in and headed down the highway toward Jump School.

My first parachute jump from a perfectly good airplane was completed. The thrill experienced was something like sex, it was as if every nerve in my body was alive and firing as I fell away from the plane and waited for the T-10 military chute to open. The chute made a loud popping sound and then a beautiful float toward the ground as it blossomed into a smooth canopy. It was a grand experience and well worth the expenditure of energy. One of my landings was pretty rough which resulted in some nasty black and blue bruises; with a shy smile Janice told me, "I'll nurse you back to health when we get back to Alabama."

Jump School ended in three days and we returned to Alabama. A trip to "Little Switzerland" had been scheduled for "members only" advanced tactical training. Shamefully my participation in the advanced training in sniper operations was cut short by my desire to see Janice. Her sister, Alana, was visiting from Arizona and the three of us drove to Gulf shores for a fantastic week on the Alabama beach. It was a week filled with healthy fun, food and companionship; it was definitely one of the best times of my life. We returned to Alabama and it was time for me to return to California. Things with Janice were moving fast; she even helped me buy a plane ticket for the trip west to see my children and to then do some philosophical thinking in the desert.

Final Philosophical Thoughts

I reached the General and took care of some domestic chores. I asked myself what had happened to my original plan, formulated in Big Sur, to develop a Formula for Life (FFL). Throughout my travels of the past few years the concept of what the Formula should look like had changed very little. It didn't matter whether I was riding in a boxcar through the slums of Chicago or contemplating the wonders of the universe from the top of the Providence Mountain Range – the Formula seemed to apply to my life. I felt that it was time for me, in writing, to summarize my attempts to explain the final development of a Formula for Life. Such an explanation would not represent the final unifying answer for my spirit but would only represent another step on my journey through life.

I started with the expression E^3OL which in longhand read, "Enlightenment, Enrichment and Enjoyment of Life." If we added to the concept of E^3OL that there was "Value in Everything" (VIE) which would then lead to Personal Growth (PG) which equaled the "Purpose of Life" (POL) and finally leading to "Total Serenity" (TS). Written as the Formula for Life it took the following form:

$$E^3OL + VIE \rightarrow PG = POL \rightarrow TS$$

E^3OL = Enlightenment, Enrichment and Enjoyment of Life
VIE = Value in Everything
PG = Personal Growth
POL = Purpose of Life
TS = Total Serenity

The Formula was a method of using logic (shown in symbols) as a way of expressing and describing a way of looking at my purpose for existing as a living, thinking, organism and the outcome of living according to such a Formula for Life. It was not meant to infer that the FFL was applicable to any other living, thinking organism. It had, however; worked for this one individual.

A more detailed explanation of the FFL might be helpful. The E^3OL component was the part most subject to manipulation by each individual attempting to reach a rational determination of the meaning of their existence (Purpose of Life). Based on my belief there did in fact exist a higher order of being (God/Creator) responsible for all creation we ponder the question as to why, for what purpose? Personal Growth (PG) seemed to be one possible answer. The growth I speak of was not only a growth which we can easily observe via external physical characteristics but growth through the absorption of energy. That was we, as living, thinking organisms were purposely designed as energy absorbers. We collected energy (the basic physical component of the universe) in the many and varied ways offered by our elaborate energy collecting machine we called our human body. Our senses and brains were part of the body and acted as the control and processing center for the energy/information absorbed from the external universe and internal stimuli. It was our personal responsibility (free will) to select and assign a value to all incoming stimuli. It could be thought of as deciding what was important to us and then remembering the Enlightenment that resulted from exposure to that particular stimulus. The identified unit of value then impacted our brain via our senses to the extent that we as thinking humans assigned it a "Space/Time Marker Value" (STMV). The resultant energy accumulation, via the absorption process, resulted in Personal Growth (PG). For me such PG seemed to be in synchronicity with the universe. Synchronicity with the universe would lead to Total Serenity (TS) which I believed to be in agreement with our Creator's wishes.

The reasoning associated with the selection of Enlightenment, Enrichment and Enjoyment as the trilogy for the purpose of my life goes as follows. Any God or force capable of creating an organism such as man and the entire universe with its untold quintillions of interrelationships must have a purpose. What was that purpose? As mentioned earlier, the design of our physical and mental capacities had made us energy processors and absorbers. We grew by absorbing energy.

I must digress slightly to establish my conceptualization of energy as it related to our ability to think and form concepts. Contrary to popular belief, a thought did have actual weight (mass) and hence when we thought and formed concepts (ideas) we were actually growing via the accumulation of what might be called "thought mass." Such mass was added to our energy base of knowledge via the process of energy absorption and was stored in the brain as energy or converted to mass in some yet, undefined way. That concept of energy being mass in motion and conversely, mass being energy at rest, was firmly based on Einstein's equation $E = mc^2$. Based on these ideas I saw in the cycle of the universe, which at this point in scientific thinking appeared to be expansion, a synchronous relationship between man and the universe. Therefore, by thinking, we were in fact expanding our store of energy and mass and we actually grew. That was the Enlightenment element of the E^3OL variable in the formula. As a result of

"Enlightenment" we become "Enriched" and that process resulted in "Enjoyment." For me the three components were the same, experience one and I experienced them all.

Returning to the concept of creation, it appeared that a being (God) advanced enough to create, or to set in motion creation, which lead to and beyond my existence must have placed us here for a reason. For me the thought was that the creator did in fact want us to enjoy our existence. The only stipulation was that we not infringe on others in our pursuit of personal growth. It was my belief there was plenty of energy (mass in motion) to supply everyone's E^3OL component. Therefore, such E^3OL could be attainable while not infringing on others rights to the same E^3OL. In looking at the "Value in Everything" (VIE) variable we saw it was a way of living life especially when we found ourselves in situations where Enlightenment, Enrichment and Enjoyment appeared to be minimal or even non-existent. Let's consider the extreme case of dying. Death was another step in the process of expansion, for at death we ultimately became more synchronous with the universe. Stored thoughts (energy and mass) did not cease to exist for we knew that energy cannot be destroyed. Our energy base of knowledge took on another form and was distributed throughout the universe as radiation. Therefore, the value in dying was the distribution of our accumulated energy throughout the universe. We then became part of everything, whether we were aware of that transition was another matter. Perhaps there was a kernel of awareness (our soul) which held together and we became keenly aware of other planes of existence. In less extreme cases, such as living day to day, we found ourselves in situations where it was difficult to identify the value at a particular moment in time. At such times we were required to think (process energy) to identify the value. At times we might feel (and rightly so) that the energy processing (assigning STMV's) was not balancing out. In other words, it took too much effort (energy expenditure) to identify the value in something to make it consistent with E^3OL. When such a situation was identified it became our responsibility to move (mentally and/or physically) to a less energy consuming environment. That was the reason that freedom of body and spirit was so important to most human beings. When considering the Purpose of Life (POL) variable we must again refer to the "Creator" and ask ourselves if a being, possessing knowledge beyond comprehension, would set in motion circumstances which would discourage growth (accumulation of energy)? I think not, our purpose was to acquire knowledge and that process was designed to be enjoyable. Once we understood there was "Value in Everything" (sometimes we might have to look hard to find the value) and then realized that it was Enriching through the Enlightenment process we could Enjoy ourselves and continue to expand toward a stage of Total Serenity (TS). Some may wait for death before they experience Total Serenity but it was the ultimate Purpose of Life. That being attained, man and all creation would have a synchronous relationship with everything (and everyone) including our Creator. To be at peace and in love with our Creator and the universe was the ultimate goal of mankind.

On the Alabama Tracks

Since figuring out the purpose of my life, I decided to head for Alabama to spend some time with Janice. I immediately understood that things were very serious when she agreed to ride the rails. Her mother dropped us off at a little used railroad siding in Woodstock, Alabama, and we waited twenty-four hours for a slow freight west. At the twenty-fourth hour we were in the bushes playing around. We struggled to get ourselves dressed as the long slow freight rolled down those Alabama tracks. I spotted an open boxcar, threw our gear on board and with a boost Janice was riding in her first boxcar. We rode the Southern freight train to the yards in Meridian, Mississippi, a trip of one hundred and fifty miles. It was hot and humid throughout the day. It was a good workout for both of us. About midnight one of the yard workers directed us to an east bound freight and we climbed aboard. It wasn't long before we were highballing down the tracks riding on the back end of a grain car. We fell asleep and didn't wake until we passed through Woodstock, McCalla, Bessemer and Birmingham. We awoke as the train was entering the yards in Irondale, northeast of Birmingham! We decided to make a jump-and-run exit from the moving train as that would qualify Janice as a full-fledged female hobo. She did just fine. Uncle Henry and her Mom came to pick up the two hobos at the Irondale train yards in the champagne-colored Mercedes Benz. We headed for the nearest restaurant where there was excited conversation about our little train adventure.

The next trip to California was made in the car with Janice. We stayed at the General for a couple of days and then headed east. In Las Vegas we picked up a marriage license and got married in the small desert community of Searchlight, Nevada. We spent our honeymoon in Laughlin and another adventure began!

Afterthought

The story told above is really about freedom. I was truly blessed to have many individuals in my life that didn't stand in the way of my exercise of extreme freedom. I had the liberty to search for the meaning of my life without interference – a rarity.

Freedom. All one has is the energy within one self-there is no more. This energy is the most valuable thing in the universe and it must be guarded. You are its keeper--you must control and guide it in a synchronous manner. You are the best and the final judge as to how your energy should be processed--this is freedom. The freedom to enlighten oneself as one chooses. We people are learning machines!

James Aldrich

About the Author

The author is a retired university statistics and research methods teacher. He taught medical biostatistics, epidemiology, business statistics and social statistics at various universities in Southern California. Aldrich has published textbooks on these subjects. He currently spends time between working on his "Juniper Art" and trying to keep current with his eight grandchildren and nine great-grandchildren.

www.ingramcontent.com/pod-product-compliance
Lightning Source LLC
Chambersburg PA
CBHW020524080526
44583CB00013B/729